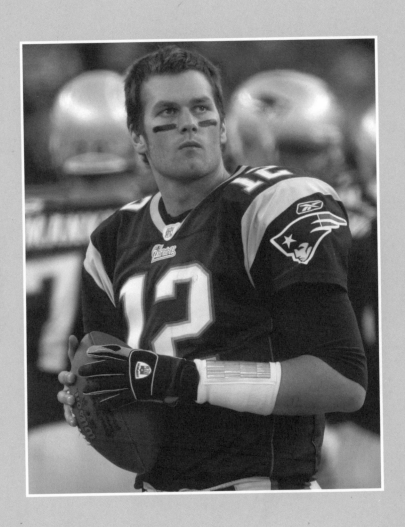

FARRAR
STRAUS
GIROUX

MOVING THE CHAINS

MOVING THE CHAINS

TOM BRADY AND THE PURSUIT

OF EVERYTHING

CHARLES P. PIERCE

FARRAR, STRAUS AND GIROUX | NEW YORK

Farrar, Straus and Giroux
19 Union Square West, New York 10003

Copyright © 2006 by Charles P. Pierce
Distributed in Canada by Douglas & McIntyre Ltd.
Printed in the United States of America
First edition, 2006

Endpaper photographs of Tom Brady: (front) © *Robert E. Klein/Icon SMI/CORBIS;*
(back) © *Brian Snyder/Reuters/CORBIS*

Library of Congress Cataloging-in-Publication Data
Pierce, Charles P.
   Moving the chains : Tom Brady and the pursuit of everything / Charles P.
Pierce.— 1st ed.
      p.   cm.
   ISBN-13: 978-0-374-29923-1 *(hardcover : alk. paper)*
   ISBN-10: 0-374-29923-4 *(hardcover : alk. paper)*
      1. Brady, Tom, 1977–   2. Football players—United States—Biography.   I. Title.

   GV939.B685P54 2006
   796.332092—dc22
   [B]   2006015869

Designed by Abby Kagan

www.fsgbooks.com

10   9   8   7   6   5   4   3   2   1

FOR DAVID BLACK, TRUE BELIEVER

ANDREA: Unhappy is the land that breeds no hero.
GALILEO: No, Andrea. Unhappy is the land that needs a hero.

—Bertolt Brecht, *Galileo*, scene 12

CONTENTS

MOVING THE CHAINS

INTRODUCTION | TWO DRIVES, THREE FACES

THE INSTRUCTOR was not optimistic. He was looking at a roomful of knuckleheads.

There were a couple of hockey players, and there were four or five baseball players—always the worst, a sense of entitlement on them as thick as pine tar on.a bat. There were a handful of football players. There even were ten unsuspecting students unaffiliated with any of the university's teams. This was a composition class at the University of Michigan, but it was stratifying by attitude into an unruly homeroom from some god-awful high school in the land of *Beavis and Butt-head*.

The instructor wasn't theorizing from the faculty lounge, sherry and contempt dripping from his lips. Eight years earlier, he'd been one of them, a scholarship offensive lineman, a grunt in the service of Big Blue, a cog in an athletic combine that had entertained more than 40 million people since the first Wolverine team went 1–0–1 in 1879. He'd sat in classes like this. He had bullied the teachers. He had blown off the reading. He'd been a dumb jock. Looking back, he thought himself a thug.

Elwood Reid was a football apostate. He'd come to Michigan from the same high school in Cleveland that produced Elvis Grbac, a quarterback who'd thrown for 6,480 yards at Michigan and had helped win the 1993 Rose Bowl over Washington before moving on to a career in the NFL. Reid arrived in Ann Arbor bursting with words and ideas, and they'd proven to be stronger in him than the pull of a sport that seemed to have little use for either one. A sport that had left him, as he put it in a magazine piece years after leaving Michigan, "with this clear-cut of a body."

Ultimately, Reid would turn his years at Michigan into a novel, *If I Don't Six*. It was a *roman* for which no *clef* was necessary. Its hero, named Elwood Riley, is a freshman offensive lineman at Michigan with a jones for Marcus Aurelius. His gradual disillusionment with football is the story's arc.

"They don't show the bumps and bruises on television," the fictional Elwood Reid says at one point, "or the long practices, cortisone needles as big as tenpenny nails, the yelling, and hours of boring film meetings where you watch the same play a dozen times until the coach feels that when you go home and close your eyeballs, the play's going to be running on the back of your eyelids."

So Reid knew what he was looking at in his classroom full of knuckleheads. He was looking at a kind of fun-house mirror in time, where the years bent and showed him the reflection of the person football had tried to make of him. The person he'd never be.

Reid noticed the skinny quarterback right off. He didn't dress the way the other jocks did—a style that could generously be described as workout casual. The quarterback was polite. He was sincere. "He'd read the material that I didn't give a shit about in that class when I took it," Reid recalls.

What was even more interesting to Reid was the reaction of the other jocks in the class. He'd seen the really heartbreaking ones—the ones who established their own territory through a kind of armored ignorance. Not only did they not do the reading, but they were also conspicuously proud that they hadn't, and openly contemptuous of anyone who had. "They make fun of you," Reid muses. "That's the way they cull you from the herd."

The quarterback was different. He spoke differently. He even brought his books to class. Reid figured that the knuckleheads would eat him alive. He thought, at best, the quarterback would get himself a reputation around Ann Arbor as a kind of drop-back Eddie Haskell. At worst, he'd get his ass kicked, literally and figuratively, for the rest of his college career.

For good and ill, football is a great leveler. In no other sport is the balance between personal achievement and collective accomplishment so exquisitely delicate. In no other sport is the conflict between the two so consistently volatile. In football, it's a dangerous business to stand out in the wrong way.

To Reid's surprise, even the most disruptive guys in the class did more than leave the quarterback alone. They seemed to look up to him. In fact, they seemed to look up to him more because he wasn't following their lead. "The pull of the pack is to act a certain way," Reid says. "And he wouldn't do it. He took things seriously, and he was very gracious, so I figured, here was a guy who was going to go through the [football] program and then go find a life for himself.

"I said to myself, look at this guy. I'm going to help this guy. I want to open his eyes. So I made sure he read all the essays. I was a little harder on him than I was on the other guys. I told him to pay attention in class, because that's the thing that I didn't do."

Five years later, in 2002, the skinny quarterback led the New England Patriots to a shocking win in the Super Bowl over the St. Louis Rams. Two years later, he did it again, this time over the Carolina Panthers. The next year, he did it a third time, defeating the Philadelphia Eagles. He became football's biggest star. He became celebrated for his ability to stand out at the top of his profession while maintaining an almost fundamentalist belief in being a teammate.

It was very strange to see played out on a vast stage the same thing that had happened in that classroom full of knuckleheads, thought Elwood Reid. It was very strange to see what had become of the kid who always brought his books to class and who never was given any shit about it, even from the people who—whether they knew it or not—already were dedicating their lives to giving shit to people about things like that. Because there was something about him that connected. Because there was something about this Brady character that was real.

"I remember that class," Tom Brady said, leaning against a fence one summer's day, as the New England Patriots rounded into the last weeks of training camp before the 2005 season. They had won two consecutive Super Bowls and were preparing to try to win their third, securing the team's place even more firmly as one of the greatest in the history of the National Football League, and Brady even more firmly in the ranks of the league's greatest quarterbacks.

Over the previous four years, Brady had been the Patriots' starting quarterback, and, in two of the three Super Bowls that they'd won, he'd been the Most Valuable Player. In that time, the team won twenty-one consecutive regular-season games, an NFL record. This success was all the more remarkable given the history of the Patriots, once so lost and bedraggled a franchise that they were forced to play a home game in Birmingham, Alabama, because no stadium around Boston would have them.

Now, though, the team drew thousands of people just to watch it train at its facility outside Gillette Stadium in Foxborough, an otherwise sleepy little town south of Boston, just about on the upper bicep where Massachusetts flexes itself into Cape Cod. They showed up, in the height of the high summer, more than 52,000 of them a week, to watch football practice, which, on its most exciting day, can fairly be said to make the main reading room of the Boston Public Library look like Mardi Gras.

They showed up, and the young girls screamed for Tom Brady the same way the fifty-year-old men did, except the pitch was higher. On the field, the team moved through its drills, grouped by position and then all together. Whenever a player, or a group of players, made a mistake, he had to run a lap around the entire field. When the various miscreants passed a grassy knoll that rises behind one end zone of the practice field, the fans sprawled thickly on the grass gave the passing screwups a standing ovation. Nothing the New England Patriots did was wrong, not even the things that were, well, wrong.

Unlike basketball, where people scrimmage, or baseball's spring training, which involves playing actual games, nobody who comes to football training camp actually sees anyone play a game of football. "When I was playing lacrosse in high school," the New England head coach, Bill Belichick, once recalled, "I couldn't wait for practice because I got to *play lacrosse*. Football practice isn't like that." Instead, football players train in crushing heat in order to perform in shattering cold. They toughen themselves for December in August. People come to training camp in order to see the players, not the game itself. It is a festival of individual attention before the season begins and the personalities of the players are subsumed by the team and by the grind.

Brady came over to the fence to discuss a book—this one, to be precise. Earlier this spring, he'd signed a six-year contract extension for $60 million. He'd hosted *Saturday Night Live*, where not only did he sing, but he also performed a skit in his underwear. He was dating a movie star. He was at the top of his profession. He was twenty-six years old.

He is a substantial presence, six-four and 225 pounds, almost 30 pounds heavier than when he sat in Elwood Reid's class at Michigan. (On page 156 of the 2005 Michigan football media guide, there is a picture of Brady, cocking his arm to throw. He appears to be wearing his big brother's jersey.) He favors the actor Matt Damon a little, but he has a Kirk Douglas cleft in his chin. More to the point, there is about him a genuine sense of the present. He has that gift for which the average politician would gladly sell the portion of his soul not yet sublet by lobbyists—the ability to make the person he is talking to feel as though the rest of the world has fallen away and there is only this one conversation happening anywhere. Asked a relatively simple question—"Do you mind having a book written about you?"—he didn't fall into easy cliché. His answer was subtle, and just worldly enough to be interesting.

"To tell you the truth," Brady said, "there's only one real problem I have with this. I don't know if I'm old enough for a book like this."

Old enough.

It's not a simple answer. It's an answer with some thought—and, therefore, some substance—behind it. It's an answer indicating that, despite his accomplishments, and despite all the extraneous celebrity sugar that's come his way, he will not be completed on anyone's terms but his own. In his answer, there's a glimpse of something restless in Tom Brady, something visceral that resists summing up, something that insists on the primacy and integrity of an individual journey. But it is an interesting answer. In fact, it is just interesting enough to make sure that the project moves forward. It's an answer that moves the chains.

Each chain is precisely ten yards long. There's an upright at either end. There is also a third upright with numbers on it. The uprights are called the "sticks." The officials who keep the uprights that are connected by a chain are called the "rod men." The official who keeps the other upright, which is called the "down indicator box," is called the "box man." Across the field are auxiliary chains and sticks, and auxiliary rod men and box men, so that players can look at either sideline and determine the state of play.

When a football team makes a first down, one rod man plants his stick in the ground parallel to where the ball has been placed. The other rod man extends the chain to indicate to the team (and the spectators) how far they have to go to another first down. Once a team passes that second stick, it gains a first down and the chains move. The object of any offense is to keep the chains moving.

It's within the movement of the chains that football finds its soul. It's within the movement of the chains that football players see most clearly how they are bound together. When an offense is moving the chains, it keeps its defense off the field, rested and ready, while exhausting the defense of the other team. When an offense is moving the chains, its success is easily defined in calibrated achievements, ten yards at a time, one after another after another again. Each player gains confidence—in himself and in what comes to be seen as an inexorable whole. This confidence can become an almost physical force—something Newtonian, like gravity or inertia: "An offense in motion tends to stay in motion, except when acted upon by an equal or opposite force, which is usually a linebacker with blood in his eye." In fact, an offense relentlessly moving the chains is often said to be going "downhill." The constant progress shortens the game. "Time of possession" is one of the most beloved statistics among football coaches. Moving the chains bends time itself to a team's will.

Tom Brady moves the chains. It's the first thing the New England Patriots and their coaches saw in him, back in 2000, when he was a sixth-round draft pick—and a fourth-string quarterback—directing the scout team with players who hadn't been around long enough yet to be considered castoffs. The scout team's job is to simulate the offense of the upcoming opponent. However, after practice, Brady and the scout team would practice the New England offense. He led, and they went with him. "They'd go through the plays, and, if somebody got something wrong, he'd correct them," recalls Belichick. "You could see them getting better. They moved on you."

Almost two years later, in the Superdome in New Orleans, playing with the starters in the biggest game of his life, at the end of a very strange football season, Tom Brady moved all the chains, literally and figuratively, transforming the Patriots and changing his life. By the end of the day, he had produced a remarkable upset that had marked a beleaguered franchise with an entirely new identity, one that resonated deeply with a country still freshly wounded, and Brady instantly personified all the change he'd helped to engineer. Along with his team, he stepped into strange new territory.

In the early evening of February 2, 2002, the Patriots were sitting on their own 17-yard line, tied at 17–17 with the heavily favored St. Louis Rams with 1:21 left in regulation time. Their defense, which had smacked the velocity out of the Ram offense all evening, was literally on its last legs, having just surrendered a touchdown on which at least one pursuing New England defender simply collapsed as though the air had gone out of him.

The smart play was to let the clock run and take a chance on winning in overtime. In fact, John Madden was recommending that very thing on national television while Brady, Belichick, and the offensive coordinator, Charlie Weis, huddled on the sideline. "It was a ten-second conversation," Weis recalls. "What we said is we would start the drive, and, if anything bad happened, we'd just run out the clock."

Belichick and Weis agreed that the Patriots should try to win the game immediately—in part because of the exhausted state of their defense, but mainly because they knew that, even if he didn't get the team a chance to win, Brady was not likely to make a mistake that would cost them the game.

The bare-bones play-by-play does not do justice to what happened next. Consider the play described as: "2-10 NE 41 (:29) T. Brady pass to T. Brown ran OB at SL 36 for 23 yards (D. McCleon, Little) Pass 14, Run 9." Brady hit receiver Troy Brown with a pass that Brown carried twenty-three yards down to the St. Louis 36-yard line before being forced out of bounds.

What's missing is the moment on the previous play that made this one possible. Brady read a blitz by a St. Louis linebacker and threw the ball away. ("T. Brady pass incomplete," says the official record.) What's missing is the fact that Brady noticed that St. Louis had rushed only three of their defensive linemen, dropping a defensive tackle into pass coverage, the way he'd seen them do it on all that film with which he'd seared his eyeballs over the previous week. What's missing is how he bought enough time for Brown to "clear" the unwieldy defensive tackle and get free, how Brady took a tiny, instinctive step up in the pocket to avoid an onrushing lineman whom he felt more than he saw, enabling him to find Brown for the completion.

"There are a lot of little things that go into it," says Bill Belichick, whose occasionally terse commentary can make the official play-by-play read like *Finnegans Wake*.

The movement is missing. There's no sense of constant forward motion, or of the burgeoning confidence that was its primary accelerant. Two plays later, with seven seconds left, Brady "spiked" the ball, deliberately tossing it to the ground in order to stop the clock so that New England would have time to kick the winning field goal. In this situation, most quarterbacks simply slam the ball to the turf and walk off the field.

However, on this occasion, Brady bounced the ball gently, caught it, and handed it to the official. ("T. Brady pass incomplete" reads the play-by-play sheet again.) Up in the luxury suites, Robert Kraft, the owner of the Patriots and the man who had redeemed the franchise from its history as one of the greatest screwball comedy acts in the history of professional sports, was stunned by the coolness of the gesture. On the next play, Adam Vinatieri came on and won the game for New England with a 48-yard field goal.

Two years later, in Reliant Stadium, deep in the industrial savanna outside Houston, Brady established himself permanently in the place where the win in New Orleans had brought him. The Patriots were favored this time, and this time Carolina could be said to have tied *them*, 29–29, on a late touchdown pass. However, New England was gifted with a bizarre kickoff that went out of bounds on their 18-yard line, giving them a minute and eight seconds to travel only about thirty-seven yards to get into position for another field goal try. The measure of the distance that Brady had come is the fact that, this time, almost everybody watching the game expected him to do it.

This time, the pivotal play came with fourteen seconds left, a third-down-and-three situation from the Carolina 40-yard line. Again, Weis and Belichick worked on a vulnerability they'd spotted earlier in the week. Carolina would play man-to-man coverage near the line of scrimmage while sending two defensive backs deep, what the coaches called "Cover Five." At the line of scrimmage, Brady read the defense and intuited the consequence: receiver Deion Branch would be open underneath the deep coverage.

Branch lined up in the slot between another wide receiver and the line of scrimmage. The cornerback was playing him to take away the middle of the field, so Branch broke out and down and away, toward the near sideline, and Brady hit him for seventeen yards and a first down. The chains moved. Vinatieri kicked another game winner. A year later, in Jacksonville, Florida, Brady and the Patriots beat the Philadelphia Eagles to win their third Super Bowl in four seasons.

The territory that had been so new in New Orleans was now the place in which he would live out the rest of his life. Brady would forever be discussed in the same conversation with the greatest quarterbacks who'd ever played. He would be held up as the ideal player on an exemplary team and, while the velocity of his life had increased exponentially, it would be assumed by others that its trajectory would remain straight and true. In the minds of many people, he could live the rest of his life on automatic pilot. He didn't have to move another step. His life could be complete if he wanted it to be.

And this is the oddest irony about moving the chains—the

quarterback is the only player anywhere on the football field whose job specifically requires him to stand still. Even the most mobile quarterback usually has to stop to throw the ball. This means that the quarterback has to perform a task made up of a half dozen finely jeweled movements while a thousand pounds of hostile beef is running around him with its hair on fire.

"Think about it," says Steve Nelson, a former Patriot linebacker. "The quarterback's the only player on the field that has to worry about his elbow pointing the right way to do his job." And the final irony is that it's what the quarterback does when he's standing still that gets the chains to move.

Ultimately, moving the chains can add up to a journey. By resisting easy summation, Tom Brady commits himself to that journey on his own terms. He declines to be defined by the limits of his profession. He declines to be the vessel for anyone else's virtue. Somehow, he has struck and kept the balance that Elwood Reid noticed in that classroom full of knuckleheads. He will live life—and be successful—on his own terms and, at the same time, he will not be culled from the herd. He will be a star and he will be a teammate. He will be smart and handsome and rich and popular and he will be one of the guys, too. He will move the chains in his life, constantly, so that he will determine its ultimate definition.

In this, he sets himself up for a journey through public life that's fueled by formidable contradiction. He will live a normal life, albeit one that includes a movie-star girlfriend and a condominium that priced out last year at $4 million. In this, he is the perfectly consonant face of the mythology that his performance has helped the New England Patriots create and market about themselves—that, in a day of stylized individualism, the Patriots and their quarterback are a team with red-state family values playing in the bluest state of all.

Can anyone be humble if he talks about being humble on *60 Minutes*?

Can anyone be a teammate when the team's success works at the same time to exalt him individually?

How can any football team be a family when a great deal of the family's success depends on grinding up some of the children and tossing them away?

There are material rewards, certainly, to football, but they come with the realization that physical destruction is as central to the sport as it ever was to boxing. (Which is why so many of the pious calls to ban the latter ring so hollow when they come from people who glorify the former.) That basic fact can lead to a soul-killing destruction, in which the player commodifies himself until the essential parts of the person grate together the way the bones in a knee will when the cartilage is removed.

Success is an anodyne. Adulation is a powerful anesthetic. It deadens the pain of that moment when the physical destruction of the sport darkens the heart and bleeds the soul. The key is to keep the adulation under control in such a way that the essential person is not lost. The key is to keep moving. Resist everything that slows you down, whether it's physical pain or the petrification of celebrity. Keep moving. Keep moving. Keep the team moving, even when you're standing still. Keep your life moving, even when you're frozen in the fondest memories of the people who watch you play.

This is the journey Tom Brady has taken on. It began in a family wherein the spirit and documents of the Second Vatican Council mean as much to his development as any playbook. It moved along to college, where the whims of incompetent coaching nearly brought it to an end. It proceeded into the NFL, where it benefited by a brutal injury to another quarterback and where it has arrived, finally, at the opening game of the 2005 season. A Thursday night at home, September 8, 2005, against the Oakland Raiders.

In its game presentation, the NFL is what the Roman Empire would have been had it invented the bass guitar and the thirty-pack. To be in the middle of it is to be deaf to many things, including irony. For example, there has to be an academic slumming out there somewhere who's willing to undertake the study of the phenomenon of sockless males—public heterosexuality and testosterone at flood tide—howling along to "YMCA" and "Rock and Roll, Part Two," the only hit for Gary Glitter, a kiddie-porn aficionado who, at the very moment his song is blasting away across Gillette Stadium, is on his way to a couple of decades in a Vietnamese prison for having transferred himself and his hobby to Southeast Asia.

Tonight, the NFL's in full voice. The rapper Kanye West was dropped at the last minute because he'd said unkind things about President George Bush's reaction to the devastation of Hurricane Katrina, but he was replaced by Santana and the Rolling Stones, and we have indeed arrived at that dark day in which the Stones are the safe play. There are fighter jets and fireworks. The teams come out onto the field as completely obscured by smoke as Cemetery Ridge was on the last day at Gettysburg.

Outside the press box at Gillette Stadium hang a series of television monitors. These enable the sportswriters to follow the action, especially the slow-motion replays, since the height and funky corner location of the press box make watching the actual play on the field problematic. One screen carries the actual television broadcast seen in people's homes. Another carries the raw feed. At this moment, Tom Brady is on both of them.

On the broadcast monitor, dressed in a knife-sharp suit, he's sitting at a table in what appears to be a high-toned restaurant, surrounded by his actual offensive linemen, who are in full uniform. It's a commercial for Visa credit cards, and the linemen are metaphors for the various forms of consumer protection offered by the card. They read their lines, straight credit-card cant, no chaser. They cut their eyes at one another from behind their facemasks, which, oddly, emphasize every change in expression rather than obscuring them, as though the cages bring their features into clearer focus. The funniest thing, of course, is that here in the restaurant, full to the gunwales with Armani and attitude, it's the offensive linemen who have individual identities, even if only as "Fraud Protection" or "Zero Liability." These are roles with greater range than those of, say, "Left Tackle" or "Right Guard," which can be the football equivalent of those movie roles identified in the closing credits as "Second Man in Elevator" or "Dead Soldier No. 3." Here, Brady's just another guy in an expensive suit, and he's the straight man.

Presented with the check for the meal, Brady delivers his one-liner: "Do metaphors pay?"

"Ha, ha," the linemen laugh in reply. "No."

On the monitor next to this one, there is a low-angle shot of Brady live on the New England sideline, with fireworks exploding far above his head. It's the kind of hero shot in which the NFL specializes. It's hard to tear your eyes away to look all the way down to the sideline at the actual person, slapping high-fives with his teammates, his face a bright burst of joy that you don't need a television to see.

This is where the journey truly happens, down on the field. Everything else is side trips and diversions—roadside amusements and reptile farms. Tom Brady fought hard to begin the journey, and he will fight just as hard to determine its direction. Ultimately, he'll determine its end. After all, in some ways, his career is already complete. He's won three Super Bowls, more than any other professional quarterback except Joe Montana. He's rich. He's famous. He will be inducted into the Pro Football Hall of Fame, even if he gives the whole thing up tomorrow and joins the Carthusians. But he won't stand still, except for those moments when he has to in order to move the chains.

"Is there a perfect game out there?" Brady muses. "It's got to be at the highest stakes. It has to be a game that means a lot, and it has to come down to the end, probably a game where you have to keep digging and digging. You don't remember the ones you win 35–17. You remember the ones you win 38–35. A two-minute drive. They score. You score. Those are the ones that are memorable. Who wants everything to come easy?"

PART 1 THE PROBLEM WITH METAPHORS

1 | ON THE AVENUE OF THE FLEAS

THE GOAT livened up the first week of the season.

Just before the opening game against Oakland, Brady was profiled in *GQ* magazine. The piece caused no little stir because, at one point, while attempting to establish his bona fides as a regular guy, Brady gave a non-denial denial to a question about whether he scanned the Internet looking for dirty pictures. This prompted a spate of TOM SURFS FOR PORN! headlines, most notably in "Inside Track," the gossip column produced by two indefatigable women in the tabloid *Boston Herald*. But the pictures accompanying the article were what were bound to bring out the inner Marx brother in any teammate—especially, it seems, in offensive linemen.

They were the usual fashion magazine photos—glossy and softly lit, and nearly recognizable as depictions of an actual human being. With someone apparently under the impression that Brady had an independent film debuting at Sundance this year, the quarterback was posed in a variety of high-end leisure clothes. He was shown dreamily doffing a yachting cap. Even more inexplicably, he was photographed holding a baby goat.

It turns out that the goat photo was something of a surprise. Brady was taken to a farm. Someone handed him a goat. Someone else took his picture. The magazine published it, and the overall effect was that of Orlando Bloom in the role of Mr. Green Jeans. His teammates noticed, as he was sure they would.

The day after the magazine hit the stands, Brady brought the team up to the line of scrimmage, only to discover that tackle Matt Light and center Dan Koppen had fastened the goat photo to the backs of their jerseys. Practice convulsed for a long moment, and nobody laughed harder than the guy with the goat.

The mastermind of the plot was probably Koppen, a redhead with a determined slouch to his jaw and middle school mischief in his eyes. A lineman as bright as he is deft, and as deft as he is strong, Koppen is Brady's backgammon rival, and one of his best friends on the team. As the center, he has to make all the calls for the offensive line, especially those regarding Brady's pass protection, so Koppen and Brady spend hours together on the practice field and in the film room trying, among other things, to keep Brady upright and intact.

Koppen's entitled, then, to these moments of hilarity with his quarterback. It wasn't the first. After Brady hosted *Saturday Night Live* the previous April, in the course of which he did one skit in his underwear, he found the Patriot locker room festooned with Jockey shorts. Koppen was the prime suspect in that caper, too.

Brady's first touchdown of the 2005 season came with 2:05 left in the first quarter against Oakland. Up until that moment, his performance had been fitful at best. Once the smoke from the pregame bombardment had cleared, he had missed open receivers on three occasions in the first quarter, including a pass to Deion Branch on which Branch had left two defenders behind on a route that took him to the middle of the field. Brady overthrew him by half a yard.

Branch is a quick, smart receiver who can turn an eight-yard pass into a twenty-yard gain. He was the Most Valuable Player in the previous season's Super Bowl, catching eleven passes for 133 yards against the Eagles, including a critical nineteen-yard reception that led to the field goal by Adam Vinatieri that proved the difference in the game. His connection on the field with Brady is not dissimilar to that between Brady and Koppen, born, as it is, from endless sessions on the practice field. On a third-down-and-eight situation from the Oakland 18-yard line, Branch broke off a sharp cut to the outside, and Brady hit him in the end zone for a 10–7 New England lead. Brady sprinted the eighteen yards in order to be one of the first to jump on Branch's head.

Oakland responded almost ten minutes later with a 73-yard pass to Randy Moss, the vastly gifted, and vastly truculent, wide receiver who'd come to Oakland after making Minnesota too hot to hold him. In many ways, Moss is the antithesis of Branch: eight inches taller, thirty pounds heavier, and explosively athletic, especially in midair. On this play, with New England defensive back Tyrone Poole stumbling in his coverage, Moss simply tapped the ball over Poole's head as though he were playing beanbag with a child. The touchdown put Oakland ahead briefly, but Brady hit Tim Dwight with a five-yarder to give New England a 17–14 halftime lead. The Patriots stretched that to 30–14 before Oakland scored a meaningless touchdown with 3:04 left to cut the final margin to 30–20. Brady threw for more than three hundred yards for the ninth time in his career, completing twenty-four of his thirty-eight passes.

Much of the talk in the locker room after the game was of the Visa commercial that had debuted on the telecast that night, and of how the offensive linemen had stolen the show from their quarterback. This is something of a karmic earthquake. After all, there is nobody simultaneously more important and more anonymous than an offensive lineman. With very rare exceptions, including John Hannah, a Hall of Fame guard for the Patriots who is reckoned to be the greatest offensive lineman ever to have played the game, even the NFL's formidable myth-making machinery breaks down on the topic, usually treating a team's offensive line as a mass of undifferentiated muscle. If the FBI really wants to hide a cooperating witness, football coaches say, it should train its canaries to trap-block.

"You have to know what's right for you," Koppen explained. "You're in high school, right? You're old enough to know, and smart enough to realize, that you don't have the physical abilities to be a receiver or anything like that. If you love to play the game, you've got to play it whenever you can.

"You pretty much fall into it. I don't think in backyard football, what are you going to do? 'Hey, I want to play center'? No, I don't think so. It's picked for you, probably. Everybody wants to grow up to be the wide receiver, or the running back, or the quarterback. But whether it's because you're bigger than the other kids at a younger age, or you just get bigger in high school, the offensive line is just someplace where they put you."

However, the commercial was different. They were all individual performers, each of them sharper and more vivid while wearing a face mask than their quarterback was in his suit. He was upstaged, and he appears to have loved it. "It was a long day, working with those five guys," Brady says. "They'll never be actors. I don't think we'll win any Emmys for that thing, but we had a lot of fun doing it. I love having those guys around. They got asked to be in the commercial, and I think that's always kind of flattering to be asked. Hopefully, it put a few bucks in their pockets.

"But those guys never pay for anything."

There are quarterbacks whose standing with their teammates never would have survived the goat photo and the *GQ* spread. There are quarterbacks whose images as matinee idols and public figures of conspicuous decency would have put their football credibility into a debt they could never repay. They would have been ridiculed, culled from a herd whose attitude toward issues of gender never has been an enlightened one. That's never happened to Tom Brady, in whom people invest themselves for reasons that seem to be beyond envy or greed, or any of the easy categories of the game.

"Tommy is a traditionalist," muses Robert Kraft, the owner of the Patriots. "But, he's a what? What do they call it now? That term they use in gossip? Metrosexual? Something like that, but at the same time, he's an old-time football player. You can connect with him and feel that you have a special bond with him. He's soft and gentle, but he can be really, really tough when he has to be. It's a terrific balance of him almost being naïve at times, but, when it comes to that border, he knows how to be pragmatic. He's such a competitor, but he can cuddle a baby, too."

It's hard to imagine, say, George Halas ever talking about his quarterback that way, and it's hard to imagine, say, Doug Atkins not laughing his head off at the old man if he did. But, almost from the start, Brady has managed to be beyond ridicule without being above it. He'll hug his sisters, or a teammate's mother, and get teased about it, and the episode will pass without hanging around his neck. In seminaries, theologians talk about charisma in ways that involve the laying on of hands. Politicians have managed to transmute the sacred into the profane, kissing babies for the cameras. Brady's is a secular charisma derived from authenticity.

Brady's toughness is beyond question. His teammates marvel at his coolness in those scrambled moments in which the quarterback has to be the only one standing still in the middle of what is really little more than an organized riot. Opponents respect his ability to take a fearful pounding and come back at them again on the next play. "I would never take a cheap shot at him," says Jason Taylor, the talented Miami defensive end who is one of Brady's best friends in the league.

"Quarterbacks," says Bill Belichick, sounding very much the way a former defensive coordinator should, "are going to get hit."

Nevertheless, given the attention that accrues automatically to the position, even the toughest quarterback can lose his teammates, most often by carrying himself above the grunts who sacrifice themselves to keep his uniform clean. Bobby Layne, the legendary hellion who quarterbacked the Detroit Lions in the 1950s, once explained to the writer Myron Cope how he'd learned to play quarterback in the fullest sense of the position.

"I learned one thing playing for the New York Bulldogs," Layne said. "I found out I wasn't gun-shy. I could stay in the pocket and get hit and it would not bother me." Layne also learned to divine the essential nexus for any quarterback between the ability to hang in the pocket to throw the ball on Sunday, and a willingness to pick up the dinner check the night before. "I was making more money than anyone else on the club so I always allocated a certain part of my money to spend on the players," he said. "I wasn't trying to be a big shot and I don't think any of them thought I was trying to be one."

In many ways, between the *GQ* article and the Visa commercial, what Elwood Reid, that former offensive lineman turned Michigan professor, identified in his classroom played out on an immensely bigger stage. This was someone with enough substance to him to render the usual methods of culling the herd irrelevant. Brady's character had moved him beyond those simple dynamics without placing him beyond the individuals who made up the herd. The herd invested in him, and he invested so much in them as individuals that their mutual investments in one another added up to a profound sense of being teammates. In every sense, including both the catholic and the Catholic ones, charisma inevitably involves someone wishing to make contact finding other people willing to receive it. And football is, after all, a contact sport.

"All I ever wanted," Tom Brady says, "was the camaraderie, to share some memories with so many other guys. I mean, if you choose to alienate yourself or put yourself apart, you know, play tennis. Play golf."

This was someone who saw deeply into the bonds that hold people together, who saw so deeply into the concept of being a teammate that he saw all the way down to that abiding confidence that is the strength of the best families. All successful teams refer to themselves as families without ever realizing the weight of what they're saying, as though "family" is merely a group of like-minded people with a common goal. And that's one of the problems with metaphors. Sometimes, they oversimplify.

The lineage of quarterbacks is as much a question of nature versus nurture as is any other genealogical spelunking. The dynastic Mannings—Archie, Peyton, and Eli—are one example, as are Bob and Brian Griese, and Phil and Chris Simms. The line that leads to Tom Brady, though, may trace itself back not to a great-grandfather calling signals for the Canton Bulldogs, but to Jim Walsh, a Catholic priest born in Cambridge, Massachusetts, on February 24, 1867. Walsh attended Boston College High School and, eventually, Boston College, where he showed promise as a debater and as a journalist. He dropped out of BC to study bookkeeping, but abandoned that and enrolled across the

Charles River at Harvard. Eventually, however, he found his way to St. John's Seminary in Brighton. He was ordained a Roman Catholic priest on May 20, 1892.

From the start of his priesthood, Walsh sparkled with missionary zeal. In 1907 he founded a magazine dedicated to the foreign missions. In 1910, at a eucharistic congress in Montreal, Walsh met a kindred soul. Thomas Price was a North Carolinian inculcated by his mother with a deep devotion to the mother of Christ. (In fact, Price credited the intercession of the Blessed Virgin with saving him from a shipwreck on his way to the seminary in Maryland.) Acting independently, both Walsh and Price recognized a need in the Church for a seminary that would train young men specifically to work overseas. In 1911 Pope Pius X formally blessed what the two priests called the Catholic Foreign Mission Society of America, which became known as Maryknoll for short, after the plot of land on which Walsh and Price had established their seminary in Ossining, New York, not far from the New York State correctional facility there—which was known, also for short, as Sing Sing.

The Maryknoll order was an immediate success. Its first missionaries set sail for China in 1918. The organization also developed an order of nuns and an order of lay missionaries. From its start, the spirit of Maryknoll was of a Catholicism that reached out to the rest of the world, that was active in that world, a spirit that was far more democratic than it was hierarchical.

Not long after the order was founded, Maryknoll opened another seminary, this one on the grounds of an estate donated to the order in Glen Ellyn, Illinois, twenty-two miles west of Chicago, a former outpost for Protestant circuit-riding preachers. It was in some ways a foreign mission itself; Glen Ellyn didn't even have a Catholic parish for the first sixty years of its existence. The Maryknoll Seminary soon became a local landmark, not merely for the grace and beauty of its grounds but also because it gave Glen Ellyn its very own ghost story. Rumor had it that a monk had hung himself in the seminary's bell tower, and that you could hear him moaning in the night. It was also rumored that, on the anniversary of the monk's death, the walls of the bell tower dripped blood.

In 1962, Thomas Brady, an eighteen-year-old Catholic schoolboy in San Francisco, found himself fascinated by Maryknoll and its mission work. He was a second-generation Californian from an intensely competitive and intensely spiritual family. "Coming up in grammar school, I learned about them, and I absolutely fell in love with them," he recalls. However, his father, Harry, had the chronic Irish problem with expressing deep emotion. He simply didn't. His son vowed not to seal himself up that way, but to raise himself and his children to be open in all ways to the world around them.

"You learn from that how not to repeat the mistakes [of your parents]," says Stephen Pope, a cousin who is now a professor of theology at Boston College. Pope's sister, Barbara, spent eight years as a Maryknoll lay missionary in a Venezuelan barrio. "It was a fairly tight-knit, but not suffocating, Irish Catholic family, and it was a fairly big one, full of vocations to the priesthood. That competitive, driving side of the Irish character? Well, the Bradys have that in spades."

In 1962, Tom and his brother Phil were both at Glen Ellyn with the intention to become Maryknoll priests. They brought with them not only their fiery competitive bent but their high spirits as well. In the yearbook for his freshman year at Glen Ellyn, amid all the timorous, anxious smiles of his classmates,

Tom Brady is grinning as if he just made a great deal on something very expensive. He played soccer and, with his brother, worked as a groundskeeper at the golf course that had remained part of the seminary's property from the time of the original bequest. There is perhaps something of the Divine Hand in the fact that Tom Brady went to a seminary where he could still get a round in.

In 1965 the changes in the Catholic Church wrought by Pope John XXIII's Second Vatican Council had reached Glen Ellyn. In calling the council, the pope famously urged that the windows of the Church be flung open to the world. Perhaps the council's most singular departure was its ultimate insistence that the Church ought to abandon its rigidly hierarchical structure and accept that it actually is what the council called "the people of God."

"Christ teaches through his whole church, not just one part of it," writes the historian Garry Wills. "The pope leads but it is within the apostolic body of bishops; the laity share the priesthood of Christ; infallibility belongs to the whole body of Christ."

Maryknoll's founding principles made the order uniquely suited to the changes coming out of the council. "The old image of Maryknoll was to go out and convert souls and save them from hell," explains Stephen Pope. "There was a transition around Vatican II in which Maryknoll made a commitment to works of social justice and to interreligious dialogue, but especially to social justice."

At almost the same time, Tom Brady was struggling with a church tradition that Vatican II had declined to change. He had no desire to remain celibate for the rest of his life. "I decided," he says, "as my old Latin teacher used to tell me, 'Mr. Brady, you ought to propagate the faithful, not propagate the faith.'"

Brady left Glen Ellyn in February 1965 and returned to California, where in April, while he was a student at the University of San Francisco, his missionary zeal undaunted but somewhat redirected, he joined the Marines. "Love of God and love of country," he says. "If I wasn't going to be a soldier of God, I was going to be a soldier of the United States." He was ticketed for Vietnam right after his graduation. However, in May, Brady tore a cartilage in his knee while working out, and he was discharged as a lance corporal.

"Yeah, it's a good thing," he muses. "So many of my friends were altered by the experience. One of my very best friends, that I was with in the seminary, came back from Vietnam and he never stopped drinking. We buried him [in 1997]." After graduation, Brady took a job selling insurance. One day, in 1968, he knocked on the door of an apartment belonging to a flight attendant named Galynn Johnson. She didn't buy any insurance. "We never even talked about it," he says.

She had been born in Browerville, Minnesota, a small town 140 very flat miles northwest of Minneapolis, the daughter of the town barber who dreamed of being a farmer. Gordon Johnson didn't much like the hustle and bustle of downtown Browerville, so little by little, at fifty cents a haircut, he saved enough to purchase his dream. He moved his family out to it when Galynn was a sophomore in high school.

"Our farm was three miles outside of Browerville," she recalls, "but, oh, it was scary. You would have thought I was moving across the country." She had an uncle and aunt who actually did move across the country, settling in Santa Ana, California, and they would come back and regale the people they'd left behind with tales of lemon trees and orange groves.

The California stories were enough to overcome whatever

trepidation Galynn had about moving. "It was always somewhere I wanted to go," she recalls. One day, while working at an advertising agency in Minneapolis, Galynn saw an ad in the paper for the stewardess program at Trans World Airlines. A month later she was at the training school in St. Louis. Galynn chose to fly domestic routes because she could live in California. (TWA's international crews were all based in New York.) That was why she was home that day when Tom Brady showed up, thinking he was there to talk about insurance. Instead, they fell into a long conversation about their families and wound up going out the following Friday.

It was a whirlwind courtship, six months from that knock on the door to the altar. Tom put his salesman's gifts to fine advantage. When Galynn's parents came out to California to meet him, he showed up at the airport with flowers for her mother. "That was it," Galynn recalls. "She was hooked."

They were married and they moved to San Mateo, a suburb south of San Francisco bisected by an old thoroughfare that has run through California since the days in which the road was merely a cow path—Alameda de las Pulgas, the "Avenue of the Fleas." All around the alameda, the neighborhoods are layered on a series of plateaus, giving the town a ladderlike effect that rises by degrees into the mountains. Down on Portola Drive, the Bradys had four children. Three daughters—Maureen, Julie, and Nancy—came first. Tommy was the caboose, born on August 3, 1977, five years younger than his oldest sister and a year younger than Nancy.

"We were all very close together," Nancy Brady says. "There was about sixteen months from one to the next." The sisters adopted Tommy almost immediately, dressing him up. As they all grew up together, Tommy learned a great deal from his sisters. They were people and they were athletes, and he would forget either fact only at his considerable peril. He learned the difference between being sensitive and being thin-skinned, and he learned how to be sensitive and still be strong, and how passions are formed in the spaces formed by those differences.

"Tommy, I think, has always been a sensitive man," Galynn Brady says. "But he's also very masculine. But, having three sisters, I think, he had to be a little sensitive to learn about women because, really, we're all pretty crazy."

However, Tommy's growing understanding of women perhaps helped him to regularly con his mother into driving him to What's On Second? for baseball cards, or ferrying him around on his paper route. "We had a Volkswagen van, and he'd throw the papers out the door," Galynn recalls. "And we'd get back and I'd say, 'Tommy, I'm not going to do it again.' And the next night, he'd be there, 'Mom?' I could never say no."

"If you ever hear him talking to anyone," says Nancy, "it's always, 'How are *you* doing?' 'How's *your* job?' That's always been part of his being a teammate. It's just such a part of his personality. I mean, it's not just his work. He's incredibly loving."

In fact, it's a family of huggers and a family of kissers. At breakfast in San Mateo, Tom Brady, Sr., will leap out of his chair to embrace a friend who's just arrived in the restaurant. And it's equally startling to see his son, after a Patriots game, win or lose, greeting old friends with a kiss on the cheek. Part of it stems from the emotional distance that the elder Tom Brady sensed in his father. Another comes from his involvement in the Cursillo movement, one of the several retreat movements that arose in the Catholic Church as part of the lay activism that exploded in the wake of Vatican II.

"Cursillo is very Latino in that it is very expressive and emotive," explains Stephen Pope. "It's about communal-oriented compassion. The way his father was has a big impact on the way Tom conducts himself around other people."

(Once, when Pope's son brought his girlfriend to a game in New England, Tom Brady, meeting her for the first time, greeted her with a hug and a kiss. "She was already a little swoony [over the quarterback] anyway," Pope says. "That's also very Californian. It's the California thing that overcomes that Irish Catholic Jansenistic fear of the body.")

With the arrival of his fourth child, Tom Brady found himself with another man in the house. "All of a sudden," he recalls, "there were four women and two men in the house, even though one of the men was only two." By the time Tommy was five, they would go off to the California Golf Club, a private, men's-only club where the elder Brady was a member. "That was kind of their way to get out of the house," Nancy says.

"We'd go out and play at six-thirty in the morning on Sundays and be home in time to go to Mass at eleven o'clock," the elder Brady says. By the time he was ten, Tommy was playing golf, and at the club, Tom Brady saw his son grow at ease with older men at an even younger age. "When he was five or six years of age, we'd sit in the grill and play liar's dice. And I'm teaching him how to play, and my friends are coming in, and we're all playing. Or playing golf with adults, and stuff like that. He learned to handle himself."

Both of his parents began to see a little bit of themselves in their son. He was friendly and outgoing, the way his father was, but without Tom's seemingly limitless irrepressibility. He didn't have the salesman's grin. There was a reservoir of caution there, a touch of his mother's Minnesotan reserve. One thing he did have was a temper. Video-game controllers were known to fly through the air when Tommy was playing, and there's still a hole in the wall of the house, a relic of a long-forgotten bad bounce or errant throw.

All of the Bradys were sports silly. There were earnest theological disquisitions as to the propriety of wearing San Francisco 49ers jerseys to Mass, but as soon as the service ended, they were off to tailgate at Candlestick Park, where Tommy Brady became a fan of Joe Montana and the 49ers. The family even would watch a replay at home of the game they'd seen in person that afternoon. Tommy never tired of watching a game on film that he'd seen with his own eyes because Montana's gift for playing his best at the most crucial times so appealed to him.

Galynn was an excellent tennis player and developed a real talent for golf, which she shared with her husband, who also was a notably enthusiastic pickup basketball player. ("He doesn't believe in that rule about charging," comments his cousin, the theologian.) The girls all played softball and soccer, and Maureen developed into a talented pitcher, throwing fourteen perfect games in high school and eventually winning a scholarship to Fresno State. Tommy played baseball and football. And not all the competition was athletic. While at Hillsdale High School, Nancy Brady became a formidable debater, practicing on her parents. "She's convinced me to change my mind on several subjects," her father says. "Even though she'd never believe it."

There was a calendar in the kitchen that kept track of the children's various games, which Galynn and/or Tom always attended. The year Tommy was in eighth grade, there were 315 games on the calendar. And one of the things Tom Brady remembers most clearly about Fresno State is that "it's 177 miles from our front door to the playing field."

"I don't think we were typical girls," says Nancy Brady. "I think we all liked to play everything the boys did, and there were about eighty or ninety kids in the neighborhood, so there was always something going on. And it was always the three Brady girls and Tommy."

Tom Brady involved himself with the basketball teams at St. Gregory's, the parochial grammar school that his son attended. He insisted that everyone on the team play in every game, which drew the ire of some of the parents. Tommy was one of the basketball team's stars, but his first talent was for baseball. He showed real ability as a catcher, particularly as a handler of pitchers. But, somehow, baseball didn't reach him. There was too much about it that was individual. He had defined his passions and his enthusiasms within the context of his family. Everything about him, and everything about how he'd been raised, shaped him to be part of something oriented around the first person plural. "Baseball, while it's ostensibly a team sport, it's totally a one-on-one sport," says his father. "In football, it's eleven guys against eleven guys."

Tommy was still playing both sports when he went up the hill, and across the Avenue of the Fleas, to Junípero Serra High School. Named for the man who brought Catholicism to California, the all-male institution was first built in 1944 on the grounds of an old elementary school right on the alameda. It moved to its present location eleven years later. It's a low, sprawling place, with its thousand-odd boys walking down corridors that wind through a campus that seems much smaller on the outside than it actually is, and that is built around a central courtyard, where a statue of the Madonna stands amid picnic tables.

Serra, as everyone who ever went there calls it, was part of the movement to the suburbs of all those immigrant Catholic children whose parents had come to this country and settled in the cities. In the 1950s, when Serra moved to San Mateo, a home in the suburbs was part of a culture of achievement, a just reward for hard work. Catholic schools sprang up in all the suburbs, often with "For God and Country" carved above the doorways. The yellow-and-white papal flag was always tucked discreetly behind the Stars and Stripes off to the side of the auditorium stage, or hanging beneath it on the wall of the gymnasium.

Athletically, Serra was primarily a baseball school. Jim Fregosi, a shortstop with the California Angels and, later, the manager of several major-league teams, graduated from there in 1959. And, almost a decade before enrolling, Tom Brady had watched a Serra Padres—of course—team that was led by a lanky outfielder named Barry Bonds. The high school's sole claim to football immortality—outside the undefeated 1949 squad, that is—was Lynn Swann, who, after graduating in 1970, went off to the University of Southern California and, thence, to a Hall of Fame career with the Pittsburgh Steelers. (Most recently, of course, Swann ran as a Republican for governor of Pennsylvania.) Tommy Brady's arrival at Serra was as unremarkable as the school's football team. Most people thought Serra simply had landed a talented catcher.

"I don't think anyone here was looking for Tommy to play football here," says Mike Peterson, a former coach who's now the vice principal at Serra. "We're not known as a football school."

"Football," says Tom MacKenzie, who coached Brady at Serra, "was always just trying to measure up here."

Brady managed his transition into high school smoothly, almost clinically, even taking a course in academic organization the summer before his freshman year to prepare for the increased workload. He succeeded in baseball immediately. But football was still drawing him, even though it didn't come to him as easily as baseball did. Between Brady's freshman and sophomore years, Serra's starting junior-varsity quarterback walked away from the team, having taken a serious pounding the previous season. This was the first time that the physical side of football had opened an opportunity for Tom Brady. It would not be the last. In that spring and summer, he and his father went to quarterback camps in Arizona—with a side trip to spring training—and at the University of California. The elder Brady also suggested they talk with a throwing guru he knew named Tom Martinez, who ran a school for quarterbacks at the College of San Mateo, up in the hills.

Martinez is one of those curious sports gurus who develop a system for teaching a specific skill extraordinarily well. Basketball has its shot doctors. Baseball has hitting consultants. Martinez has dedicated himself to studying every delicate action that makes up the art of throwing the football. He has broken down every part of the act of throwing a forward pass—from the number of steps the quarterback takes to the position of his hand before the throw—into its components. And he has developed his own training techniques along the way. If a quarterback comes to him with an inefficient sidearm motion, Martinez will have him throw while standing at arm's length from a fence or a brick wall, so that a series of skinned knuckles will themselves explain to the quarterback that it is better to throw the ball overhand.

A craggy-faced pedagogue with enormous, meaty hands, Martinez played at San Francisco State in the middle of the riots during the 1960s. He developed his coaching style while teaching high school mathematics. "My students would ask me a question," he says, "and I'd say, 'You do it that way because I told you.' Then I'd go home that night and think, You know, they probably deserved a better answer than that. At that point, I began to challenge *my* knowledge of the things I was teaching. I mean, I was fiery. I was a motivator, but I didn't know what the hell I was doing." In young Tom Brady, Martinez found a student as devoted to the "why" of things as he'd become.

Martinez worked with Brady on every aspect of what a quarterback should do. He explained, in pointillist detail, how a quarterback should start his drop into the pocket with his dominant foot—the foot corresponding with his throwing hand—forward, to make it easier to pivot and retreat, thereby gaining distance quickly and, thus, more time to read the defense and throw the ball. He also explained why Bill Walsh of the 49ers had coached Montana and his other quarterbacks to take little steps forward in the pocket. (Walsh even timed his receivers' routes to take this shuffling into account.) Martinez gave all his students, including Brady, the option of shuffling or standing still, and he emphasized a short, powerful stride with the throw, arguing that a wide stride—what he calls a "long lever"—results in a short-armed throw.

Martinez also explained the difference between a C throw and a U throw, the names coming from the position of the hand on the ball at release. If you're holding the ball by its side when you throw, your hand makes a C. If you hold the ball underneath, your fingers would make a U. Which is how most people throw a football, Martinez explains. "If you just handed someone a football and stood behind them, you'd see a U, and there's less control of the ball, so it wobbles," he says. "There's a tendency to be underneath it because that's the only way most people can hold it and throw it."

The level of detail in Martinez's coaching appealed to the side of Brady that had driven him to take an organizational course in his summer before high school. He took copious notes, to which he refers even today. Also important for Brady was the fact that Martinez could explain why things worked. And Brady appreciated the amount of personal attention he received. "You get Tommy to work best," his father says, "by supporting him and not by derogatory comments or whatever other techniques that coaches use. When Tommy has somebody on his side, he'll do anything to make the guy look good."

When Brady's confidence broke down on the eve of his first junior-varsity game, during his sophomore year in high school, his father drove immediately back up into the hills. Martinez walked out of a coaches' meeting, and he and Brady spent a few minutes reviewing what Martinez had taught him over the summer. "Tommy's eyes lit up," his father recalls, "and he was totally confident again. It was all about having someone who was confident in him be able to reassure him, because you don't forget how to throw, you just don't believe you remember how to throw."

Brady was finally moving decisively toward football as his primary sport. His devotion to belonging was satisfied more by football than by baseball, which, by comparison, seemed to be a pile of pretty leaves pretending to be a tree. In addition, playing quarterback engaged his abiding curiosity about figuring things out, something that his teachers had noticed about him straightaway.

Brady liked to know the why of things, as well as the who and the what. He found himself gravitating toward classes like geometry—and to an architecture course taught by his baseball coach, Pete Jensen—that required a developed sense of precision. He also gravitated to classes in which give-and-take was encouraged, taking the lead in one course on Catholic ethics in which the moral issues of the day were earnestly debated. His competitive side was engaged after his JV season, when Tom

MacKenzie told his father that Tommy had "a Division I arm, but a Division 5 lower body."

"That was all it took," says MacKenzie. "Tom Brady is the only student athlete I ever saw who took advantage of every opportunity that was provided to him." Seeing that MacKenzie was enamored of a tedious footwork drill called the Five Dots, which most of his players loathed, Brady set up the Five Dots in his backyard, working his way through the drill every morning before school.

"I've never been real fleet of foot," he says today. "I enjoyed the struggle of it. I gained a lot out of it, in terms of mental toughness."

Brady's days fell into a pattern. He would rush home from school to dispatch his homework, then go off with friends to work out, usually at the Pacific Athletic Club in Redwood City, where some of the 49ers trained as well. He did not have a job, preferring to work out three or four hours a day. He was well-liked and romantically popular. Having been raised in a houseful of women, Brady never lacked the ability to connect with women to whom he did not happen to be related. He was the starting high school quarterback, which no doubt helped him personally, but he didn't create anything like the circus that Serra had been when Barry Bonds was there.

"He didn't do things to draw attention to himself, the way Barry did," recalls Mike Peterson. "Tommy was this good, smart kid that people liked, but he wasn't bigger than life, the way Barry was."

And, of course, the football Padres were nothing particularly special, either, kicking around the break-even point in wins and losses over Brady's four-year varsity career. At one point in his junior season, the Padres lost consecutive games by a combined 110–6. He ended his career as a senior with two consecutive losses, a tailspin that knocked Serra out of the postseason playoffs. For his career, Brady completed 52.8 percent of his passes, for 3,702 yards and thirteen touchdowns.

And, while he wasn't the marching band that Bonds had been, Brady brought baseball scouts to Serra. He was still a good enough catcher to be drafted by the Montreal Expos in the eighteenth round of the 1995 Major League Baseball draft; he even hit a home run during his tryout at the Kingdome in Seattle. But football had connected with him on too many levels, and he and his father turned the Expos down. Now, his only choice regarding his immediate athletic future was to find a college where he could play. His performance at various football summer camps—including one run by Tom Martinez—earned him increased attention from the assistant coaches who did the recruiting for the major college programs.

The Bradys put together a videotape of Tom's games and sent it to fifty-five universities. They got fifty-two replies. Only Arizona, Nebraska, and Hawaii turned Tom down out of hand, probably because they did not run the kind of passing offense best suited to his abilities. However, nobody was as persistent a believer as an assistant coach from the University of Southern California named Mike Riley. Brady's team responded to him, Riley noted, even though it wasn't really very good. Brady threw a good, solid pass, made very few mistakes, and seemed quick to read defenses and react to them. That he was skinny and immobile was all many of the assistants saw, but Riley thought he saw something the rest were missing.

As USC's offensive coordinator, Riley dragged himself north from Los Angeles every week. He liked the poise with which Brady maneuvered in the pocket, holding the ball until the last possible second, allowing his receivers to run their full routes before delivering. He loved the strength—and, more important, the nerve—with which Brady threw the deep out ball.

The deep out is the true measure of a passer. The receiver goes straight downfield and then breaks toward the sideline. The quarterback must throw an instant before the receiver breaks so that the ball will coincide with the receiver's turn back toward the line of scrimmage. It's a moment fraught with peril. If the quarterback throws the ball too soon, or too softly, the defensive back will be there to "jump the route," which is to say catch the ball on the dead run, going in the opposite direction, often for an easy touchdown. The deep out is so critical to the passing game that it even affects the way professional teams evaluate prospective defensive backs. They are judged on their "closing speed"—how fast they can cover the ground to a receiver in a burst from a standing start. One badly executed deep out, thrown toward a cornerback with superior closing speed, can end a season. A few of them can end a quarterback's career.

Riley saw Brady throw the deep out with an immense amount of confidence, both in his personal technique and in his teammates' ability to run their routes correctly and catch the ball. There was something about Tom Brady in which Riley believed, even though it wasn't anything he could time with a stopwatch or write down on a three-by-five card. There was no line on any form for loyalty or devotion, or the kind of charisma that engenders either one. Mike Riley loved football, and he loved football players; to him, that was explanation enough for why he wanted to recruit Tom Brady. He fit all the categories that were hardest to define.

Riley went back to USC and argued his case, over and over again, with the head coach, John Robinson. However, Robinson had already recruited two quarterbacks and wasn't in the market for another one. Riley pleaded his case vigorously, but in vain. Then he had to go back to San Mateo and tell the Bradys what had happened. He knew he was right, but nobody would listen. This wouldn't be the first time this happened to Mike Riley, who would spend the next five years as the Cassandra of Tom Brady's career. "I'll always think of him as the lost opportunity of my career," Riley says with a sigh.

Meanwhile, the recruiting process ground on. UCLA was interested for a while, but, while Brady was still deciding, they signed a quarterback named Cade McNown, so the Bradys eliminated the Bruins. The University of California seemed to have everything Tom wanted, and it was close enough that he and his father could keep their regular Sunday golf date. Tom was also interested in Illinois, but the campus looked gray and cold during his visit in December. So it was something of a surprise to his father when, a month later, Tom called him extolling the charm of Ann Arbor, Michigan, in January.

"I checked The Weather Channel," the elder Brady recalls. "And it was dreary and it was desolate, and it was snowy, and Tommy calls from the airport and says, 'Dad, this place is fabulous.' And I said, 'What?' I mean, in the winter, how is that different from Champaign, Illinois?"

Michigan had entered the picture late, probably because Illinois, also in the Big 10 Conference, had pursued Brady so ardently. At the start, the Bradys had mailed a tape to Michigan solely on the basis of its football program's undeniable historic aura—"those frigging winged helmets were so cool," Tom, Sr., says with a laugh. So, when a Wolverine defensive coordinator named Bill Harris began to recruit Tom, the family had taken him very seriously. The visit clinched it for Tom. All the lore surrounding Michigan football, and the fact that he would be competing at the top level with at least four other quarterbacks, made for an appealing challenge to his sharpened competitive instinct. The head coach, Gary Moeller, flew out to San Mateo to close the deal. Tom Brady signed a letter of intent to play at the University of Michigan; his father pretty much fell apart.

"My son," he says today, "my golfing partner, you know, he's cutting out. When he decided to go there, I started crying, and I cried for like forty-eight hours. It was like, 'He's turning his back on me and I still want to play golf on Sunday mornings.'

"So, two days later, we held hands and I said, 'Tommy, this is going to change our relationship.' And he says, 'Dad, I know. It has to.' I mean, he's fine, and this is so painful I have to go see a counselor for eight weeks. It was hard for me to let him make the decision to do that, but it was his life, he had to make the decision.

"But Michigan? You know, they've got six quarterbacks, you know? You're going to have to compete against the best. Cal says you'll start as a sophomore, junior, and as a senior. I'm saying to him that that's a no-brainer for me. But, if he'd have gone to Cal, he'd probably be a stockbroker today." And Tom Brady had this inscribed under his picture in the 1995 Junípero Serra High School yearbook: "If you want to play with the big boys, you've got to learn to play in the tall grass."

And, far away from the Avenue of the Fleas, on a wall in the Schembechler Room at the University of Michigan, the place where they bring in recruits like Tom Brady and drown them in mystique, as if in reply, there was a sign that read: THOSE WHO STAY WILL BE CHAMPIONS.

SEPTEMBER 18, 2005: CAROLINA 27, NEW ENGLAND 17
SEPTEMBER 25, 2005: NEW ENGLAND 23, PITTSBURGH 20
RECORD: 2-1

A professional game arrives first in its ancillary activities. Get there early enough in the day at a place such as Heinz Field in

Pittsburgh, with the fog just clearing the tops of the mountains and the propane fumes not yet rising from the parking lots, and you can see something like a city coming to life. Gradually, the music rises from a thousand corners, mingled in a cacophonous welter with the voices of all-sports talk radio as the sound of manufactured outrage mixes with the rising scent of barbecued meat. Footballs fly and flutter all around the petrified remains of a city's industrial base. (No C throws here, alas. All U grips and wobbly passes, tossed by men holding bottles in their other hands.) Old machine shops and loading docks, mottled with graffiti, stand mute witness to their new function as holding areas for the entertainment economy.

You don't need a tailgate to tailgate. The open trunk of your car will do just fine, or the top of a beer cooler, or a card table, or even a hibachi, right there on the asphalt. Only the people who park closest to the stadium, as early as they can, ever see the buses that bring the teams to play. The arrival of the team buses is almost an afterthought. Football teams arrive much more quietly than their game does.

It was the third game of the 2005 season, and already rather a critical one. A week earlier, the Patriots had lost, 27–17, at the Carolina Panthers. The New England offense had been an unbalanced mess, rushing for only thirty-nine yards. Brady had been forced to pass forty-four times. He spent most of the second half passing out of a shotgun offense, a formation in which the quarterback stands five yards behind the center rather than retreating into the pocket from under center.

He stands alone in the middle of the field. He's not bent over the offensive line, his bobbing head barely distinguishable from theirs, which must remain still or cost the team a false-start penalty. Just about the only thing you can do from a shotgun formation is pass, so the quarterback is never so distant from his teammates as he is in the shotgun, his importance not only emphasized, but also as stark and obvious as a tree in a pasture.

The shotgun was an innovation of the 1960s. The San Francisco 49ers won four of their first five games of the 1961 season with it, then lost their next one, and the shotgun was briefly dismissed as a gimmick. A decade later, however, Tom Landry brought it back in order to take advantage of the skills of Roger Staubach, and the shotgun became a staple part of most offenses at every level of the game. Quarterbacks now usually enter the NFL having played at least part of the time in the shotgun ever since high school.

"We saw Tom play some in the 'gun' at Michigan," Bill Belichick says. "It was usually in two-minute situations and like that. He was really good at reading coverages back there, and at adapting what he needed to do. Under center, you take five steps to throw the ball, and in the shotgun, you take two, to get the same timing on the route, provided that the ball is snapped where the quarterback can handle it."

Belichick sees the shotgun as a modern manifestation of the old single-wing formation. "It's what they used to call a short-punt formation," he explains. He also sees the advantages to it as well as its drawbacks. It does give the quarterback extra time to read the defenses and make his throw, but putting the quarterback in the shotgun is all but declaring that you've abandoned the idea of rushing the ball. And, in the mind of the defensive lineman, this is like ringing the dinner bell.

In the third quarter against Carolina, playing out of the shotgun at his own 33-yard line, Brady fumbled after being belted by Carolina defensive end Mike Rucker, who'd come roaring from the left side. On the replay, you could see Rucker dip his shoulder and then spin, speed following power following speed. He covered the ground to Brady stunningly fast and still had enough strength to deliver a fearful hit. The fumble led to the final Carolina touchdown. But Rucker was able to commit wholly to the effort only because he knew the Patriots were going to pass.

"Anytime you get one-dimensional," Brady explained, "it becomes too difficult to do anything. You can talk to any defense, and what they want to do first is to stop the run, because when you run the ball, you can control the tempo of the game."

One of the many gimcracks that the NFL employs to maintain "competitive balance" is giving winning teams in one season tough schedules in the next—and, conversely, giving weaker teams an easier ride. Seven of New England's first eight games were against teams that had made the playoffs the previous season. Today, in Pittsburgh, they were playing the team they'd defeated for the AFC championship the previous January. Losing to Pittsburgh after losing to Carolina would have put the Patriots in a deep hole right at the beginning of what had been reckoned to be one of the toughest schedules ever handed a defending Super Bowl champion.

The running game stalled again, and Brady had to throw the ball twenty-one times in the first half. Worse, in the course of the game, the Patriots suffered two critical injuries, losing two of their most important players for the season. Safety Rodney Harrison, a brutal, reckless hitter whose play had run through the defense for two seasons like an electric current, blew out his left knee. On television, you could see Brady on the sideline wince behind his face mask. Harrison was carted off, waving, on a truck.

The Patriots are notorious around the NFL for being shell-mouthed about injuries. Players are forbidden to discuss even their own. Other teams in the league complain that the Pats' required weekly injury reports usually are masterpieces of soggy generalizations. In the press box, when Harrison's injury was announced as a "leg," and his return as "questionable," the joke was that, had the Patriots been in charge at Ford's Theatre, Abraham Lincoln's wound would have been reported as "Head. His return is doubtful."

Then, in the second quarter, New England running back Kevin Faulk took a pitch from Brady toward the left side and then cut back to the middle for a short gain. Left tackle Matt Light got tangled up and went down, his leg broken. Adding to the tension, Belichick got into a strange wrangle with the Pittsburgh medical staff, angrily waving them away from his fallen player. The cart came out and ferried Light off, too. His return was likewise said to be "questionable."

For a right-handed quarterback, the left tackle is the most critical part of his pass protection, because the left tackle protects the quarterback's blind side from marauding defensive ends. Moreover, Light was a veteran, and one of the best-liked players on the team. It was Light who still remembered all his lines from the Visa commercial.

Now, the job of left tackle would be handed to Nick Kaczur, a huge rookie out of the University of Toledo who'd grown up playing hockey in the same town in Ontario that had produced Wayne Gretzky. That football was not as important in Kaczur's town as it is in this country is best illustrated by the fact that he lost most of his senior season to a teachers' strike. In, say, Texas, they probably would have fired all the teachers and played out the season anyway.

The left guard was another rookie, Logan Mankins, the team's first-round draft pick out of Fresno State, a cowpuncher off an enormous family spread deep in California's Catheys

Valley. For the foreseeable future, Brady's blind side would be protected by two rookies with four NFL games between them. By the beginning of the fourth quarter, the Patriots trailed the Steelers, 13–10, and Brady had been sacked three times. Then he got hot.

It began with a deep out to David Givens on the left side for fourteen yards. Then, Brady waited just long enough for Deion Branch to clear and hit him for eight more. A deep crossing route to Troy Brown got the Patriots into Pittsburgh territory at the 45-yard line, and then Brady hit Brown again for five more. The Patriots ran Corey Dillon up the middle, and then, with Brady in the shotgun, Dillon flattened a blitzing Steeler linebacker and gave Brady enough time to find Givens deep down the left sideline for thirty yards at the Pittsburgh 7. Dillon cracked over from there to give New England a 17–13 lead.

Brady was five for five on the drive for seventy-six yards. Moreover, the offensive line had seemingly found the downhill slope on the field. Brady put the ball in one spot, and then in another, and then in another again, always at the right time and always where the receivers could catch the ball, turn, and make a play. There was something inexorable about it, and the Pittsburgh defense looked flustered and helpless, caught in what seemed like a natural vortex. The acceleration increased when, after the Steelers couldn't move the ball, Brady hit four more passes in a row to set up Adam Vinatieri for a 35-yard field goal that pushed the Patriot lead to a full touchdown, at 20–13.

To its credit, the Steeler offense, with their second-year quarterback, Ben Roethlisberger, operating exclusively out of the shotgun, answered in kind. Pittsburgh took advantage of a long return of the ensuing Patriot kickoff, and of a pass interference play by New England's Chad Scott, to tie the game at 20–20 with a four-yard pass to Hines Ward with 1:25 left. On the Pittsburgh bench, running back Jerome Bettis looked at the clock and thought the Steelers had left Tom Brady too much time.

Starting at his own 38-yard line, Brady hit three more passes, giving him twelve in a row for the quarter, and moved the team just far enough so that Vinatieri could win the game from forty-three yards away, 23–20, the eighteenth game-winning field goal of Vinatieri's career, two of which, of course, won Super Bowls. There hadn't been such a happy marriage of mutual interest between a kicker and a quarterback in the NFL since old George Blanda, who used to kick and play quarterback for the Oakland Raiders, practiced alone.

"Honestly," Dan Koppen said, "in those situations, losing doesn't even come into our minds. We know [Tom's] going to make plays to get us victories. We know we have 12 back there and we just have to get him to good field position and get in range for Number 4."

It was a virtuoso performance—twelve for twelve with an important game on the line. But, with the running game balky and Light apparently gone for the year, this was shaping up as a season in which Tom Brady would be forced into a position contrary to the competitive persona he'd built for himself, consciously, one teammate at a time and then one team at a time. He would have to be so individually excellent that his teammates might be overlooked. That was not the place he'd carved out. Another problem with metaphors is that, at the worst times, they'll break down on you.

2 | THE BIG HOUSE

OCTOBER 2, 2005: SAN DIEGO 41, NEW ENGLAND 17
OCTOBER 9, 2005: NEW ENGLAND 31, ATLANTA 28
RECORD: 3-2

A WEEK AFTER Adam Vinatieri beat the Steelers, the Patriots played the San Diego Chargers at home in Foxborough. They had won twenty-one consecutive games in Foxborough's Gillette Stadium, a monument to the persistence of the team's owners, the Kraft family.

It's a big, angular place, full of terraces and decks, and wide patios where people congregate when they find the walk back to their seats from the beer stands too taxing. Most newer American stadiums have these huge open areas, so, at odd moments during the game, there are always a considerable number of open seats because the people who paid $150 for them are milling about somewhere else in the complex. Between the club-seat dilettantes and the corporate cowboys in the luxury suites, and the ordinary ticket holders wandering and mooing about in the various open spaces, the average professional football game in the average professional football stadium can look almost like an afterthought. But it's one whose patrons are as rigidly segregated by class as were the people who sailed on the *Titanic*—except that, in this case, the steerage folks are on top, way up in the thin air, where not even the beer vendors dare wander.

This stratification can have a deadening effect on the atmosphere, so much so that some fundamentalist Patriots fans have taken to summoning up muted nostalgia for Gillette's predecessor, a dog-ugly pile of concrete and steel thrown up virtually overnight in 1970 for $6.7 million. It had three names—Schaefer Stadium, Sullivan Stadium, and Foxboro Stadium—because the team's economic status fluctuated so wildly through the years. Only 5,000-odd patrons got to sit in actual seats. The remaining 55,000 were relegated to fifteen miles of aluminum benches, a true proctological delight during games in the winter. The cheap stadium inspired cheap behavior. In 1976, during a Monday night game against the New York Jets, one fan collapsed with a heart attack. While paramedics were treating the man, another fan urinated on them. The local town fathers had always had their doubts about their biweekly visits from the region's Ostrogothic class, and now Foxborough was a national embarrassment. They howled so loudly that the franchise was effectively banned from ABC's *Monday Night Football* package for more than a decade.

When the Krafts bought the team, they made a concerted effort to run the barbarians out of the joint. The stadium remained an architectural grotesque, but there was less mutant behavior to turn a bad experience into a miserable one. In fact, the best night in that house of horrors was its last one, when New England played Oakland in an AFC divisional playoff game on January 19, 2002. Coincidentally, it was also this game that cemented the reputations of both Adam Vinatieri and Tom Brady, as though one of the the first things they could do as Patriots was to absolve the stadium, and the franchise it held, from all their bad fortune and all their past sins.

It snowed throughout the game, softening the edges of the ungainly old corral. However, the conditions made actual football a perilous business. By halftime, the favored Raiders had hacked out a 7–0 lead, and both teams had combined for only 238 yards total offense. In the third quarter, Oakland managed two field goals to New England's one and led 13–3 going into the final fifteen minutes of the game.

At this point, Brady began to play at another level—one only a couple of inches above the snowy turf. It was as though he had found some inner traction while everyone around him still struggled simply to stay upright. On New England's next possession, he completed nine straight passes, none of them for more than fourteen yards, to move the Patriots from their own 33-yard line to the Oakland 6. He then burst up the middle himself for a touchdown, losing his footing only when he spiked the ball ferociously in the end zone and ended up looking like a goat on ice skates.

With the score a dodgy 13–10 and the weather worsening by the moment, the two teams essentially fell on each other for the next five minutes, until New England got the ball back on its own 46-yard line with 2:06 to play. Operating out of the shotgun, a dicey proposition in the snow, Brady hit one pass, then ran for a first down at the Oakland 42. On the next play, and with less than two minutes left, Raider defensive back Charles Woodson came through untouched and clobbered Brady. The ball popped away, and linebacker Greg Biekert fell on it, apparently salting the game away for the Raiders. Barring, of course, an outburst of authentic NFL gibberish.

The Patriots appealed the play, and a referee named Walt Coleman ducked under a tiny awning—it was one way to get out of the snow, at any rate—to watch it again. It seemed that Brady had been bringing his arm forward, and that he had not "tucked" it back against his body. It didn't matter how much it looked like a fumble. It didn't matter that you could have shown the tape to cannibal tribesmen in New Guinea and *they* would have thought it was a fumble. Under the penumbral clauses of something called the "tuck rule," it was determined that Brady had thrown an incomplete pass. Coleman reversed the ruling on the field, and New England got the ball back. Brady hit receiver David Patten for thirteen yards, and, after Brady had pushed the ball forward another yard by himself, Vinatieri hit one of the greatest field goals in NFL history, a 45-yarder that cut a low line through the snow and over the crossbar to tie the game and send it into overtime.

Oakland never got the ball. The Patriots won the coin toss and moved sixty-one yards in the next 8:29. Brady hit six in a row. His receivers—especially a little running back named J. R. Redmond—suddenly seemed to be playing with him just above the snowy surface. The Patriots moved all the way to the Oakland 5-yard line, and, when Vinatieri hit another field goal to win the game, center Lonie Paxton ran into the end zone and, flat on his back, began making frenzied snow angels. The Patriots spent their final moments in the old stadium like kids set loose on the playground during a snow day. The last memories of the joint were happy ones. They sold the old aluminum benches for big money that went to charity.

Four years later, on the first weekend of October, there was bright sunshine and it was seventy-three degrees, and people left their seats to walk around. There wasn't much to watch anyway. San Diego came in and took the Patriots for a ride, 41–17. The game was tied, 17–17, at halftime, but the New England defense simply broke down thereafter, surrendering 134 yards to the Chargers' star running back, LaDainian Tomlinson. The San Diego running game chewed up the clock; the Chargers put the game out of reach with two drives that took up almost nine minutes of the third quarter.

Brady hit nineteen of thirty-two passes for 224 yards and a touchdown, but he was less relevant to the game than was the New England defense, which found itself on the field for far too long a time. Midway through the fourth quarter, Brady missed David Givens and found San Diego defensive back Bhawoh Jue. The interception meant little—New England was trailing 34–17 at the time—but it ended Brady's day. The magnitude of the loss might have accounted for a strange interlude three days later.

In his postgame press conference, San Diego's head coach, Marty Schottenheimer, by way of expressing admiration for the Patriots' ability to replace key players they had lost over the previous three seasons, innocently wondered how long New England could keep doing it. However, seventy-two hours later, at his usual Wednesday press conference, Brady still appeared nettled by what had seemed to most people who heard it a kind of compliment to the Patriot franchise from a coach whose team had just pummeled New England in its own stadium.

"When an opposing coach comes out and says stuff in the fourth game of the season," Brady said, "you take it for what it's worth. We won three of the last four Super Bowls, and I think we realize what we're all about. If people want to write us off, that's fine by us—go for it—but I don't think that's the wisest thing to do, I think we have too many guys with too much character."

He looked dead serious, his eyes alive beneath a Patriots baseball cap. "I just assumed you talk about your own team," Brady continued. "You don't talk about our team. He has no business talking about our team. He's not our coach. We'll let our coach talk about our team."

Either Brady completely misunderstood Schottenheimer or he was using the moment to send a message to the people in his own locker room. He doesn't respect us. Nobody respects us. On the face of it, it was absurd. Ever since Brady and the Patriots began their remarkable run in 2001, New England has been singled out, not merely as a model sports franchise but also as a model business operation. In her book *Confidence: How Winning Streaks and Losing Streaks Begin and End*, Rosabeth Moss Kanter of the Harvard Business School writes, "Sports is an ideal realm in which to see confidence at work, in the games themselves and in the businesses that surround them," and she repeatedly cites the Patriots as an example of how success breeds upon itself. To say that the Patriots had been disrespected, or that in complimenting the New England front office, Marty Schottenheimer was denigrating the players on the field was preposterous on its face.

But "respect" has become a useful trope in ginning up one's teammates. It is the sporty equivalent of all those politicians who campaign as common folk against the "elitists" on the other ticket. Every team plays more freely as an underdog, and under Brady, for so many years an underdog himself, the Patriots made their first statement by overcoming long odds, particularly against St. Louis in their January 2002 Super Bowl victory. This is still an essential part of the team's competitive DNA, for good and ill, three world championships later. But it also seems to resonate deeply in their quarterback. There's an echo of another time and another place, where all talk of respect wasn't rhetorical at all. A place in an old industrial city in Michigan, where muscle labor gradually gave way to higher education, and where football seems like the regularly scheduled eruption of some natural force from the earth.

Professional football stadiums seem to have been dropped where they are. You can see their enormity right from the sidewalk. Even the ones—such as Heinz Field in Pittsburgh—that are tucked into urban neighborhoods appear to have been placed there by some heedless outside force. At best, a pro football team is bestowed upon a city. At worst, it's inflicted.

In college towns, though, like Ann Arbor, the stadiums seem to rise organically from the earth. From the sidewalk, Michigan Stadium looks broad but unremarkable. The press box is only a short distance up from the sidewalk. Once you are inside, however, the size of the place is nearly surreal. It goes almost straight down into the earth, far enough these days to seat 107,501 people. Ringed by tall and gentle hillocks, the stadium seems part of the essential geology of the place, a city long-buried and brought to light.

On game days, particularly the bright ones, before winter comes behind the gray and muscled skies of the upper Midwest, the old Victorian piles that used to house the millworkers and now bear the Greek monograms of fraternities are beer-loud and raucous, even five hours before kickoff. Dyspeptic alt rockers contend with—and invariably lose to—the brachiosaurs of classic rock. (In a concert hall, Uncle Tupelo might play AC/DC to a draw, but off the tailgate of a car while people drink beer out of funnels, it's absolutely no contest.) And, above it all, the stentorian opening notes of the greatest college fight song of all:

Hail! to the victors valiant
Hail! to the conqu'ring heroes . . .

It booms out of open windows and from the insides of pickup trucks. It echoes down the alleys. It rises and falls and rises again, dozens of simultaneous choruses from dozens of different places, as ubiquitous as the breezes that carry it as you walk up the hill toward the stadium. And, at an abandoned rail yard at the intersection of Fifth and Hill, somebody cranks it up as a bus turns the corner. Inside, burly young men, uncomfortable in their shirts and ties as the sun floods through the windows of the bus, look stolidly ahead and turn up the volume of their iPods while the people on the sidewalk sing all the louder.

This is where Tom Brady came to play quarterback—an old college town where, on five or six Saturdays each year, everything surrenders to football in such a massive and gloriously romantic way that the brutal pragmatism inherent in the sport can get lost in the autumn sunshine and drowned out entirely by the marching band. The promise of a Saturday afternoon like this one is that you can beat the game that beats on you the rest of the week, and it is a golden promise.

"My head feels like it's full of blood and cotton," says the protagonist of *If I Don't Six*, the football novel by Elwood Reid. "I've got one over on them, taken their best shot and walked away. Suddenly, I love this whole fucking game and I know why I'm doing this. Because I can."

Brady was looking for tall grass and big dogs, and he found more of both than he'd even planned. When he and his parents went east to Michigan at the beginning of his freshman year, they stopped for dinner in a campus joint richly festooned with pictures of Michigan football greats. "He told me that, one day, he was going to have people in that place know who he was," Galynn Brady recalls. And, one day, they would, but destiny doesn't always walk a straight line.

The whole thing started to get strange the summer before Brady came to Ann Arbor. His father got a phone call from Bill Harris, the assistant coach who'd recruited Tommy for the Wolverines. "Bill says to me, well, I've got good news and bad news," the elder Brady recalls. "The good news is that we're going to play golf sooner than this next summer, and the bad news is that I'm no longer here at Michigan." Harris had taken a job as the defensive coordinator at Stanford. A month later Gary Moeller, the head coach, got in a bizarre saloon hooley with his wife and was fired. Brady hadn't yet thrown a pass or lifted a weight at Michigan, and he'd already lost the coach who'd sold him on the place and the coach on whose behalf he'd been sold.

"This is a month after he signed, and the two people that wanted him there are gone," says his father. "And he's screwed, but he didn't know how screwed he was."

Moeller's replacement was Lloyd Carr, a Michigan lifer, an All-State quarterback who'd left Riverview High School to play at Missouri, staying there just long enough to be the backup quarterback on the team that won the 1966 Sugar Bowl. However, Carr ultimately had transferred back to Northern Michigan University. After graduating in 1968, he'd coached at a number of high schools around the state, and as an assistant at both Eastern Michigan and Illinois before joining Bo Schembechler's staff at Ann Arbor in 1979.

"My first recollection of Tom was during a scrimmage in fall practice, and he was with the third team," says Carr. "They kept blitzing him and he kept standing in there and throwing the ball right on the money. I don't know what he weighed back then—185 maybe. But he got beat up pretty good that day, and you could tell he was really competitive and real tough."

Brady sat out his first year at Michigan as a redshirt. In 1996, in what was his freshman season of eligibility, he played in only two games, completing three of the five passes he threw for a total of twenty-six yards. The first pass he ever threw as a college quarterback was to a UCLA linebacker who brought it all the way back for a touchdown.

At the same time, Brady was settling into the university and, as would be the case throughout his life, building around him a community of people who found themselves invested in him on a number of levels beyond the athletic. "I first met him as a freshman in August 1995," recalls Brad Canale, an Ann Arbor businessman who works in a mentoring program that Michigan sets up for its athletes. Brady had been assigned to Canale when he arrived at the university. "We met the first day he was on campus, and it was obvious that he was smart, but he had a certain awareness of what was going on around him. I didn't get that sense of pullback that you get from young athletes when you meet them for the first time. Over that Labor Day weekend, I called and left him a message, and he called me back, which is fairly unusual for an eighteen-year-old, and he apologized for the delay in calling me back, which is *very* unusual for an eighteen-year-old."

Before what would be his sophomore year as a football player, as he prepared to make a run at the starting quarterback's position, Brady suffered an attack of appendicitis that required him to be hospitalized. He wound up losing thirty pounds that he could not afford to lose. He was sick, and he was emotionally battered. As a freshman, he'd been assigned to Greg Harden, a counselor in the athletic department.

"My first impression was that Tom was a classic quarterback, maybe a little prettier than most," says Harden. "I knew him as well as I knew any of my first-year students. A year later, as he was trying to make his breakthrough into the lineup, he walks into my office and he says, 'I need help.' And I say, Well, *that's* different. He said that he'd been quitting and giving up on himself, and he said, 'That's not me.' He's using all the resources here, and that's not the norm for football players. So he tells me that he's going to be the starting quarterback at Michigan, and I'm looking at him, and I'm thinking, Okay, I'm not going to rain on his parade, but he's all broke down, and emotionally worn out. So I tell him that what I could do was promise that you'll never quit on yourself."

More than anything else, Brady was looking for someone with whom he could create a plan, someone to demonstrate the techniques he could use to solve his own problems, the way Tom Martinez had shown him the techniques for throwing the ball that he had worked so diligently to hone, the way his father had shown him the techniques for dealing with men who were older than he was.

"The kid shows up here, and it's a dark time," Harden says. "All I could tell him was the truth. He had to decide for himself that he was going to be the best quarterback on the team and that he would have to do it for himself. And, when I tell him that our work is going to be centered on the man he was going to become, this guy begins to believe without proof that I can make him a better man."

Brady was looking for something that worked, and someone who could show him how it worked. Harden was more than willing to invest himself in someone who was obviously ready to invest so much of himself. "He commits wholeheartedly to the program, and I can think of only two players that did that— Tom Brady and Desmond Howard [a receiver and kick returner who won the Heisman Trophy at Michigan in 1991]."

In that year's spring camp, Brady found himself slotted in behind the starter, Scott Dreisbach, and the backup, Brian Griese, whose father, Bob, had been the star quarterback for the Miami Dolphins during that dynastic period in the 1970s when the Dolphins became the only team in NFL history to finish an entire season, including the Super Bowl, without a loss.

The competition at the camp was ferocious. The coaches again were struck by Brady's ability to move the chains, and by his willingness to hang in the pocket until the precise moment the ball needed to be thrown. (This sold him to his teammates on a more visceral level. The fundamental bona fides for any player is his willingness to risk injury to finish the play.) He clearly beat out Dreisbach, and when Griese got suspended for throwing a barstool through a saloon window in the middle of camp, it seemed the starting job was his.

"He competed very well in the spring," says Lloyd Carr.

Carr's situation was both unique and uncomfortable. He had gotten the job under bizarre circumstances, and was far from secure in it. At Michigan, at least since Bo Schembechler left the sidelines, coaching positions were very much temp jobs. In 1989, for example, when the basketball coach, Bill Frieder, was revealed to have been negotiating during the season with Arizona State, Schembechler fired him on the spot, elevating Steve Fisher to the position of interim head coach. Fisher didn't get the job permanently until after he'd led the Wolverines to that season's national championship. Carr was learning his new job on the fly, and it's clear that he never found a way that was both smart and graceful to finesse the matter of the quarterback position.

To Brady's considerable surprise, Griese was designated the Michigan starter. There were rumors that his father, who'd moved on to become ABC's lead college football color commentator, had thrown his weight around. This shook Brady, whose view of football as essentially a meritocratic enterprise is profound. For the first time in his career, a hint of being a disposable commodity rather than a football player had appeared, and it worried him. He didn't quite know how to express his dissatisfaction, and, perhaps making the whole matter even more difficult, he was not without his allies within the Michigan athletic department.

"The problem here was that Tom was always a lot smarter than the people who were coaching him," says Brad Canale. On more than one occasion, Brady would say, he would be called to the sidelines by Carr between plays.

"He's telling me stuff I already know," Brady would tell Canale.

With Griese starting and Brady as his backup, the Wolverines went 12–0 in 1997, edging Washington in the Rose Bowl and winning the school's first national football championship in forty-nine years. Brady appeared in four games that season. He completed twelve of fifteen passes for 103 yards. Griese was graduating, and the starting job apparently was Brady's if he wanted it. By now, though, he wasn't sure that he did. While Brady never had complained to his parents, he eventually told his father that he thought he might be stymied at Michigan. Brady even talked to Carr about it in the middle of the championship season. "In college," explains his father, who often sounds like a man who's brought his faith along as a not altogether adequate guide to something as secular as football, "you don't expect to have several sets of rules. You expect to be treated like everyone else."

Brady began talking about transferring home to Cal. His father was torn. On the one hand, if Tommy transferred to Cal, he'd get his Sunday golf partner back. On the other hand, his son seemed to like Michigan as a school as much as he liked it for football. He was enjoying his classes, moving toward a concentration in business. (In a 2001 interview, Brady's friend and teammate Jason Kapsner recalled Brady fuming at a grade that came in lower than he'd expected.) He was doing volunteer work at Mott's Children's Hospital the way a number of Michigan athletes (including Brian Griese) had done before. His social life was vast and impressive. As they talked, his father realized that, whatever might happen in the locker room, Tommy still wanted to go to school at the University of Michigan.

Tom already had rehearsed a speech to give his son, although his son had kept playing him out of the opportunity to deliver it. You can still hear the echoes of it, however, years later. "You know," Tom Brady, Sr., says, "people's careers come to an end at various times. Some come to an end in sixth grade, and some come to an end after nine years in the pros. But they're all going to come to an end. So the end of an athletic career isn't the end of the world. It was Tommy's original goal to get through an academic institution and be treated fairly." He left the decision to remain at Michigan up to his son who, ultimately, would have to judge the fairness of it all himself.

Lloyd Carr wasn't so sure which way Brady was leaning. "I was in a staff meeting, and I told people, you know, Tom's going to leave," Carr recalls. "And he comes in and he tells me that he's going to stay and show me what kind of quarterback he is.

"Later, in a conversation with his dad, I found out that, while I thought his dad would say, Okay, leave and come home, his father had told him, 'It's your decision, and whatever decision you make, I'll support.' I always thought that was a remarkable thing for a father to do. In most cases, the father is saying, 'Leave.'"

It was all the more remarkable because neither Tom nor Galynn was entirely sure what Carr was up to regarding their son. They'd been coming to Michigan from San Mateo for as many games as they could manage, often just to watch Tommy warm up on the sideline. They were getting much the same education in the icy-hearted side of football that their son was, and not just because the physical risks of the game seemed to grow geometrically with the size of the players and the size of the crowds. (Once they watched Tommy get carried groggily off the field, and Galynn Brady remembers that moment as the one in which watching her son play football stopped being what she'd describe as fun.)

Nevertheless, at home in the spring and summer of 1998, preparing for his junior season, Brady was clearly the Michigan starter. There was an extra edge to the way he prepared himself. The faculty at Serra regularly saw him in the mornings, running with his headphones down the alameda. In addition, Tom Brady added discreet breaking and entering to his training regimen.

Driving back to Ann Arbor after a former teammate's wedding in Chicago, Brady realized that Michigan would open the upcoming season at Notre Dame—not an ordinary road game. A football Saturday at Notre Dame is what the Roman Catholic Church does for lunatic alumni now that it no longer launches Crusades. Brady had no intention of being deafened by echoes rung down from Wherever. He would not be blindsided by lore. He decided to stop in South Bend in order to get the feel of Notre Dame Stadium.

Arriving in the early evening, he found a gate unlocked and walked in, roaming the old concrete staircases all the way to the topmost rim. Brady then walked back down to the gate through which he'd entered. It was locked. He tried all the gates. They were all locked. He realized he was facing a future of unfortunate headlines: MICHIGAN QUARTERBACK ARRESTED AT NOTRE DAME was the best of them.

Brady wandered the stadium as night fell, looking for some other way out. Finally, risking an even worse headline— MICHIGAN QUARTERBACK FALLS TO DEATH FROM NOTRE DAME STADIUM—he slung a ladder over a wall, hopped onto a small roof, and leaped from there to the ground. He beat it out of town very quickly. He returned to the scene of the crime on September 5, and the Wolverines lost, probably on the merits, 36–20.

Even as Brady and the Michigan team struggled in defense of their national championship, both he and the team found themselves entangled in the kind of politics that have nothing to do with football, but everything to do with a major college's football program. Having patiently waited behind Brian Griese after a competition that at least had begun as a fair fight, Brady was battling for his job again, this time against booster yokel- ism and the shadowy attraction of a local high school reputa- tion. It would be almost two full seasons before the increasingly strange battle ended.

Drew Henson had been a phenom from Brighton, not far from Ann Arbor. Already the subject of a profile in *Sports Illus- trated*, Henson was a good enough quarterback that a number of college coaches promised in their recruitment of him not to bring in another quarterback for at least two years. (Now, nobody should ever trust a promise made by a coach during recruiting any further than that person can throw Michigan Stadium, but the coaches bent to Henson's demands, a prece- dent that would haunt both them and Tom Brady.) He also was good enough that star high school receivers—including a big, flashy kid from Chicago named David Terrell—committed to Michigan specifically to play with Henson.

Moreover, Henson was a good enough baseball player that the New York Yankees signed him to a $4.5 million deal that would kick in whenever his career at Michigan was over. The talk around campus was that Michigan had promised Henson the starting job as a way to keep from losing a local hero to the undeniable blandishments of George Steinbrenner's wallet. There was also tremendous pressure being brought to bear on Carr and his staff to elevate the local hero over Brady before Henson had ever played a game. The coaching staff was in a public dither; Carr did neither his team nor himself any favors when, shortly before the Notre Dame game, he said in a press conference that Henson "is without question the most talented quarterback I've been around."

Most football coaches do everything they can to avoid "quarterback controversies." The position is central to everything the team does. Everyone—coaches and teammates alike—has to invest so much trust that uncertainty over the quarterback can rupture a team's entire fabric. And the easiest way to undermine it is for whispers to start in the locker room—and then for those whispers to be amplified in the general public—that the incumbent quarterback isn't up to the job, that maybe it's time to give the other guy a chance. It's for this reason that coaches ruefully comment there's never anyone more popular than a backup quarterback.

Quarterback controversies tear even veteran teams apart. In fact, just as Tom Brady was beginning his career at Serra, the team at Washington State University nearly came to blows when the locker room was split between one group of players who supported a pair of veteran quarterbacks and another group who had aligned themselves with a gifted freshman named Drew Bledsoe.

Not even professional teams are immune. In New England, for example, Steve Grogan played long enough to have been cast in both roles. He started out as the young quarterback who people demanded replace the battered veteran Jim Plunkett, and became the battered veteran some wished young Tony Eason would replace. And, as an added twist, when Eason evinced a tendency to turn turtle in the face of a pass rush, there were cries for his head from inside and outside the Patriot locker room, and loud calls for Eason to be replaced by the tough, plucky veteran—Steve Grogan.

This is the kind of destructive nonsense that whipsawed Carr and his staff. Having done nothing to quell the rising controversy, the Michigan staff seemed unable—or unwilling—to deal with the forces they'd unleashed. Michigan followed up the loss to Notre Dame with another loss, this one at home to Syracuse. Brady threw an interception early in the game and was immediately benched by Carr as 107,000 fans cheered. The Orange quarterback, Donovan McNabb, personally took the Wolverines apart. Henson rolled up some meaningless yardage in the fourth quarter of the rout.

Though at the center of it all, Brady kept his own counsel and started for the rest of the season. However, it was significant that his teammates were vocally (if anonymously) in his corner, occasionally venting to the student-run *Michigan Daily* on his behalf. The season turned for good in a November game against Penn State. During the preceding week, Brady, ordinarily a smiling encyclopedia of banality concerning his opponents, spent a good deal of time lamenting the difficulties he suspected Michigan would have moving the ball against the Nittany Lions. On Saturday, however, he and the Wolverines crushed Penn State, 27–0, the first time the Lions had been shut out in eleven years. Michigan put the game away near the end of the first half when Brady hit four passes in a row for sixty-six yards to lead a long touchdown drive, including a delicate touch pass to Tai Streets, who'd run a fade pattern toward the far corner of the Penn State end zone.

"This," Brady told the press later, "was the most enthusiastic we've been in eight weeks. We were sick of people saying we couldn't do things." That he had been one of those people as recently as the previous Wednesday passed largely without comment. He was beginning to develop a canny gift for talking past his immediate audience and into the locker room. The press, as Sherlock Holmes once advised Dr. Watson, is a useful instrument, if one knows how to use it.

While Michigan failed to defend its national championship, it put up a respectable 10–3 record. Brady completed 61 percent of his passes for 2,636 yards and fifteen touchdowns, and he set Michigan records for both attempts and completions. Against Ohio State, Michigan's traditional rival, Brady put the ball in the air a school record fifty-six times, completing thirty-one of those passes in a 31–16 loss.

At one point in that game, when Michigan had closed to within eleven points of the Buckeyes, Brady loudly reminded the Ohio State players that Michigan had beaten them eight of the previous nine years, despite the fact that the Buckeyes had been favored in most of those games. Michigan lost anyway, but, clearly, in woofing on behalf of his team, Brady felt confident that he'd established himself, finally, as the starting quarterback for the rest of his time at Michigan. The brief Drew Henson experiment seemed to be over. But nobody had reckoned with the possibility that Lloyd Carr and his staff could take an uncomfortable situation and make it an impossible one.

It began in the Citrus Bowl, in which Michigan would face Arkansas, a quick, mobile bunch who'd played much better than had been expected in the Southeastern Conference. Suddenly, Arkansas's speed on defense seemed to reenergize the debate concerning the Michigan quarterbacks. Henson was considered more mobile than Brady. He certainly was faster in a sprint. (Almost anyone on the roster was.) On the first Michigan possession, Brady drove the team into position for a field goal. Then, like a manager changing pitchers, Carr benched Brady in favor of Henson on the next possession, just long enough for a gimmick play to fail. The next time Michigan had the ball, Brady was back under center.

He played the rest of the game, throwing two damaging interceptions but driving the Wolverines twice for touchdowns in the face of his own mistakes and a 31–24 deficit. Ironically, given the pregame punditry, on the first of the critical drives Brady made key plays with his legs—first by stepping out of what appeared to be a sure sack and completing a crucial pass, then by running the ball himself to convert another third-down play. Even the Arkansas players were struck by how deeply Brady involved himself in the game. At one point, after a Razorback defensive lineman named Sacha Lancaster smacked down a Michigan runner, Brady helped Lancaster up. "Good hit," Brady said. Lancaster was so struck by the moment that he talked about it extensively after the game.

The game-winning touchdown was a pass to DiAllo Johnson. Brady, standing in the shotgun, noticed that two men had lined up in coverage against Johnson. He correctly determined that one of the two men was going to come after him on a blitz, thereby leaving one man to stay with Johnson down the sideline. Hit just as he threw the ball, Brady feathered the pass to Johnson, who described it as being "like a loaf of bread" descending into his hands, right at the goal line for a 21-yard touchdown. Scoring 21 points in the game's final four minutes, Michigan won, 45–31.

However, Henson's brief appearance early in the game was enough to set off the quarterback controversy once again. Throughout the off-season, there were a number of stories floated, all of them anonymous, that Henson's game had made great strides while Brady's had stayed pretty much the same. The pressure from influential alumni to play Henson intensified. Spring practice occasioned stories on the situation in a number of national publications, including *Sports Illustrated*. Nothing helped. Even Brady's election as a tri-captain that August was interpreted—probably correctly—as a vote of confidence from his teammates and against Henson.

Matters got worse when Carr and his staff devised a plan for the upcoming season that seemed surreal. Brady would start every game. Henson would play the second quarter. Then, at halftime, the coaches would decide who had earned the right to play the rest of the game. It was an invitation to disaster that seemed to have been borrowed from the playbook the Marx Brothers put together for the final reel of *Horse Feathers*.

Tom Brady was hurt, the way he had been when Griese had gotten the job. But this time he also was bristling with righteous anger. Which was nothing compared with what happened back home. The Bradys lost whatever use they'd had left for Lloyd Carr. "That was bullshit," says his father. "How do I say that nicely? Again, he was screwed." In Ann Arbor, the support system with which Tom Brady had surrounded himself was agog.

"I had become biased toward Tom, and I saw how painful this was for him," recalls Greg Harden, Brady's athletic counselor. "We saw that all he could do was to establish for the record that, when he was on the field, there was nobody better. We talked about how he had to trust his instincts, and how he had to fight back against any feelings of betrayal. For any human being, that's when it gets tough. All he'd fought back against—losing the starting job, and appendicitis, being deep down the depth chart because he weighed 160 pounds or whatever."

Once again, Brady and Harden devised strategies that kept Brady focused on what he needed to do on the field while avoiding the kind of corrosive bitterness that could change Brady into a person he would not recognize.

"So, on Fridays, before Saturday games, we'd have a come-to-Jesus meeting," Harden recalls, "because he thinks he might play tentatively because he could lose the job, and he's acting like somebody's doing him a favor, and that allowed me to challenge him and say, 'This is your team. Start acting like it.'"

At that moment, it was within Tom Brady's power to blow up the Michigan team. He had earned the respect of most of his teammates, and most football observers believed the system Carr had devised, ostensibly to keep both quarterbacks happy, was guaranteed to please neither one of them. There was now a blazing controversy, searching only for a focal point around which to organize itself. To the surprise of many people, and the great relief of Lloyd Carr, Brady turned down the role.

"I don't think either of them was happy with it," says Lloyd Carr. "I expected they would handle it in a way that wouldn't divide the team, but Tom, as a captain and as a fifth-year senior, I know it had to be tougher on him. I wouldn't have done it that way if I didn't know the kind of person he was."

In retrospect, Carr seems to have been thrown into a crash course in all the political pressures that go along with running a football program the size of Michigan's, many of which have nothing to do with what goes on between the sidelines. (If Drew Henson had been from Brighton, Texas, it's unlikely the heat on Carr would have been half as intense.) It just happened to be Tom Brady who nearly got hung up forever on Lloyd Carr's learning curve.

"I think the only word for what he did was 'grace,'" says Brad Canale, Brady's mentor at Michigan. "I'm sure it has to do with how he was raised and so forth, but I don't think he had it in him to disrupt the team. I don't think he'd even consider it."

Brady went on being a teammate, grinding in the film room, and maintaining an even public disposition, but the weird experiment imposed upon him took a toll. Oddly enough, the difficult position further cemented his standing among his peers. At some level, all football players are in tacit alliance with one another against their coaches, and the unfairness with which Brady was treated made him more deeply one of them. They admired his ability to continue to work as hard as he did in the face of what seemed not only a glaring personal inequity but also a tactical football bungle, and they respected his efforts to keep the controversy to a minimum. His family, however, felt no such restraint.

"Tommy has a very highly developed sense of deserving what you work for," says his sister Nancy. "He'd pretty plainly earned the job."

"The way he was getting jacked around," his father recalls, "I didn't really consider, seriously, the possibility of his having an NFL career. I just wanted him to have a good college career, so he'd look back and say, 'That was a happy experience.' Once in a while, piecemeal, things would come out that, if I'd been there, and I'd have known about it, I would have punched Lloyd Carr in the nose."

The experiment lasted five weeks. Every time Henson took the field, he got an ovation from the local fans. It looked as if Carr had won his gamble. With Brady as the second-half starter in most of the games, the Wolverines stood at 5–0, having kicked off the season by beating Notre Dame in Ann Arbor. In the sixth week, they played Michigan State, their in-state rival from just up the road in East Lansing. For this game, Carr reversed his pattern, starting Brady in the first half and Henson in the second. The latter threw an interception that put Michigan down 27–10, and, in the fourth quarter, Carr brought Brady back in to try to salvage the game. The chains began to move. Brady nearly pulled Michigan all the way back, hitting thirty of forty-one passes for 285 yards as the Wolverines suffered their first loss of the season, 34–31.

Almost immutably, with Brady as its catalyst, the chemistry

had established itself. Whatever Henson's obvious athletic abilities, it was Brady in whom most of the team had invested their confidence. He was the one Carr rode hardest when a practice went sour, and, when that happened, it was Brady who would ride his teammates, who took it because he was so completely one of them.

At the same time, he wasn't full of himself. He'd do an imitation of Al Pacino's Tony Montana that sounded like Donald Duck, and he'd laugh at himself as loudly as they would. Once, in a game against Penn State, Brady faked an injury to buy time, a football trick dating back to leather helmets and coaches named Pudge. Brady buried himself in the part, wandering off toward the Michigan sideline like a man with a wooden leg. His teammates tried hard not to convulse. This guy, they thought, better make it to the NFL because he'd never get work as an actor.

They'd watched him work. They'd watched him handle an unprecedented career path without disrupting what they were trying to accomplish. They'd watched the way the team moved when he was running it. An unspoken emotional plebiscite was taken, and there was a landslide winner. Even David Terrell, the hyperemotional wide receiver who'd come to Ann Arbor specifically to catch passes from Drew Henson, was struck by Brady's coolness in the huddle where, now, there was no controversy over who the Michigan quarterback should be.

"The way I looked at it," Brady says today, "I was getting a chance to play, which I hadn't had my first two years. All I wanted was the opportunity, and I still had that. All I wanted was the chance to play, and to share some camaraderie, to share some memories with so many other guys."

Carr stayed with his grand design for one more game—a 35–29 loss to Illinois in Ann Arbor in which Henson again made a critical error. Afterward, it was announced that Tom Brady would be the starting Michigan quarterback for the rest of the season. The team won its last four regular-season games, coming from behind in the last two of them—a tough win at Penn State and a victory at home, 24–17 over Ohio State, in what would be Brady's last trip through that annual ritualized collision. His teammates noticed in the latter game that, at some point, Brady had begun calling the plays he wanted to call and dismissing ones he didn't with a signifying glare at the sideline. Nobody in his huddle questioned that he'd earned the right.

Michigan was invited to play in the Orange Bowl on New Year's Day against Alabama. The Wolverines were something of an underdog. The Crimson Tide was a speedy, veteran team—not unlike Arkansas from the previous season but manifestly more talented—and they were led by All-American running back Shaun Alexander. By comparison, Michigan was reckoned a bunch of plodders, easily exploited to the outside and deep through their secondary. Their best chance, it was said, was to hold the score down by slowing the pace of the game. At its start, Alabama stacked the line of scrimmage, daring Brady and the Wolverines to pass.

In response, Brady determined to use Terrell as a weapon. He hit him for 57 yards and a touchdown in the first half, and then twice more, for 27 and 20 yards, respectively. The game turned ragged and high-scoring. (Alexander would run for 161 yards and three touchdowns.) Twice, Alabama built fourteen-point leads, and twice Brady erased them, chopping the Crimson Tide defense apart with short, precise passes, moving the chains so fast it was hard to keep up with him. He was so wrought up that he was vomiting on the sidelines between possessions. In the stands, his father was worried that he'd collapse. Tied at 28, Michigan had a chance to win the game in regulation, but Alabama blocked a Wolverine field goal in the final seconds, sending the two teams into overtime.

In college football, games are not settled by sudden death. One team gets the ball on the other's 25-yard line. If that team scores, on either a touchdown or a field goal, the other team gets an identical opportunity. This process continues until one team either scores unanswered points or outscores the other on consecutive possessions. Occasionally, this results in final scores more suited to the NCAA's basketball tournament. As football, it resembles nothing more than a pickup game on a suburban street with telephone poles marking the end zone.

Michigan won the coin toss, and, on the very first play of the overtime, Brady read the Alabama defense and found the tight end Shawn Thompson over the middle for a touchdown. The extra point gave the Wolverines a 35–28 lead. Alabama got the ball for what now might be its only shot to win the game. Alexander picked up four yards on the first play. Then, on second down, a backup quarterback named Andrew Zow threw a touchdown pass to Antonio Carter, and it seemed that the game would go on. However, Alabama kicker Ryan Pflugner pushed the extra-point try off to the right. Shockingly, Michigan had won the game, and Brady had decimated the Orange Bowl record book.

He set new marks for passing attempts (forty-six), completions (thirty-one), yardage (369), and touchdowns (four). He broke old records—the passing yardage mark had stood since 1945—and he broke new ones, his four touchdowns surpassing the three that Danny Kanell had put up only three years earlier. More important, he'd vindicated the confidence invested in him not only by his teammates but also by the community that had developed around him in Ann Arbor.

In the tunnel after the game, he couldn't even lift his equipment bag. His father carried it for him. On the way out, they ran into Stan Parrish, the Michigan quarterback coach, who'd been caught in the middle of an untenable situation for two seasons. What Brady had gone through, Parrish told them, would have broken most players.

Later, in the middle of a joyful scrum of well-wishers, one of them recalled a moment earlier that season, right in the middle of the misbegotten two-headed quarterback experiment, when Henson had played well in a close-run win at Syracuse. After the game, as was the custom, the team captains led a chorus of the Michigan fight song:

> Hail! to the victors valiant
> Hail! to the conqu'ring heroes . . .

His friend remembered how clearly he could hear Brady's voice that day. Now, Brady finally had the moment he'd earned, and he had it all to himself. On the way, he had learned something about the line that is drawn, not often brightly, between confidence and arrogance, which is a political lesson that not even many career politicians learn. He'd also learned something about opportunities—that they are there to be grasped, but that they must be infinitely renewable. They can be more attainable than they are durable. The effort to seize them is only the beginning of the effort to hold on to them, and that effort doesn't need to be a selfish one, although, at its worst, it can be.

Somebody asked him about his time at the University of Michigan, coming to an end late this night in Florida. Tom Brady had a saga to tell, full of twists and turns and heartbreak and struggle. He thought for a moment, and decided to let its ending tell the tale for him.

"It was a storybook career," Tom Brady said.

■ ■ ■

From the inside, all domed stadiums look unfinished. No matter how hard the people in marketing try, they can't hang neon on everything in the Georgia Dome. There's only so much even the best sales staff can do with concrete walls and cement outcroppings and metal abutments. The gladiatorial frisson inherent in any NFL game grows particularly intense when you can't see the sky. In addition, in an enclosed facility, your "game presentation"—that twenty-first-century term of art that means indoor pyrotechnics, thumping Jumbotron cheerleading, and more heavy metal than they're going to play at Ozzy Osbourne's funeral—becomes increasingly less like family entertainment and more and more like the strategy they used to pry Manuel Noriega out of Panama. With twenty seconds left in the game, and the ball on the 11-yard line of the Atlanta Falcons, Adam Vinatieri stood in the middle of a hurricane of electronic foofaraw and tried to win himself and the Patriots another football game.

It had been an odd week since New England was crushed at home by San Diego. The rout had been such a thorough one that representatives of the national media came to town to suss out what was going wrong with the defending champions. There was some grumbling about how Doug Flutie, the backup quarterback who'd come to the Patriots this season from the Chargers, was seen socializing with his former teammates before the game. Belichick clung so tightly to his Zen insistence that the world exists one game at a time that it seemed his knuckles were white. "All I'm saying," he explained, "is wherever our team is now, I don't think we were necessarily there two weeks ago, one week ago, three weeks ago. I don't think it's apples to apples here."

At Brady's weekly news conference, he'd been defensive about the shot he'd taken at Marty Schottenheimer, and he'd been thrown completely by a question from a reporter representing a newspaper catering to Irish Americans and recent Irish émigrés, which apparently had named him one of the most prominent Irish Americans. What did Brady know, the fellow asked, about his Irish heritage?

"I have to be cued up on this one," Brady said, as the assembled media chuckled. "My Irish heritage? Can you come back tomorrow for a better answer on this? Well, my father's all Irish, and I'm half Irish. I don't know. You stumped me. I wish I had a better answer." There was a moment of doubt, just the slightest hesitation, before the grin came back. He was off-balance, briefly, caught between the temptation to go for the easy answer and palpable intrigue at the oddball question.

In Atlanta, the Patriots were desperately searching for a balance on offense and plugging holes on defense. In addition to the loss of Rodney Harrison, Richard Seymour, the team's most talented defensive player, would miss the game with a leg injury, although that fact was kept secret until almost game time—as was the fact that Michael Vick, the superbly athletic Atlanta quarterback, also would not play. In Vick's place was a raw-boned second-year player named Matt Schaub. As the Falcons went through training camp, there was some inevitable stirring in the media that Schaub perhaps ought to be playing ahead of the heralded Vick.

Brady had kept the Patriots ahead, with some help from running back Corey Dillon. During the previous season, Dillon had come to New England from the Cincinnati Bengals, one of the NFL's most chronic landfills, with a reputation as a strong runner and a public malcontent. (During one of Cincinnati's dismally customary losing streaks, Dillon went to the sideline and ripped off his jersey in what even some NFL traditionalists accepted as an understandable public act of civil disobedience.) A dead ringer for the late Sonny Liston, Dillon had been a vital part of New England's third Super Bowl win. Now, though, he seemed to be showing the effects of age and the accelerated physical breakdown characteristic of the NFL, and, if he were still prone to demonstrations of public frustration, this would appear to be the time for one.

"I know you guys are just waiting for this big eruption and it's not going to happen," he said. "I'm telling you, that volcano done blew its top a long time ago."

Against Atlanta, Dillon cracked through for 106 yards, with no run longer than 12 yards. An actual running game allowed Brady to go deep three times for touchdowns, including a magnificent 55-yard pass down the left sideline to Bethel Johnson, a wide receiver of dazzling speed who'd been the bane of the New England coaching staff, and of Tom Brady, for two seasons. Johnson was fragile, and he'd had the devil's own time learning to run his routes correctly. He couldn't fit his obvious gifts into the context of the team's offense, and it so frustrated Brady that he once told his father a ball that Johnson dropped had been his own fault for having thrown it to Johnson in the first place.

This time, though, Johnson's route was a simple one. He only had to run straight down the field, past Falcon cornerback Jason Webster, and Brady put just enough air under the ball so that Johnson was able to accelerate farther away from the defender in order to track it down. That last burst of speed is what kept Brady and the New England coaches hoping for the best about Bethel Johnson.

"It was just a perfect pass," Johnson said. "Tom gave me a chance to accelerate and make the plays. That's what he does. That's what he has the feel for—if the guys are close up on us, he'll lay it up and let us make plays. If he lets it go, you've got to find that other gear and go make the play. He knows who's tall and who's fast, and what they need to go do their jobs. He knows his guys."

There was an urgency to the game that was intensified by the claustrophobic atmosphere of the Georgia Dome. A squabble over an out-of-bounds call had New England linebacker Mike Vrabel yelling at the Atlanta head coach, Jim Mora, Jr., and Belichick visibly fuming on the other sideline. Through it all, however, the Patriots couldn't hold a 28–13 lead. Schaub threw two touchdown passes in the fourth quarter, the first after a short pass by Brady was deflected, and then intercepted. His short toss to wide receiver Brian Finneran for a two-point conversion after the second touchdown tied the game at 28–28 with a little under four minutes to go.

New England held the ball for the rest of the game. It wasn't their smoothest drive, nothing at all like their remorseless progress down the field two weeks earlier in Pittsburgh. They committed two penalties on the first two plays of the drive. A false start by young tight end Ben Watson that probably owed everything to the inhuman noise in the dome was followed by a holding call that knocked out one Brady completion. His next two passes were incomplete. On the second of these, though, Atlanta cornerback Allen Rossum completely handcuffed Deion Branch, and the interference penalty gained the Patriots thirty yards. Four running plays later, the last a one-yard quarterback sneak by Brady to center the ball on the field, and Adam Vinatieri was lining up another field goal at the end of another close-run game.

Vinatieri's is a unique career, even by NFL standards. Kickers are reckoned necessary evils. Their importance is undeniable, yet only one of their number, Jan Stenerud of the Kansas

City Chiefs, is in the Pro Football Hall of Fame. For a long time, placekicking was simply an extra skill for gifted players to have. Back in those dim times, every back was expected to drop-kick placements from anywhere on the field, which was one of the last bits of fossil record tracing football's descent from rugby and soccer. Don Chandler, who kicked for Vince Lombardi's Green Bay Packers, was a perfectly adequate wide receiver, and Chandler's backup was Jerry Kramer, an All-Pro offensive guard.

As football became increasingly specialized, any other skill a kicker might possess had become vestigial, like the ability of penguins to fly or pitchers to hit. The final stage in the evolution of the position became glaringly obvious in the 1972 Super Bowl, when Garo Yepremian, the Cypriot placekicker for the Miami Dolphins, tried to throw a pass out of a botched field goal attempt and looked for all the world like a sea lion tossing a bowling pin with its nose.

Vinatieri, however, may be the great exception to the glib dismissal of kickers as football players, and not just because Bill Belichick always makes sure to remind people that he is "not just a kicker. He's a player." He has made more critical kicks at more critical times in more different critical contexts than anyone in the history of the NFL. He's made them indoors and outdoors, in the sun and in the rain and, most memorably, in the snow.

Adam, a descendant of General Custer's bandmaster, grew up in Rapid City, South Dakota. He battled learning disabilities throughout his primary and secondary school days, and did so determinedly enough to win an appointment to West Point. However, Adam hated the hazing of plebe summer so much that he came home, graduating from South Dakota State in 1994, just as Tom Brady was leaving Serra High School. Undrafted, Vinatieri sold himself to NFL franchises by buying twenty dol-

lars' worth of blank videotapes at Wal-Mart and putting together his own audition tape, which was pretty much the same
thing the Bradys were doing in San Mateo on Tom's behalf for
the benefit of the colleges recruiting him. The tapes landed
Vinatieri a chance to kick for the Amsterdam Admirals in the
NFL's World League in Europe.

(It turns out that, what with the indigenous passion for what
they call football, Europe is one of the few spots on the globe
where placekickers get the kind of respect usually reserved for
quarterbacks. The fans there may not know a fade route from a
croissant, but they know what's going on when a soccer-style
kicker lines one up. Every kick Vinatieri made in Amsterdam
occasioned bells and whistles and joyous singing.)

The Patriots found Vinatieri in 1996 when Bill Parcells was
reviving the credibility of the franchise for good and all. Since
then, of course, after the kicks in the snow against Oakland,
and the Super Bowl winners against St. Louis and Carolina, and
the one that turned out to be the winning margin against the
Eagles in the previous Super Bowl, and the fifteen other game
winners besides, including the one that had beaten the Steelers
two weeks earlier, Vinatieri had established a body of work
reckoned to be more than enough to put him into the Hall of
Fame with Stenerud. He added to it this day, nailing a kick to
beat the Falcons, 31–28.

"When they got that two-point conversion, I thought it
might come down to myself or their kicker," Vinatieri said. "It's
fun to be out there to put the icing on the cake after the other
guys work out there all day long. Tom and the offense will move
the ball down the field, and get it as close as we possibly can. I
know if it's any kind of realistic yardage, we're going to take the
kick, no matter what the distance is, unless it's just ungodly
long and we have to throw a 'Hail Mary' into the end zone."

Kickers are the game's greatest opportunists. They survive, always, on completing the work begun by people who pay a vastly higher physical price. They have to perform a simple task freighted with outlandish import. If they do it badly, they stand out there alone. If they do it right, they get carried off the field by exhausted teammates.

"You know," Vinatieri said, "when you're kicking into the net on the sidelines, you can sort of see them going down the field but, no, the noise and everything, you just try to forget everything around you.

"I guess Tom and I complement each other pretty good. I'll be glad to ride his coattails."

3 | AN INSTINCT FOR COMMUNION

FOOTBALL CAREERS are a wilderness of clipboards, some seen and some unseen. What happens on the field gets put on a clipboard, and what's put on the clipboard gets put in a file, and a career exists as much on the clipboard and in the file as it does in the locker room or on the field. High school players know that colleges are watching, and college players know that every muscle pull and every dropped pass is, somewhere, marked down or checked off or otherwise fed into the faceless machinery of professional scouting.

For his whole career, David Givens knew that they were out there, watching. When he was the star at Humble High School in Humble, Texas—which sounds a bit oxymoronic until you realize that the town took its name from the Humble Oil Company—Givens could almost hear the scratching of the pens at universities like Texas, and Arkansas, and Notre Dame, where he finally went to play. While he was there, Givens was injured just often enough for it to be noted, and he looked at every trip to the trainer's room and every minute on the sidelines as something like the milk bottle that used to represent the soul in the old Baltimore Catechism. Every tweaked hamstring, every second of actual football lost, was another black mark on a record he could not see. He always took a long view of things, and he was always smart enough to be concerned.

"I had a kind of injury halo over my head," says Givens, "and you know it's affecting your draft status. I thought about that all the time my senior year. I got hurt a few times, and I knew people were watching, and I knew it was hurting my draft status and hurting the team, too."

The Patriots took him in the seventh round of the 2002 NFL draft. "You're talking about a guy who played running back in high school and essentially played wingback in college," explains Bill Belichick. "His first year in our offense, he was basically a running back trying to be a wide receiver. One of the strengths that David has is running with the ball after the catch."

Givens caught nine passes his first year and thirty-four his second. He had fifty-six catches in 2004. He quickly caught on to the subleties of the New England short passing game, becoming particularly adept at plays on which Brady would notice that Givens's defender was playing back off of him a few steps. Seeing this, Brady would adjust the play at the line, trusting that Givens would catch on. He usually did, popping up right at the line, catching the ball while isolated on a defender already back on his heels. Givens then could make a play himself to gain yardage. It's a play based on instant recognition that is born of hours of practice. It is a play based on a great number of things that do not fit neatly onto a clipboard.

"We do a lot of film study," Givens says. "You see the tendencies, the leverages that the DBs play. You watch that film and you take it onto the field." Like most teams, the Patriots also take Polaroid photographs of the defense during the game and study them on the sidelines.

"It's not the 1940s," Givens says. "It's a technological game now. You have to be ready for anything."

This season, Givens once again was playing in both the present and the future. He was in the last year of his contract with the Patriots, so he would be a free agent at the end of the season. He didn't know whether he'd be staying on in New England or whether he'd be playing somewhere else. But he knew, again, that somewhere, somebody he didn't even know was watching him. The only defense against being intimidated by this distant, invisible audience is to cling to all those things for which the vocabulary of the clipboard is insufficient, to play freely from that place where all those things that can't be timed or measured lie. Among them is the wisdom to know that football careers are fragile things. Almost anything can break them. The luckiest players are the ones who learn that lesson young.

In the spring of 2000, Tom Brady left Michigan with a business degree in organizational studies. He played well in the East-West Shrine Game back home in San Francisco. After the season, when Michigan hosted pro scouts at its annual Pro Day, Brady came to the attention of Dick Rehbein, the quarterback coach of the New England Patriots. Rehbein and his new boss, Bill Belichick, were looking for someone to back up Drew Bledsoe, the franchise quarterback who'd helped turn around the fortunes of a team that had walked through most of its history in clown shoes. The team also wanted to get out from under the contract of John Friesz, a veteran NFL backup making veteran NFL money. First, Rehbein went to Louisiana to look at a rocket-armed specimen named Tim Rattay, who ultimately would play quarterback with the 49ers. Then he went up to Ann Arbor.

Rehbein grew up in football under Bart Starr, the leader of Vince Lombardi's dynastic Green Bay teams of the 1960s and the Green Bay head coach from 1975 to 1983. Starr was noted for his ability to make big plays at big moments, and to perform despite the fact that most of the glory accrued to the superstar in the camel hair coat who stalked the sidelines. While Starr was coaching the Packers, he hired Rehbein as an aide when the latter was still in his twenties. Now, more than a decade later, Rehbein looked at Brady, talked to his Michigan teammates, and came away convinced that he had found something more than a backup. He'd found himself another Bart Starr.

While Rehbein began touting him in New England, Brady spent some time at a performance clinic in Louisiana, trying to pick up just a little more foot speed. Then he went off to the NFL Combine, a weeklong orgy dedicated to the empiricism of the clipboard that seems to owe as much to Aldous Huxley as it does to Vince Lombardi. Everything about the prospective draftees is measured, from their speed in the forty-yard dash to their intellectual and emotional ability to play the game professionally. Ben Watson, the young and gifted New England tight end, once told Jerome Solomon of *The Boston Globe* about an episode during his time at the Combine in which Watson found himself experiencing an interrogation straight out of a 1950s cop melodrama.

Brady scored high on those portions of the aptitude test concerned with organization and leadership. He talked a lot about watching Joe Montana and the 49ers, which drew the attention of Dwight Clark, the Cleveland general manager. In 1982 Clark had caught the most famous touchdown pass in 49er history, from Montana—"The Catch," which beat the Cowboys in the NFC championship game. On the Huxley side of things, Brady also was asked if he'd ever kicked a cat, and whether or not he liked *Alice in Wonderland*, although that might have been an overly subtle form of drug testing.

"No," he later told *The Detroit News*, "I'm not a cat-kicker." It's probably for the best that the NFL people didn't include a question about tossing video-game controllers.

Gradually, the first professional profile of Tom Brady began to emerge. He was a slender kid who threw a nice, catchable ball and had greater arm strength than anyone might guess from looking at him. He was smart, and he worked hard, and other players seemed to respond to him. Still, most of the clipboards had him marked as a gamble. The most prominent of them, Mel Kiper, Jr., a man with the statistical mind of a savant beneath the immovable coiffure of a lounge act, commented that Brady "didn't have the total package of skills," which frosted Brady so hard that he later snapped back at all draft pundits in an interview.

Some teams, such as the Patriots, thought Brady was worth a pick. Some teams, such as his hometown 49ers, didn't. In fact, San Francisco's offensive coordinator, Marty Mornhinweg, delivered a devastatingly average assessment of Brady's abilities—citing, among other things, the fact that Brady had never been able to establish himself at Michigan. (This, of course, without noting that he would have had to lock Lloyd Carr in a steamer trunk to have done so.) It cost the 49ers the loyalty of the entire Brady family, who'd spent every Sunday of the preceding decade cheering for the team.

Then there were the San Diego Chargers, who'd mortgaged their future to a crackpot quarterback named Ryan Leaf, who was on his way to becoming synonymous with expensive self-destruction. Leaf had missed a season due to an injury, the Chargers were floundering, and their head coach, Mike Riley, saw himself with a second opportunity to work with Tom Brady. Riley had been the assistant who'd been unable to convince Southern California that Brady could start there.

"We were going to take a quarterback in that draft," Riley

recalls. "I liked his poise, and I always liked the way he threw the ball." Unfortunately, the San Diego general manager, Bobby Beathard, was less enthusiastic. If Brady was still around in the later rounds, the Chargers might take a chance on the skinny quarterback who didn't run well. Riley felt as though he were banging his head against a very familiar wall. He didn't understand why people thought Brady was such a risk. He never would. "People recruit and sign people in a box," Riley explains. "That box doesn't include the intangibles of playing a position. People draft safely."

(Which is a pretty far piece from the days in which scouting for an NFL team was a risky business requiring a roll of quarters and a pay phone. "So they would have a [draft] pick coming up, and they'd run out to a payphone and drop two dollars and twenty-five cents in," Tex Schramm, the legendary talent hound for the Dallas Cowboys, explained to the author Michael MacCambridge, "and call Pappy Lewis at West Virginia. 'Pappy who is the best offensive lineman that you played against last year?' And that's how this kind of stuff took place, as recently as the late '50s.")

Meanwhile, Dick Rehbein continued to push for the Patriots to take Brady, making all the points that Riley was making in San Diego, but in Foxborough, they were listening. Bill Belichick's father was a coach. More important, Steve Belichick had been a scout and he'd educated his son in all those things that didn't fit into the boxes on a clipboard. Bill had been appalled by the culture of entitlement that had grown up around the Patriots under his predecessor, Pete Carroll. When Rehbein pointed out that, among Brady's other attributes, Michigan had gone 20–5 under his direction, Belichick listened. Also, in a perfect obverse of what the 49ers believed, Belichick was shrewd enough to see Lloyd Carr's great experiment as a point in Brady's favor.

"We talked a lot about his production his senior year at Michigan, when they rotated Henson in, and there was a problem, and they ended up bringing Brady back," Belichick says. "Most of the time, he'd fix the problem and move the team into position where it could win. The way he handled it was good, but I think what was better was what he did with the opportunities he had.

"Our vision wasn't that Tom was our franchise quarterback but that Tom had been in situations—both in playing-time and game-management situations, tight games against good competition—and he'd handled all of them pretty well."

On April 20, 2000, all the Bradys were gathered in the house on Portola Avenue, watching the draft on ESPN, which has turned what was once a small gathering of white men sitting around a table and smoking like East St. Louis into a two-day extravaganza of hype, bombast, and grown men in replica jerseys. In contrast to the dancing loons on the screen, there was realism along the Avenue of the Fleas. Tommy would get drafted, not highly but certainly sometime during the first day.

"We're all anticipating the kickoff of the draft, and it's really exciting, you know?" recalls Nancy Brady. "And it started, and it's just so slow." Every team takes its full five minutes, and the first round goes on for hours. Eventually, probably just to get out of the house, Brady went off to the San Francisco Giants baseball game. His sisters stayed home and monitored the television. Round after round went by, and Tommy's name wasn't called. He came back from the baseball game just before the first day ended.

"He was really disappointed," Nancy says. "By then, my sisters and I were just watching the names on the ticker and saying, 'Okay, so who's he?'"

In the San Diego offices, Mike Riley failed, once again, to convince anyone to take a chance on Tom Brady. The Chargers drafted JaJuan Seider of Florida A&M, who, ultimately, would fail to make the team. With the sixty-fifth pick in the draft, San Francisco took a quarterback from Hofstra named Giovanni Carmazzi, who would become a Rhodes Scholar but never a 49er. As the draft ground along, Dick Rehbein and, increasingly, Bill Belichick, expressed surprise that Brady's name was still on their board.

The second day of the draft was miasmic. Perhaps the nadir came when Cleveland drafted a quarterback named Spergon Wynn, who had completed 47 percent of his passes at North Texas State. This sent the elder Brady over the edge. This was Dwight Clark, for whom all the Bradys had cheered, drafting on behalf of Carmen Policy, who'd helped build all those San Francisco teams on which Clark had caught passes from Joe Montana.

"Dwight Clark—unbelievable," the elder Brady says to this day. "It just killed us. Tommy was sitting there, and he was like, 'I don't understand this. I do *not* understand this.'"

It was worse than what had happened at Michigan. There, Brady had discovered, he could play his way onto the field. But this was different. This wasn't about how he played. It was about how he might play, one day, if he ever got the chance. By the fourth round, the calls began to come in from teams asking if he'd like to come to their camps as a free agent, the kiss of death for any football player but most assuredly for a quarterback. If a team doesn't draft you and then sign you to a deal with at least some bonus money, then nobody on the team—not the general manager, whose reputation is made by the players he drafts, or the owner, who's already cut you a check—has any kind of investment in you.

"We were all starting to feel really horrible now," his father says.

The fifth round passed. The Patriots took a tight end named Dave Stachelski. At about this time, Brady told his family he was going to take a walk. The house was silent. "I remember him going upstairs, and he was so angry and so hurt," Nancy Brady says. "What with what happened at Michigan, and now having this infuriating and disappointing couple of days, he just wanted to take a walk, and he grabbed a bat."

His sisters tried to explain why a bat probably wasn't a good idea at this point. He took it with him anyway, and fungoed whatever he could find in the yard. In Foxborough, Belichick mused to his assistants that Brady's name shouldn't still be out there. Not long after that, the phone on Portola Avenue rang.

"You don't want to say, 'Well, he's not around,'" says Brady's father. "I'm trying to cover this thing as fast as I can, so I said, 'Well, he's in the shower.' And they say, 'Well, Coach Belichick would like to talk to him for a second or two.'" Brady, and his bat, came back in the house and took the call. In the sixth round, with the 199th pick in the draft, Brady became a New England Patriot. It was exactly one pick sooner than the one the Green Bay Packers had used in 1959 to take a quarterback from Alabama named Bart Starr, who later would come to hire an enthusiastic young assistant named Dick Rehbein.

Brady got sixth-round money—$298,000 a year, with a $38,000 signing bonus—and he came onto the roster as the team's fourth-string quarterback. Bledsoe was the starter, Friesz was still there, and so was Michael Bishop, New England's prototype of the new, running NFL quarterback, in the mold of Philadelphia's Donovan McNabb. In fact, there was already a bit of a quarterback controversy brewing in New England, at least in that part of it waiting on hold for a chance to talk on the radio, as to whether or not the mobile Bishop should replace Bledsoe. The latter had an unfortunate tendency to be sacked, and an equally unfortunate gift for making exactly the wrong mistake at exactly the wrong time. However, for the moment anyway, Bishop's partisans remained limited largely to the airwaves. The Patriots had too much invested in Bledsoe, who, with Bill Parcells, had helped the team get to Super Bowl XXXI in 1997, a season that buried forever the franchise's history as a burlesque. Bledsoe would be the team's starting quarterback until he dropped.

Brady reported for training camp that spring knowing the 2000 season was essentially going to be a redshirt year for him. He anticipated hardly any playing time, but he determined to take the long view of his career. One evening, as he was leaving the team's practice facility with a pizza under his arm, he ran into Robert Kraft, the team's owner. Kraft is a billionaire businessman, and he's become one of the NFL's most influential owners, but he's also a fan, sometimes arguably to the point of public gaucherie. This day he was just leaving his office at about 7:45.

"So this skinny beanpole guy walks out, and he comes up to me and he says, 'Mr. Kraft? I'm Tom Brady. We haven't met yet, but I'm the best decision this franchise has ever made.'

"And it was weird the way he said it, you know? It wasn't like he was arrogant, but it was more like he was very confident. It was almost matter-of-fact the way he said it. I wasn't offended at all."

For the historical record, of the six quarterbacks picked ahead of Brady in the 2000 NFL draft, only two were still in the NFL at the start of the 2005 season. Three of them, including Spergon Wynn, who had hooked on with the British Columbia Lions, began the season in the Canadian Football League.

■ ■ ■

After Vinatieri's kick beat Atlanta, the Patriots went to Denver to play the Broncos. It was their last week before the annual "bye" week built into every NFL team's schedule. New England came out as though it had taken its bye a week early. Corey Dillon was out with a nagging leg injury, and the Patriots' running game took no pressure off Brady. Worse, the makeshift offensive line began to come apart and, without Dillon, a formidable blocker in the backfield, Brady took shots from all sides all day.

Denver was reckless and bold, jamming the New England receivers at the line of scrimmage and daring Brady to beat them deep, which he could not do because he spent most of the time running for his life, usually backward. The Broncos took a 14–3 lead early in the game, and they forced Brady into hurried throws that ended the next two possessions. At the 10:36 mark, Mike Anderson scored from two yards out to give Denver a 28–3 lead.

Football is a different game on television—smaller and more immediate, much more character-driven than the game is from the press box or from the highest deck of the stadium. The quarterback is as central to the television program that is the average NFL game as Tony Soprano is to *The Sopranos*. The camera loves him, follows him everywhere, even to the sideline, where, stunned, he can be caught trying to figure out from where the next blitz is coming. There's no place to hide. If you want to throw your helmet, or even kick a cat, you will do it on television in front of millions and that's simply the way of things. You are an athlete and a television performer all at the same time, and the same medium that casts you as the unflappable field general can instantly cast you as its opposite if you begin to play that way.

The technology has improved so much that you can now plainly read a player's eyes even deep in the gloom of his helmet.

Twenty-five points down, Brady was visibly furious. At the same time you could read his wariness as the big deficit gave Denver's defense the opportunity to come at him even harder. He tried to bring New England all the way back, and he nearly did. He drove them to a Vinatieri field goal, and then, on the next drive, David Givens made a dazzling third-down catch to keep alive a drive that ended with a New England touchdown. The next time they got the ball, Brady drove the Patriots seventy-one yards in a little more than three minutes. Givens caught the touchdown, a leaping grab from eight yards out that cut the Denver lead to 28–20. The game got no closer, however. On New England's last drive, Brady hit both Givens and Deion Branch with critical passes that the receivers dropped. In between, he got called for intentionally grounding the ball in the face of a huge Denver rush. New England lost.

A pattern had developed. They would win a game and then lose one. They were 3–3 coming into the bye week. Brady blamed himself for not making plays. He didn't say anything about the balls that Branch and Givens had dropped, or the threadbare protection he'd received throughout the game. Nobody played well. Everybody lost.

Two weeks after the Denver game, Tom and Galynn Brady came east to visit Tommy and Nancy, their daughter who worked as a pharmaceutical sales representative near Boston. Tom also arranged to visit Father Joe Waters, the pastor at Our Lady of Good Counsel church in Lawrence. It's an aging parish on the side of a hill in an old mill town, a parish that has served several generations of immigrants. The signs on the buildings around the church are all in Spanish now. On this Sunday morning, a small group of men in front of the bodega across the street ducked inside when a soft rain began to fall.

Tom agreed to give a talk as part of a Sunday afternoon fundraiser at Our Lady's. The program also included a silent auction featuring a number of Patriots-related items. Tom brought along a couple of his son's Super Bowl rings. Children lined up to have their pictures taken wearing the preposterous baubles. The younger ones could barely lift their hands.

Tom got up to speak. He talked about his seminary days, and he talked about how even the Brady family had its stresses and strains, how hard it was that Maureen had had a child without being married (as would her sister Julie later that year). His tone was soft. There was no edge of judgment to it. He talked about how he and Galynn had gone through the Marriage Encounter program together. "It was the kind of thing where my wife would tell me what her issues are, and I wanted to be the macho man and never shared my issues with her. It must have been pretty tough for her to be married to God. At that time, I was able to start to become more of a whole man."

There was a sharing in what he said, the kind of thing that draws the listener into what can only be called communion with the speaker. The smallish crowd, shifting in their metal folding chairs, found themselves involved in what Tom Brady was saying because he had allowed them into his life and asked, gently, to be part of theirs.

"One of the things about Tom is that there is an idealism of love there, and not an idealism of judgment," says Stephen Pope, the Boston College theologian who's also a Brady cousin. "Tom finds it very troubling when people in the Church don't represent the face of Christ. They represent the face of an institution that tries to stereotype, and pigeonhole, and judge people, so part of the thing with Maureen and with Julie is to know that, hey, people are a mess and they're loved by God anyway, especially when it's close to the bone. If you can't be merciful yourself, you can't expect anyone to be merciful to you. [Tom] has enormous intergrity in his compassion."

"How do I live my life as a man of faith?" Tom Brady asks the people in the parish hall, competing with the smell of lasagna and the bustling of children trying to hoist his son's rings. "I'm always reminded of my mother's dictum—pride and arrogance always come before the fall. Numerous times in my life, when we kind of had things going, it would all get knocked out from under me. Pride goeth before the fall. It's as true in life as it is in religion as it is in sports.

"I think the thing we need to get back to is really our core values—taking care of our brothers and sisters as we take care of ourselves. You think the Church is on top? *We're* the Church, and we should worry about taking care of our sisters and brothers."

There are echoes of Vatican II in this, a lost summons for what it had called the People of God. The Council, which opened just as Tom Brady was leaving Maryknoll, unleashed something in the Roman Catholic Church that stubbornly refuses to be controlled. Listening to traditionalist Catholics talk about Vatican II is very much like listening to conservative politicians quote Martin Luther King. Vatican II did more than what's contained in its documents. It wrought a profound change within the laypeople of the Church. As the historian Garry Wills makes clear, "They are what the council called them—witnesses to the faith, guided directly by the Spirit, who is shed on the entire people of God."

Vatican II knocked the laity out of lockstep with the hierarchy, creating what its opponents now deride as "cafeteria Catholics." But it produced a laity intent to, as Wills puts it, live the Council and not argue about it. It freed them within their own consciences to disagree with their nominal leaders, to call for a hierarchy that directs but does not rule. When, along about the time that the younger Tom Brady was winning his first Super Bowl, the Archdiocese of Boston came apart in a scandal of abuse and ecclesiastical omertà that would have embarrassed the Gambinos, it was the laity who chased the hapless Bernard Cardinal Law out of the country, all the while remaining as Catholic as they believed themselves to be. "They do not reject authority in general," Wills points out, "but recognize an authority at odds, on some points, with the pope."

Rain began to fall again outside the church. Tom Brady, Sr., was closing his speech. "Our faith story is all about how the closer we can stay together, the tougher it will be to become disillusioned or disenfranchised," he said. "The Holy Spirit has given me and my family the grace to overcome disenfranchisement."

The biggest problem with metaphors is that you can stretch them too far. Teams are not families. Teams are not churches. But within all three of them is always the question of the source of authority. Does it come from the top down, by dictum, its effective morality depending wholly upon the person or group who exercises it? Or does it rise from something that gathers itself from many sources into a single power and then lends itself and its direction, carefully, to a common good?

Tom Brady is not the conspicuous Catholic that his father is, but there is in him an instinct for communion. It was stronger than the capricious authority under which he played at Michigan. Something innate sensed that the real authority was what was loaned to him by his teammates through their respect and, especially, through the way they played when he was on the field. Vatican II created change, controversy, and perhaps a couple of saints along the way. Within one of the most profane contexts imaginable, its spirit also may have helped create a quarterback.

PART 2 THE UNIVERSE OF QUARTERBACKS

4 | THE CLOWN COLLEGE

THE OLD RECEIVER coached here once, and he got the New England Patriots to their first Super Bowl in 1986, but the old receiver is a visitor this day in the stadium press box, and he's talking about being a receiver, and the first things you notice about him are his hands. There are odd bumps and twists to the fingers, but they are wiry and solid. Renaissance sculptors would have died to create these hands.

Raymond Berry is in the Hall of Fame. He was a tough coach's kid from Paris, Texas, and he was already an established star when the Baltimore Colts came to training camp in 1956. The starting Baltimore quarterback was George Shaw, a number one draft pick out of the University of Oregon who'd been the NFL's Rookie of the Year the previous season. Also in camp was a refugee from the sandlots named John Unitas, whom Baltimore had brought in as a backup. "Weeb Ewbank [the Colts' head coach] came up to me, and he told me to keep working with this guy," Berry recalls. "Weeb already recognized that he had something there that was special, but he couldn't put him in as a starter, not with Shaw being Rookie of the Year and a starter."

Instead, Berry and Unitas pushed themselves every day after

practice. Unitas threw Berry thousands of passes, most of them short- and medium-range balls that would move the chains and eat the clock. They developed a checklist to organize their workouts together. They began to be able to read each other's minds.

In the first game of the 1956 regular season, a Chicago Bear named Fred Williams blew out the knee of George Shaw. Unitas came in, and the first pass he threw in the NFL was brought back the other way for a touchdown by Chicago's J. C. Caroline. "John hit him right in stride," Berry says. "But John came back and had a pretty decent day. That was the first tip-off on Unitas—that he was tough-minded, and that he was confident."

Shaw never got his job back. Berry and Unitas continued to work together. One time, they decided to work on what was then called an "L pattern," on which Berry would run a short, quick square-in cut toward the center of the field. "What we wanted to do was to decide what we should do if I had a linebacker in my face," Berry recalls. "We decided that, if that happened, we'd change the L pattern to a slant." They worked every day on the pass, and on the unspoken communication required to make the play work. The problem was that nobody ever lined up that way against Berry all season. Then, the Colts played the New York Giants in the 1958 NFL championship game, the overtime thriller that's now recognized as the "Greatest Game Ever Played," and the single game that gave professional football the last big push toward the dominance it now enjoys among American sports.

"We're down 17–14 with about a minute and a half, and we're eighty yards out," Berry explains. "John's got the L pattern called, and their outside linebacker comes out on me, and we'd never seen the Giants do that before. I'm not sure John and I ever talked about them doing that before. But there he is, so

I look at John and he looks at me, and he's got the play called. I did what we'd talked about, and he executed it, and we pick up about thirty yards. We kick the field goal and send the game into overtime.

"There was one time in our career together that this happened—once, you know? What's at stake? Why do you work on these little things? Because they ain't little. They get big pretty quick."

Berry's team isn't even in Baltimore anymore. In the dead of winter in 1983 they were moved lock, stock, and shoulder pads to Indianapolis because the city fathers there were willing to hand the keys to the civic treasury over to a brigand of an owner named Bob Irsay. Now the Indianapolis Colts train on a bright, breezy plain just north of the city. In the first week of November, there are still enough golden leaves on the trees to soften the place, even when the inevitable unmarked security car comes up behind you and, from the other side of tinted glass, somebody instructs you that you've parked in the wrong place.

Even before the events of September 11, 2001, which would prove critical to the development of the public image of the New England Patriots under the leadership of Tom Brady, NFL teams wrapped themselves in security. It comes from the top down. In *America's Game*, his magisterial history of the NFL, Michael MacCambridge writes that one of the first things the league did when its popularity exploded in the 1950s was to put a former FBI agent on retainer in each NFL city. (According to MacCambridge, this policy was designed by a former G-man with the impossibly Dashiell Hammett name of Austin Gunsel, who also served as the league's first treasurer.) Each decade added new threats to the old—from gamblers and drug dealers to Osama bin Laden—and each new threat brought a new level of security, until the average NFL game became one of the most militarized entertainment spectacles this side of the Blue Angels.

The teams followed the league's lead until, now, every NFL camp is an obstacle course, and they all seem to have been designed by whatever it is that school-crossing guards have for a Special Forces. In addition, each team has a further motivation for secrecy—the desire to keep the other teams from obtaining useful information, especially through the public prints. In this, under Belichick, the Patriots have become notorious. In public, they are so taciturn about injuries that even the tightly wound NFL office has taken notice. The team regularly keeps track of the number of stories written about the Patriots as opposed to those about the Red Sox, an unfair measure as it presumes to compare enthusiasm with mania, but nonetheless an unmistakable indication of a hypersensitivity on the part of the football team. Among other things, this practice has led to a kind of low-level feud between the Patriots and *The Boston Globe*, New England's largest newspaper and, as Patriots officials occasionally whisper, a property of the New York Times Company, which also owns a piece of—wait for it—the Boston Red Sox.

Belichick's daily press conferences take place in a windowless bunker inside Gillette Stadium. These are tightly controlled affairs, which occasionally can be quite enlightening. Belichick is a brilliant historian of the game, and, when he's of a mind to do so, he can deliver a seminar on, say, defensive secondary play that's as detailed as any lecture at MIT. However, on the subject of the game immediately ahead of him, Belichick can be little more than a walking catechism of perfunctory cliché.

In *The Education of a Coach*, his 2005 study of Belichick, David Halberstam attributed this to a public persona that Belichick chose to adopt when he first became a head coach, in Cleveland in 1991. Among other things, Belichick moved quickly to restrict and control what had been fairly free access to the team, even once calling a Cleveland beat reporter to complain about an accurate story concerning an injured Browns receiver, based on information the reporter had gotten from the team's owner.

As difficult as they can be with the home press, the Patriots and Belichick can be impossible on the weekly conference calls they're required to make to the reporters in the city of that week's opponent. On the Wednesday before the Patriots and the Colts played on Monday night, November 7, Belichick's answers to the Indianapolis writers were succinct, accurate, and almost completely useless. Then, the Patriots chose linebacker Willie McGinest to represent the team's players. McGinest is a smart veteran player, who once sealed a win over Indianapolis by personally stuffing the All-Pro running back Edgerrin James on the New England one-foot line with eleven seconds left in the game. But he wasn't the story of this upcoming game any more than he was the mayor of Indianapolis.

Over the five years Brady had played in the NFL, these two teams had developed a rivalry that was as ferocious as it was one-sided. New England had won fourteen of the previous sixteen games it had played against Indianapolis, including the last six in a row. Two of them were playoff games, including the previous season's AFC divisional playoff. Moreover, both teams had become defined, as most football teams are for good or ill, by their quarterbacks.

In his autobiography, Knute Rockne—who, with his Notre Dame teammate Gus Dorais, is widely credited with inventing the forward pass, although Rockne insisted the honor belonged to Eddie Cochem—makes it quite plain that the game changed once coaches realized the football could be moved down the field by throwing it just as well as by carrying it. "The pass," writes Rockne, "complicated matters too much for old-fashioned coaches who preferred to rely on bull-strength and Lady Luck." Moreover, it began the process by which the quarterback would become the first among equals, which is why Bobby Layne always set aside beer money for teammates who didn't make as much as he did. It's also why this upcoming Monday night game between Indianapolis and New England was framed as Peyton Manning against Tom Brady.

Sometimes, quarterbacks run in families. Manning's brother is a quarterback with the New York Giants, and his father was a quarterback, too, a fire-haired legend from the University of Mississippi, where he is still so beloved that the speed limit on the Ole Miss campus is forever kept at 18 miles per hour, the number Archie Manning wore when he played for the Rebels back in the turbulent mid-1960s.

"How do you decide to become a quarterback?" Archie Manning laughs. "I don't know how it happens these days, because kids don't go out and just play, but in my day it just kind of happened. When I played with the older fellas, I just played where they told me to play. The first organized football I played was in seventh grade, and we had a new coach and he just lined us up and told you where you were going to play. Me? I got put at wide receiver. I was as heartbroken as I'd ever been in my life. One of my friends was picked as the quarterback, and I wouldn't even speak to him."

Archie bounced back, wooed and married an Ole Miss homecoming queen named Olivia Williams, and even survived the horror of his father's suicide. He played for some terrible New Orleans Saints teams and was nearly crippled for his trouble. He and Olivia raised three sons in a big house in the Garden District in New Orleans, and the second one, named Peyton, was a precocious kid. "He couldn't have been more than four," says his father, "and he could do a dropback. His brother used to show him off a little—you know, 'Do a dropback, Peyton.' And he would." Peyton grew into a great quarterback. In 2004, he'd had a towering season, throwing forty-nine touchdowns, breaking Dan Marino's NFL record by one. However, his season ended on a cold January day in Foxborough when Bill Belichick and the Patriots made him look like a child for the second year in a row.

In the 2003 AFC title game, Manning threw four interceptions. A year later, he threw only one, but he couldn't move the Colts offense at all. Meanwhile, Brady and the Patriots steadily ground out the yardage and wore out the clock. They went to the Super Bowl. For the sixth time in a row, a team quarterbacked by Peyton Manning had lost to a team quarterbacked by Tom Brady.

The rivalry got nasty, and it reached all the way into the executive suites. After the 2003 playoff game, in which Manning had thrown those four interceptions, the Indianapolis president, Bill Polian, howled to anybody in the league who would listen that the New England defensive backs had been allowed to manhandle his team's receivers. The NFL's competition committee subsequently adjusted the rules on pass coverage, making it more difficult for defensive backs to muscle up on receivers. It escaped nobody's attention in Foxborough that Polian himself sat on that very committee. Sooner or later, as it always does, the focus of the spat became the teams' respective quarterbacks.

Somehow, the two men—and through them, the two teams—had come to symbolize polar opposites. Manning was the high-priced quarterback who couldn't win. In the spring, he'd signed a new seven-year contract that totaled, with a $34.5 million signing bonus, $98 million. The deal was widely said to have paralyzed the team with regard to the NFL salary cap. Meanwhile, Brady, who'd never lost to a team led by Manning, and with three Super Bowl championships besides, accepted a six-year, $60 million extension of his contract. Brady wouldn't be selling apples on the street, but his contract was considered something of a discount because it allowed the Patriots more roster flexibility than the Colts now had. Only in the giddy economics of sports can accepting a $60 million deal be considered in any way selfless, but it seemed to be another critical symbolic difference between the two quarterbacks.

Many New England fans—especially those who could make their way to a computer keyboard, or to a telephone in order to call a sports-talk station—had come to regard Manning as little more than a statistical show pony. Comparatively, they saw in their hometown quarterback every virtue, which, truth be told, made him more than a little queasy.

"Almost every discussion on the site," says Aaron Schatz, who runs a popular football Web site called Football Outsiders, "turned into Brady versus Manning. There is this image of Tom Brady as sort of this knight in shining armor and Peyton Manning as this prissy little nancy boy whose only concern is the money he makes." At his site, and many others, the quarterback controversy rages on behalf of figures made of cyberstraw.

"From Indianapolis, it's the exact opposite," Schatz explains. "Brady is never going to be as good as Manning, and his defense helps him win the games anyway. But, there, Brady is not held nearly as negative as Manning is [in New England]. I don't know either of these two guys, and neither do most people. I have no clue what they're like as people. I'm a statistical analyst, and I think this whole Brady-versus-Manning thing is incredibly disrespectful to, among other things, the New England defense."

As it turned out, the 2005 edition of the rivalry was more important to the Patriots than it was to the Colts, who had won their first seven games of the season. After losing to Denver, the Patriots again had moved one game above the .500 mark at 4–3 by beating the Buffalo Bills at home in a game that had marked the return of linebacker Tedy Bruschi, whose career had been thought to be over when he suffered a stroke shortly after the Super Bowl the previous winter. However, even with Bruschi's return, the New England defense was still a mess. Richard Seymour, the team's best defensive player, wouldn't play against the Colts because of a mysterious knee injury suffered when Belichick put Seymour in on offense to block on a goal-line play. This is the kind of risky maneuver that only having won three Super Bowls immunizes a coach from being parboiled for by his fans.

The New England injuries had put a reverse spin on the comparison of the two quarterbacks. The Colts were healthy and running a balanced offense, and Manning was throwing less than he ever had before. Meanwhile, with his defense in tatters, Brady had thrown for a whopping 2,020 yards in the first seven games. He was on his way to his first 4,000-yard passing season. Manning already had six of those, and, according to the received wisdom of New England's partisans, all of them were a perfect indication of Manning's fundamental inferiority as a quarterback.

Of course, Brady and Manning are perfectly cordial to each other. (Both of them, it turns out, are friendly with Philadelphia's Donovan McNabb.) "He doesn't give out the company secrets," Brady says, laughing. "He kind of likes to keep those under wraps." They talk, mostly about the curious lives they lead. Neither is the sum of his public image. Neither trusts the symbolic life that has been constructed on his behalf.

"He's proven himself, year in and year out. You can rattle off statistics, but he sets the standard for quarterback play," Brady continues. "Obviously, the quarterbacks don't compete against each other, but, as a team, you're competing against the team that he leads. We have quite a rivalry, going back to the days when they were in our division. Even when I first started, those were fun games."

"These are the kind of games you like to play in," Manning said. "When the game is on the cover of the national magazines before the game, that tells you it's a pretty big game. [*Sports Illustrated* put Brady and Manning on that week's cover under the headline THE DUEL.] This is why you play in the NFL."

Brady is the more imposing—square-shouldered and visibly bigger, the beanpole of Michigan a memory for all but readers of that university's media guide. At first glance, this gives him an apparent physical advantage over Manning, whose shoulders are long and down-running. Neither is strikingly athletic in his play; Manning runs even more awkwardly than Brady does. The differences in how they throw the ball result largely from the differences in the respective offenses they are asked to lead.

"They're more similar than they are different," explains the Indianapolis head coach, Tony Dungy. "Both are guys with great leadership, great presence. They're not what you'd call 'athletic,' but they don't get sacked much. Games hinge on quarterbacks, or they seem to hinge on quarterbacks. That's the nature of the position, and they all know that going in."

Here, on a bright day with the last of the autumn colors blowing around, the Indianapolis Colts looked bright and new and more than a little bit anxious. From the perspective of the Indianapolis training facility, the New England Patriots were a smooth and faceless monolith standing directly in the path of the Colts. New England fans would be surprised how much their football team—*that* football team—looked, at this remove, like the New York Yankees.

It was the autumn of 1970, and Bob Gladieux had bars to close, dozens of them, in Boston's Back Bay. Neighborhood joints and restaurant lounges and what were only then becoming known as "singles bars." Bob Gladieux was going to close every one of them, from Massachusetts Avenue up the slow rise toward Beacon Hill. Like Hillary on Everest, Gladieux was going to establish base camp and then make a steady assault on the summit, which in this case would be the golden dome of the Massachusetts State House. There were bars up around there, too. "I closed the city down, three nights running," he recalls.

He had a right to this historic bender. He was angry, and he had a right to be that, too. Gladieux was no slouch. A tough running back at Notre Dame—he had scored the Irish touchdown in the legendary 10–10 tie with Michigan State in 1966—he'd signed on in 1969 with what were then called the Boston Patriots of the American Football League. The AFL was just on the verge of its improbable triumph; less than a decade after its scruffy beginnings, it was about to force a merger with the lordly NFL. This revolution had succeeded the way Benjamin Franklin had said all revolutions do—like bastard children, half improvised and half compromised. However, the Boston patriots with whom Franklin had worked knew their business. If he had been dealing with the Boston Patriots whom Bob Gladieux joined, we might all be singing "God Save the Queen" before our football games.

One of the AFL's charter franchises, the Patriots were bedraggled right from the start. Most of the problems stemmed from the fact that their owner, Billy Sullivan, a former Boston College publicist and president of the Metropolitan Petroleum Company, was of a different financial phylum from many of his fellow owners. Even though the AFL seemed a risky proposition at the start, its owners included the extremely wealthy Bud Adams in Houston and the ludicrously wealthy (and hideously reactionary) Lamar Hunt in Dallas. (Perhaps Sullivan's job as head of the MPC made him the closest thing to an oilman Adams and Hunt could find in Boston.) Even by the penurious standards of the early AFL, the Patriots were cheap. Once, in Buffalo, they told their players to sleep on top of their beds to avoid the housekeeping charge in their motel.

Worst of all, however, was the team's chronic inability to find a home. When the Patriots were founded, the city of Boston had just gone through a series of highly volatile fights over urban renewal, the bloodiest of which occurred in the mid-1950s and concerned the demolition of a neighborhood on the far side of Beacon Hill called the West End. The resentment lingers in city politics to this day. In the 1960s, when the Patriots were looking for someone to build them a stadium, it was still raw, and no local politician wanted to get in the middle of the next West End fight. For the first eleven years of their existence, the Patriots were orphans.

They played at Fenway Park, the football field ridiculously catty-cornered to the old park's baseball layout, with bleachers in front of the famous left-field wall. They played at Boston University in a stadium left behind when the Braves blew town. Boston College hosted the team for a few games but threw them out after Patriots fans got too rowdy. In 1968, they played—and lost—a home game in Birmingham, Alabama. In 1970 Harvard was grudgingly hosting the team, whose new stadium was finally being built in Foxborough. Which is how Bob Gladieux came to believe he would be playing at Harvard Stadium when the Patriots opened the 1970 season against the Miami Dolphins.

Except that he wouldn't be.

On the Wednesday night before the game, Gladieux was summoned by Clive Rush, the new Boston coach. Rush's hiring was perfectly consonant with Patriots history. The team had determined that it would hire one of two assistants off the staff of Weeb Ewbank, whose New York Jets had just won their epochal Super Bowl over the Baltimore Colts. One was Chuck Noll. The other was Clive Rush. The Patriots hired Rush. Noll, of course, went on to win four Super Bowls with the Pittsburgh Steelers. Rush was nearly electrocuted by a faulty microphone at his introductory press conference and, eventually, went completely around the bend, ending up in Massachusetts General Hospital. On this day, however, he told Gladieux that he had been cut from the team.

Gladieux knew what was going on. He was owed a two-thousand-dollar incentive bonus if he made the club. Furious, he headed into Boston and proceeded on his quest to drain the Back Bay dry again. Eventually, he found his way to the apartment of a friend, and the two of them decided to go to the game at Harvard. "He had a six-pack of Schlitz in the car, and a bottle of rum," Gladieux recalls. They got to the stadium, an old concrete corral on the banks of the Charles River that recently had become nationally famous again when Ryan O'Neal and Ali MacGraw had cavorted around it in the snow in the movie *Love Story*. His friend went off to the concession stand to buy the first round of beers.

"So, I'm sitting there, and the PA guy announces, 'Bob Gladieux, please report to the trainer's room,'" he says. "I'm still fully loaded, as you know."

Once he got to the area under the stands where the Patriots were dressing, Gladieux found Rush and was told, quite seriously, that the Patriots would like to activate him for the game, which was now less than a half hour away. Some of Gladieux's teammates warned him not to take the offer, since the team transparently had devised this weird scenario to keep from paying him the bonus he was owed. (Since Gladieux hadn't "made the team" in training camp, management had ducked through what was admittedly a very cheesy loophole.) However, Gladieux, a free spirit whose wild hair had his teammates calling him Harpo, wanted to play. He accepted the offer. Then the team threw him out there to cover the opening kickoff.

"I'm running out there, and I'm thinking, Jesus, Mary, and Joseph, what's going to happen now? I was just looking for someplace to hide," he recalls. "My first thought was, Whatever you do, protect yourself. Bob and weave! Avoid all contact!

"So I run down, and I see the wedge form to the right, and I'm on the left, so I feel good, and then Jake Scott [the Miami kick returner] makes this mistake. He runs away from the wedge and right towards me."

Gladieux's companion was just at that moment returning from the concession stand with the afternoon's first round of beers, blissfully unaware that anything had happened in his absence. A great cheer went up around him.

"Tackle by Number 24, Bob Gladieux," said the PA announcer.

His friend drank all the beers.

It remains an iconic moment in the history of a team that was as beset by misfortune as it was by the lack of a home field on which to play. It wasn't just that bad and crazy things happened to the Patriots. It was that monumentally bad and crazy things happened to the Patriots. The Patriots were on *Monday*

Night Football the night John Lennon was shot. A Tufts professor got infatuated with a hooker from Boston's Combat Zone, beat her to death with a hammer, and Patriot players got called in to his trial because they'd been part of her client base, too. They finally got a stadium built, and, shortly before the first game, some concerns about the plumbing arose and the team's entire administrative staff was dragooned to flush all the stadium's toilets at once to make sure they could handle the pressure of a capacity crowd. And, within five years, the stadium had the reputation of being the NFL's preeminent bucket o' blood.

"I was there for the third or fourth year of the stadium," says Steve Nelson, who played thirteen years at linebacker for the Patriots. "We were never on TV. We had blacked-out games all the time. You'd have to drive to New Hampshire to watch us play." In his rookie season, Nelson was invited to a birthday party for one of his veteran teammates. The next day, the head coach, Chuck Fairbanks, called Nelson into his office. The coach told Nelson to watch himself. The Drug Enforcement Administration had been watching that player's house, and the Feds probably had Nelson in a file somewhere now. "I was young and I was from North Dakota," Nelson says with a laugh. "I didn't know anything about that stuff."

Nor did success necessarily mean good fortune for the Patriots. In 1978, when they had what Nelson reckons to have been one of the best teams on which he ever played, Fairbanks secretly negotiated a pasha's package to become the head coach at the University of Colorado. Patriot president Billy Sullivan suspended him in the locker room before the final regular-season game with Houston, which the Patriots lost. They made their first Super Bowl in 1986, becoming the first NFL team ever to win three consecutive playoff games on the road. Not only were they slaughtered, 46–10, by the Chicago Bears, but they were greeted at home by stories about rampant drug use on the team. A decade later, Bill Parcells got them back to New Orleans and the Super Bowl, only to have it revealed the day after the game that he'd gone down the Fairbanks road; he'd been negotiating with the New York Jets to take over as their coach the following season. His move started a media free-for-all between Parcells and the Kraft family that was probably the biggest reason Bill Belichick wound up as the Patriots' coach. "Sometimes," Nelson says, "it seemed like being good was the worst thing that could happen to us."

Bob Kraft was a fan for all those seasons. He and his family went to Foxborough and sat on the metal benches and froze. "I was there with my sons, and my wife was home, doing the *New York Times* crossword puzzle and going to all those artsy movies that I would never go to," Kraft says. "She loved Sundays. I loved the Patriots, even though they embarrassed me sometimes."

The genealogy of the quarterback position is probably the best guide through the team's bumptious history. In 1970, just as the old Foxboro Stadium was opening, the Patriots were led by Jim Plunkett, a Heisman Trophy winner at Stanford and a legitimate college superstar. Plunkett played five seasons with what had been renamed the New England Patriots. The team never finished better than 7–7, and Plunkett was demolished weekly behind threadbare offensive lines. Eventually, Fairbanks tried to make him an option quarterback, but Plunkett's legs were shot. He was booed unmercifully, and there were calls for him to be replaced by his backup, a leathery young man from Kansas State named Steve Grogan. "My first day of training camp here I weighed 188 pounds," Grogan says. "I would have blown away in a hurricane."

Grogan played sixteen seasons, all with the Patriots. He

threw for 26,886 yards, and he ran for 2,176 more. He played through a staggering array of injuries, from broken legs to neck injuries so bad that he played wearing a cervical collar, like a whiplash victim. In 1983, in an attempt to upgrade the position, the Patriots drafted Tony Eason, a blond Californian from the University of Illinois. It was a move that, over the next several seasons, presaged the events that would make Tom Brady the quarterback of the Patriots in 2001.

Eason was a smooth and fluid passer. However, his work ethic didn't impress his teammates, who preferred the more rugged and workmanlike Grogan. For his part, Grogan fought to keep the position as hard as he fought to play it. Once, when Grogan was at the stadium lifting weights, Eason asked him why he was doing that. Grogan looked at him as though Eason had asked him something in Finnish.

"I don't like big egos," Grogan says. "I don't like people who have them, and I wouldn't have liked me if I'd had one. But Tony, coming in as a first-round draft pick, well, I thought I'd earned the position."

It all came to a head during the Super Bowl game in 1986. Eason had been sick the night before, a development for which few of his teammates gave him the benefit of the doubt. As the game began, and as it became plain that the Chicago pass rush was virtually unstoppable, Eason missed on his first six throws and was obviously looking for a place to lie down on every play. It was the first quarter, and the New England head coach, Raymond Berry, had a near-mutiny on his hands. The players were demanding that Grogan take over. Berry made the change.

"I had visions of turning things around and pulling the game out, but it didn't happen," says Grogan. "We got the crap kicked out of us, but I was out there, and it was fun." He retired, finally, in 1990, after a season in which the Patriots finished 1–15.

Two years earlier, Billy Sullivan and his family had been drowning in debt. In the final chapter of the exceedingly strange history of his New England Patriots, one of Sullivan's sons, Chuck, had come up with the brilliant notion of investing in a rock-and-roll tour in partnership with Don King, the noted boxing carnivore. The tour was such a catastrophe that Chuck Sullivan briefly found himself living in a luxury box at the stadium. Finally, after some serious prodding from the NFL, the Sullivans took $80 million for their majority stake in the team from Victor Kiam, the president and CEO of the Gillette razor company.

Kiam turned out to be something of a public lout; when various Patriots players sexually harassed a *Boston Herald* reporter named Lisa Olson, setting off a firestorm within the NFL, Kiam made a joke about the players and their "Patriot missiles," which sent his fellow owners into a towering rage. At roughly the same time, Robert Kraft and his K-Corp had shrewdly bought the old stadium in Foxborough, which seemed a much better investment than the team that played in it but which also got Kraft's foot in the door in case he ever chose to buy the team.

On the field, the Patriots cratered. They won nine games in the three seasons between 1990 and 1992. In January 1993, almost at the end of his tether and beginning to entertain seriously the thought of moving the franchise to St. Louis, James Orthwein, who'd bought the team from the hapless Kiam a year earlier, brought Parcells out of retirement to coach. Parcells had won two Super Bowls with the New York Giants, and he gave an instant shot of credibility to the Patriots.

In April, New England drafted Drew Bledsoe, a tall, gun-slinging quarterback from Washington State, who as a freshman had faced down a rebellion by senior members of the Cougars when he was named the team's quarterback. Between them, Parcells and Bledsoe brought enough credibility to the franchise that Kraft made the move he'd been waiting to make.

In January 1994, he bought the team for $172 million. Kraft now owned the team, the stadium, and all the land around it, on which he could build his own stadium if he so desired. But while the clown college that was the New England Patriots seemed to have closed for good, nothing would come easily for the team. In fact, New England lost the first playoff game it played under Kraft's ownership, 20–13, to a Cleveland Browns team coached by Parcells's old defensive coordinator from the Giants, Bill Belichick.

The relationship between Kraft and Parcells hopelessly deteriorated. Parcells resented what he saw as meddling by Kraft, most notably in personnel matters. It was this, he later said, that prompted him to take the job with the Jets, where, as he memorably put it, he would be allowed not only to cook the dinner but also "to shop for the groceries." When Parcells departed in the immediate aftermath of New England's 35–21 loss to Green Bay in Super Bowl XXXI, it prompted a spate of stories about discord within the franchise. The local media chose up sides. The two men seemed unable to disengage from each other; a year later, Parcells gleefully scooped up New England's free-agent running back Curtis Martin.

Parcells's replacement, a former Jets coach named Pete Carroll, was a likable, enthusiastic sort, but he seemed unwilling or unable to assume complete command of his players. In fact, he couldn't even keep them from making back-channel visits to the team's front office to complain about him. Carroll's three seasons ended with the Patriots losing six of their last eight games in

1999. At this point, Kraft began to fasten his eyes on the heart of Parcells's inner circle.

Belichick had been crucial to the success Parcells enjoyed with the Giants. (In fact, Parcells has never won a Super Bowl without Belichick on his staff.) Belichick's defensive scheming was several levels above that of most coaches in the league. According to David Halberstam, when all of them were in New England during Parcells's tenure there, it had been Belichick who'd been the liaison between the coach and the owner as their relationship fell apart. Now, though, having been fired in Cleveland, Belichick had rejoined Parcells for one season in New England before moving with him to the Jets. Belichick found his relationship with Parcells fraying. (Halberstam describes a nasty incident on the Jets sideline in which Parcells cruelly cited Belichick's failure as a head coach during a disagreement in which Belichick was in the right.) When Kraft began to talk to Belichick about replacing Pete Carroll in New England, Belichick was more than ready to listen.

Something of a comic opera ensued. Parcells wanted Belichick to succeed him in New York, so he "retired" and "appointed" Belichick his successor. It was an act of unbearable paternalism. Parcells seemed to believe he had first call on the direction of Belichick's career. For his part, Belichick was whipsawed between his longtime friendship with Parcells and the staggering presumption with which he was now being treated. He dithered for a few days. At a press conference so strange that many people wondered if Belichick had come unglued, he resigned as coach of the Jets, who released a note to the media in which Belichick wrote that he was quitting as "HC of the NYJ." It wasn't until Parcells and Kraft got together on a compensation package—Belichick cost the Patriots three draft choices, including a first-rounder—that Belichick finally was free to take the job in New England.

The effort it took to land his coach was nothing compared with what Kraft went through to get his team a new stadium. He'd bought the team in 1994 believing that the then Massachusetts governor William Weld had promised to deliver public money for a downtown "megaplex" facility in Boston. There is some question about whether Weld, an eccentric politician even by the considerable standards of the Commonwealth and so flighty that he made Mayor McCheese look like Benjamin Disraeli, ever had either the intention or the clout to deliver. At the same time, there was a national backlash against spending public money for private sports facilities. In any case, an old-fashioned Massachusetts pissing match ensued for the next six years.

Several Boston proposals died aborning, including one on the South Boston waterfront that Kraft proposed paying for himself. Concocted in secret, again on Weld's advice, the plan inevitably leaked and fell victim to neighborhood outrage. A Rhode Island plan took wing briefly, then crashed; Kraft accused the mayor of Boston of having "an elevator that doesn't go all the way to the top"; the speaker of the Massachusetts House called Kraft "a whiny multimillionaire"; the Krafts made guarded comments about veiled anti-Semitism and wondered why the Red Sox, run at that time by a man named John Harrington, seemed to get their calls returned. It was a lovely war. Then, in 1998, Bob Kraft appeared to have found the king of the suckers.

John Rowland, the governor of Connecticut and a man who eventually would go to jail, at least in part for having state employees paint his vacation home, proposed to make a new stadium part of a $1 billion renovation of a spot called Adriaen's Landing, an industrial wasteland along the Connecticut River in downtown Hartford where a power plant had been built atop the site of some old tanneries. Rowland said the state would build the Patriots a $375 million stadium along with a $15 million practice facility, and it guaranteed the team the sale of 125 luxury boxes and six thousand club seats. It was the sweetheart deal to end all sweetheart deals. It was a farce from the start.

Leaving aside the economic insanity of the proposal—one legislative audit priced the cost to Connecticut taxpayers out at $257 million over five years—the site seemed to be both an ecological disaster and an archaeological treasure trove, an unusual parlay that added up to yet more reasons why the whole project could be delayed for God alone knew how long. Once the deal came to light, the state exploded. Connecticut native Ralph Nader began chewing on Rowland's leg. According to the agreement Rowland had signed with Kraft, the stadium was supposed to be ready by 2001. Once the details became public, and every interest group from taxpayer associations to environmental activists began to weigh in, it became clear that Rowland might as well have offered Kraft a snow-white unicorn on which to ride to the new stadium's opening.

In photographs taken when the Hartford deal was signed, Kraft looks as if he'd rather be anywhere else, even though he was being handed the Connecticut state treasury as a piñata. However, the deal did start things stirring in Boston again. The Massachusetts legislature began talking about supplying "infrastructure improvements" in Foxborough if Kraft was willing to build a new stadium for his team on land he already owned. The NFL intervened as well, and Kraft said he would never move the team from Massachusetts. Business leaders in Connecticut howled that Kraft was somehow reneging on a promise to rob their state blind. On June 15, 2000, the first cement was poured in Foxborough for the foundation of the new home of the New England Patriots. Not long after that, leaving work for the day,

Bob Kraft encountered a skinny quarterback carrying a pizza out to the players' parking lot. And, finally, the team was ready to lay to rest the ghost of Harpo Gladieux.

From the start, Kraft has insisted that the Patriots be not only a model football franchise, but also a public demonstration of good corporate citizenship. He wanted as much of a "family values" operation as can be built in the ruthless context of professional football, where it often becomes necessary to cast out members of the "family" when they become too old or injured to carry their weight, or when their salaries become too high for the "family" budget. The family values of the average NFL team owe more to those of the Corleones than they do to those of the Waltons, but Kraft was determined to try. On this particular topic, Kraft can induce his audience, as Dorothy Parker might have put it, "to fwow up." He is indomitable about it, though.

(Parker also once famously said, "If you want to know what God thinks of money, look at the people he gives it to." But, in truth, Kraft and his family remain formidable philanthropists in and around the Boston area, their charity both creative and ecumenical. Not long ago, they simultaneously endowed a chair in Christian studies at Brandeis University and one in Judaic studies at the College of the Holy Cross.)

"Our goal," he says, "was always to try and do things in a way that would bring a championship to New England and, at the same time, use the team as a vehicle to try and help bring the community together. I used to say that, if I could do anything, we'd run the team in a certain way. We've tried to set a value system of things we'd accept and things we wouldn't accept. Our family name is on this team. I'm not saying we're holier than thou, but we do try to run this team the way we run our other businesses."

When Tom Brady arrived in Foxborough, he was a fourth-string quarterback, struggling to make the team in what was essentially the equivalent of the redshirt year he'd spent at Michigan. Nevertheless, he was happier than he'd ever been in college. When training camp ended, he called his father, who'd gone on a golf outing to Ireland. He caught him at dinner. "Dad," Brady said, "I made the team." The whole dining room cheered the news.

He wasn't even on the scout team. He practiced mainly with a group of rookies, many of whom already had one foot in a liquor distributorship back home. Almost from the moment he joined them, however, Brady caught the eye of Charlie Weis, the New England offensive coordinator.

Weis was a huge man, another coach out of the extended family that traced back to Bill Parcells. Like all New England assistants, his public profile was a low one. (It is Belichick's policy that assistant coaches are not available for interviews.) However, given the nature of his job, Charlie Weis was theoretically visible every time the Patriots ran a play, especially the "gadget" stuff—reverses and tossbacks to the quarterback—for which Weis had a conspicuous liking. Watching Brady with the rookies, Weis noticed that these inherently disposable players seemed to get better. Brady had taken what he had been given, and out of it he was creating a team around him.

"He kind of took them over, like he was the leader of the group," says Weis. "And you just watched that whole group mature around him. It wasn't that they all could play. You just watched them all mature because he would always strive to be the best there, because he'd work harder than anyone else in the weight room."

Belichick noticed this as well. He watched Brady work endlessly with Weis and with the quarterback coach, Dick Rehbein, on refining the techniques that Tom Martinez had taught him back at home. Belichick also saw the improvement that Brady had wrought in the scrub team with whom he was practicing. "He would take the young players at the end of practice, and they'd run through our entire offense, which they never ran because they were always running the other team's stuff," Belichick recalls. "If somebody ran something wrong, he'd correct them. He developed an understanding not only of his position but of the entire offense. In his leadership style, he was able to do that.

"As they moved along, you could see the whole team getting better. These guys weren't necessarily playing; we were trying to make them better and get them ready to play. Tom showed a lot of maturity and I would say leadership. By the end of the year, he was a leader of that class."

Still, Brady remained a practice player. He got into one game, a 34–9 loss in Detroit on Thanksgiving Day. In his professional return to the state of Michigan, Brady completed one out of three passes for a total of six yards. The first one he threw was very nearly intercepted and returned for a touchdown, a step up from the first pass he'd thrown at Michigan, which actually was. New England finished the season at 5–11, and there were rumblings that Belichick's job might be on the line throughout the following season and that, if it was, it would hang on the arm of Drew Bledsoe, the quarterback who'd helped the Patriots finally achieve some sort of stability and to whom the Krafts had just given a ten-year, $103 million contract extension.

And it was no secret around the team that Belichick didn't trust Bledsoe as his quarterback. After all, both as a head coach in Cleveland and as a defensive coordinator with the Jets, Belichick had found in Bledsoe a quarterback against whom he could easily scheme. Bledsoe neither thought nor moved quickly. He would try to ram the ball into a primary receiver rather than "check down" through his other options. He took brainless penalties at terrible times. He took sacks because he was neither fast enough to escape the pocket nor quick enough to escape within it. In an offense designed on timing patterns, and on a team designed around ball control and defense, Drew Bledsoe looked not so much incompetent as miscast.

Brady threw himself into the off-season workouts, attending all of them even if he wasn't required to be there. He noticed that Bledsoe wasn't around. So did the coaching staff. Brady stayed in Foxborough even after the workouts were done, returning to San Mateo only briefly for the Fourth of July holiday. During his time at home, he and his father drove to the California Golf Club to play a round. As they were pulling into the parking lot, Brady took a call from Charlie Weis on his cell phone.

Weis was teasing him, wondering why he was slacking off at home and when he was going to be back. "Don't worry about me," Tom Brady heard his son say. "I'll be there, and, by the way, when I come back, I'm not coming there as a backup."

"It was like a shot across the bow," the elder Brady recalls. "He was telling them that he was coming back to compete."

Before the 2001 season, the Patriots had signed the veteran Damon Huard as Bledsoe's backup. The team gave Huard a million dollars just to sign. The displaced Michael Bishop went off to NFL Europe, never to return. However, the situation had to have resonated with Brady. He'd been through all of this at Michigan. A chance would open up, and circumstance would close it.

At the time, he was rooming—in a condominium that once

belonged to New England's All-Pro safety Ty Law—with Dave Nugent, a defensive end from Purdue who'd been selected two picks after Brady. In an interview given to Rich Wolfe as part of an oral history of the 2001 season, Nugent said Brady had been struck by the similarities between what he was going through with the Patriots and all that had occurred in Ann Arbor. Nugent also noticed how Brady had constructed strategies to cope with it, which likely were the product of all those come-to-Jesus Friday night meetings Brady had sat through with Greg Harden back in college. There was one significant difference. This time, the coaches seemed to be paying attention.

Even given the team's expensive investment in Huard, it was increasingly dawning on both Weis and Belichick that Brady might be more than a third-string quarterback. "Bill and I talked," Weis recalls, "and I said that maybe we ought to give Brady an opportunity to beat this guy out."

That year's training camp turned out to be both tragic and pivotal for Brady and the Patriots. On August 6, Dick Rehbein, who'd been Brady's quarterback coach since he'd convinced New England to draft him, died suddenly of a heart attack. While it was left for Bledsoe, as the team's starter and most visible player, to make public comment on the loss, Brady felt unmoored. He'd lost not only a friend, but his staunchest advocate, right from the first day he'd seen Brady at Michigan's Pro Day. "That," his father recalls, "was a tough one for him."

By the time of Rehbein's death, Huard was having a good camp. Brady was having a better one. "Now," says Weis, "Tommy didn't beat him out by a lot." Belichick agrees and credits Huard with taking his demotion with considerable grace. "It was a big decision, but it wasn't a hard decision," Belichick says. "The only thing that happened was that Brady played better in the preseason, so he got more snaps in practice because we felt like we needed to see him play. You evaluate players with the same grading scale, but they don't get the same opportunities. Some guys get fifty snaps. Other guys get a hundred. Damon [Huard] was great. He wasn't real happy about it, but there are certain decisions that are out of your control."

Brady was now the team's backup quarterback, and he began to realize that he had found the kind of meritocracy in the professional game that he'd always been promised in college. In fact, some people watching the team, and a number of the people who covered it, were openly wondering if he might still be one slot too low on the depth chart. And thus began the last great quarterback controversy of Tom Brady's career, one that would play itself out through a season that was surpassingly surreal.

New England lost its first game, 23–17, in Cincinnati to the Bengals, on September 9, 2001. Two days later, terrorists of the al-Qaeda network slammed airplanes into the World Trade Center in New York and into the Pentagon. A fourth plane, probably aimed at the Capitol dome in Washington, went down in a field in Pennsylvania after passengers stormed the cockpit. The nation convulsed, the National Football League along with it. In his history of the league, Michael MacCambridge poignantly describes NFL staffers, two of whom lost spouses in the attack, walking down the block from NFL headquarters to St. Patrick's Cathedral.

Fear was there at the bottom of everything, even the hottest anger, the strangest explanations, and the loudest demonstrations of public patriotism. There was fear laced through all of it. Nothing seemed sure or solid anymore. The oceans, we were told, no longer could protect us. No matter that the statement was historically absurd in a country that had lived for a half century with the threat of thousands of Soviet ICBMs—for that matter, the oceans hadn't done much to protect the Aztecs—the fear made it substantive and real.

No entertainment enterprise was as closely tied in to the country's centers of power as the NFL. Commissioner Paul Tagliabue, whose résumé included three years working in the Pentagon, made the determination—while the building where he'd once worked was still burning—that the NFL would not play the following weekend. Tagliabue thereby neatly side-stepped the kind of public-relations catastrophe that had be-fallen his predecessor, Pete Rozelle, who'd pushed forward with a full slate of games two days after President John F. Kennedy was gunned down in Dallas. In 2001, all the country's major sports operations followed the NFL's lead.

The Patriots didn't play again for two weeks, and then they lost their home opener to the New York Jets, 10–3. It was the worst day of Drew Bledsoe's career. He played spectacularly poorly, booting one Patriot drive by taking an inexcusable delay-of-game penalty on a fourth-and-goal from the New York 1-yard line, an egregious gaffe not only because it cost the Patriots points but also because it made both Belichick and Weis look like idiots for having declined, however briefly, an easy field goal. Headsets flew on the New England sideline. Then, late in the game and deep in his own territory, Bledsoe was chased out of the pocket, and he went galumphing up the right sideline. New York linebacker Mo Lewis had a perfect angle and murder in his eye. It sounded like a train hitting a deer. Standing nearby, Brady thought it was the loudest collision he'd ever heard on a football field. "TV does it no justice," Brady says today. "I re-member somebody finding Drew's helmet and tromping on it, trying to straighten it out."

Lewis had hit Bledsoe so hard that he'd sheared a blood vessel in the quarterback's chest. Bledsoe, who'd almost died as a young quarterback from a lacerated liver, would be hospitalized for nearly a week. Brady came on in his relief but couldn't win the game. New England split their next two contests, beating Indianapolis and being routed in Miami. That left the team at 1–3. The season seemed to be slipping away as they prepared for a home game against the San Diego Chargers.

"That was the game," Charlie Weis remembers, "when everything changed."

Within the New England locker room, the transition went smoothly. Brady, it seemed, had developed with the team's starters the same kind of relationship he'd developed when he was playing with that group of rookies in his first season. He was assertive but not obnoxious. He spent hours studying film, and he ragged on people in the weight room, driving them to work as hard as he did, but never in such a way as to alienate them. He had an innate ability to form a team around him without ever giving the impression that he was trying to do it.

"The thing is, he goes out of his way to involve everyone," Weis explains. "He's not the quarterback who hangs just with the wide receivers. He'll hang with the offensive linemen. He'll hang with the DBs. And that's very unusual in today's game. Usually, when quarterbacks have guys that their livelihoods depend on, they turn to them. Tommy works the whole team."

In fact, his best friend on the team was Lawyer Milloy, a hard-hitting safety out of the University of Washington. On the surface, Milloy couldn't have been more different from Brady, the suburban kid with the devoted family. Milloy grew up in Tacoma in an area so overrun by drugs and guns that CBS News showed up to document the carnage. A retired Green Beret living in the neighborhood took to shooting at drug dealers from his front porch. One day, while Milloy was at basketball practice, he got a phone call from the Tacoma police telling him that his mother and father had been busted together in a crack house. Milloy then moved in with the family of a teammate. It was a long way from the Avenue of the Fleas.

However, Brady and Milloy connected almost at once. They were both ferociously competitive, and they ran together at night around Boston's young singles scene, especially a string of nightclubs that had sprung up near some condominiums built in an old marina in Quincy, south of the city.

Brady spoke up in front of the team. He asserted himself in meetings. Veteran linebacker Ted Johnson was struck one day during a film session when Brady not only spoke up but disagreed with Belichick, which briefly caused Johnson to wonder when the second-year quarterback would be struck down by lightning. Publicly, he fairly burbled with enthusiasm. During one press conference, he interrupted a discussion of an opponent's secondary to interject, "Hey, guys, isn't this great?" At another, when a young reporter mentioned "Tommy" to linebacker Mike Vrabel, Vrabel, a notoriously unimpressable sort, laughed. "Oh, so it's *Tommy* now?" By degrees, the Patriots were becoming Tom Brady's team.

Against San Diego, which was now coached by Mike Riley, the coach who'd failed to get either his college boss or his professional employer interested in Tom Brady, Brady threw his first NFL touchdown pass, a twenty-one-yarder to wide receiver Terry Glenn. But with nine minutes left on the clock, New England had fallen behind and was trailing, 26–16. Brady began to click, and he got the Patriots into position to score the field goal and the touchdown they needed to send the game into overtime.

All that week, Weis and Brady had drilled themselves on one particular blitz alignment of which the San Diego defense was fond. They agreed that, if he saw this rush coming, Brady would change the play at the line and throw an "out-go" ball to receiver David Patten, on which Patten would break sharply to the sideline and then race straight up the field.

After the Chargers failed to move the ball on the first series of the overtime, they punted, and, as the Patriots lined up for their first play, Brady read the blitz. He checked off the play, Patten adjusted the route, and, completely fooled, a San Diego defender interfered with him fifty yards down the field, giving New England enough yardage for Adam Vinatieri to win it with a 44-yard field goal.

Weis was ecstatic. "It wasn't just the ten points he'd gotten us to tie," he says. "It was the fact that we'd gone through sixty or seventy plays on offense, and here it is, the first play of the overtime, and an inexperienced quarterback in his first year of really playing, saw it coming and checked to the play. There are a lot of veteran players that wouldn't see that, and a lot of them wouldn't be able to get it done if they saw it."

At midfield after the game, Brady found himself in an embrace with the San Diego coach. "I wasn't happy," says Riley, "but we had a good laugh about it."

In a mad way, Riley had seen this moment coming. This was what he had tried to explain to John Robinson at USC and to Bobby Beathard, who was now his boss. This was why he had driven up to San Mateo on all those Friday afternoons. This was it, right here, what had just smacked him in the face, beating him in a game that would turn the Chargers' season for the worse. San Diego lost its last nine games in 2001 and Bobby Beathard fired Mike Riley at the end of the season. As for the Patriots, Charlie Weis says, "It was the game that turned it all around for us."

The Patriots lost only two games the rest of the season: the first at Denver, in which Brady threw his first career interception after 162 straight passes without an interception, and at home against St. Louis, a surprisingly close-run game in which New England battered the Rams' vaunted offense. This game not only planted in Bill Belichick's mind the notion that St. Louis—the alleged "Greatest Show on Turf"—was beatable but also forced his hand on the biggest decision of his life.

Drew Bledsoe, the doctors said, was healthy again. He could play against St. Louis. In the week before the game, Bledsoe and Brady had shared the practice plays. The former had been the signature player in the revival of a moribund franchise. More than any other player, Bledsoe was responsible for the new stadium that was being built, for the willingness of the state of Connecticut to flirt with putting itself in hock, for the revival of interest in the Patriots all around New England. In addition, he had been a starting NFL quarterback, and he had left the lineup with an injury. There was talk—serious football talk by serious football people—of a "code" by which a veteran player could not lose his job because of injury. It was Bledsoe's perception that Belichick had told him he would honor that unwritten rule, at least so far as promising that Bledsoe would have a fair chance to compete for his old job.

Against that, Brady was winning games. He didn't get sacked at bad times. He didn't throw game-killing interceptions. He could even get up and give speeches—that sounded hopelessly corny if you wrote them down—to which the team responded. There was an undeniable mutual trust that was maturing by the day into a kind of unshakable loyalty between the players. There was a confidence that didn't so much glow on Brady as radiate out, from him to each teammate, until it suffused them all.

Belichick had been here before. In 1993, the defining act of his tenure as head coach of the Browns came when he cut Bernie

Kosar, the iconic Cleveland quarterback. Objectively, Belichick made the right move. Kosar was at the end of the road. In fact, a year later, behind Kosar's replacement, Vinny Testaverde, the Browns went 11–5, defeating in the playoffs a New England team led by Drew Bledsoe, whom Cleveland intercepted three times. Nevertheless, Belichick had released Kosar in such a clinical fashion that the Browns fans never quite forgave him for the apparent ruthlessness. This time, though, Belichick was benching Bledsoe, not completely defenestrating him. And, even though there was a devoted cadre faithful to the old quarterback, Brady had become a popular favorite, thanks in no small part to the fact that the team was playing so much better with him. Shortly after the St. Louis game, Belichick told Bledsoe that Brady was his starting quarterback.

While the controversy raged on the airwaves and in print, within the New England locker room, where it could have had its most destructive impact, everyone struggled to do the right thing. Bledsoe was privately furious at what he considered Belichick's duplicity. Brady was trying to remain focused on the job at hand while remaining a good teammate to everyone, especially Bledsoe, whom he praised publicly at every turn. Still, there was an undeniable awkwardness in the meeting rooms and in the film sessions, an awkwardness that seemed ironically to intensify with every game the Patriots won. It was possible to interpret each win as an implicit rebuke to Bledsoe. It was possible for success to have a little poison in it. The more people talked about how little friction there was, the more friction there seemed to be.

Charlie Weis was caught in the middle. He had to work with both men in the context of Belichick's decision. For his liaison, Weis turned to Damon Huard, the veteran quarterback whom Brady had beaten out in training camp to be Bledsoe's backup.

"Damon was a godsend," Weis recalls. "Damon was the biggest supporter of Tom, but he was also the one who kept peace in the meeting room. He'd go and hang out with one of them, then he'd go hang out with the other one, just to keep the friction as low as it could be. There were things that I wanted to say but couldn't, so Damon would say them for me. The most critical person in that whole deal was Damon Huard, because it really could have been awful."

The St. Louis game was the last game the Patriots lost that year. Most of the five consecutive wins with which they closed the regular season were tight ones. They even got lucky, which had rarely happened before. In a critical moment during a win at Buffalo, one of Brady's passes was ruled complete, partly because the ball had come to rest at the feet of the receiver, whose head fell out of bounds when he was knocked unconscious.

Brady continued to belie his years, coolly leading the Patriots through the ends of close contests. He was surprised, really, at how normal it all seemed. He did his work during the week. He watched all the films. He asked questions in the meetings. He asserted himself with increasing confidence. Then, on Sunday, it all came together the way it was supposed to. For Brady, who'd spent entire afternoons at Michigan looking over his shoulder to see if Drew Henson was putting on a helmet, the fact that he could feel free enough to succeed at the highest level made him nearly giddy. His whole career had been a struggle for self-definition, a fight to prove to other people that he was in fact the player and the person he knew himself to be. Now he was doing it on his own, fashioning a persona for himself, one win at a time. And his persona was becoming that of the New England Patriots. He found professional success liberating in a way few young quarterbacks would.

"I give myself credit for realizing what he could handle and when he could handle it," Weis says, "and for relinquishing more power to him as his mental ability and experience dictated. That's the only kudos that I deserve. And I did it in such a way where we had a good relationship. It wasn't like we didn't argue. We argued plenty. He's not the most open-minded person in the world, contrary to popular opinion. I'm not, either. But he knows what he knows."

As the Patriots moved into the playoffs, the atmosphere around the NFL remained curious. Security was clamped down in an understandable reaction to the 9/11 attacks, and every game was a statement of the wounded patriotism that had come to suffuse the nation. The United States of America, the last superpower, had been rendered a victim. There was an underdog spirit abroad, and a hunger for the kind of mythic national unity that evinces itself in signs and wonders.

That the instantly martial spirit in the country infused itself into football had to do with more than simply the fact that the attacks had taken place in the fall. Football has always been used as a restorative during those periods in which America gets the public vapors about what it considers its imperiled traditional masculinity. In his book *King Football: Sport and Spectacle in the Golden Age of Radio and Newsreels, Movies and Magazines, the Weekly and the Daily Press*, Michael Oriard, who played at Notre Dame and briefly for the Kansas City Chiefs, cites one memorable quote from 1925 in which Grantland Rice writes that football puts "iron in the soul and steel in the heart." Rice saw the game as an antidote to gin, jazz, and what he called "the softness, and the comfortable ease that money can buy." Of course, the Homer of the Polo Grounds found his Odysseus in Notre Dame's Knute Rockne, for whom football players were society's last line of defense against a plague of what Rockne disdained as "those rumble-seat cowboys."

And Oriard was talking exclusively about college football. The dynamic is even more powerful in the NFL, which has long possessed a capacity for self-mythology that would have embarrassed the Borgia popes. Author Michael MacCambridge notes that Steve Sabol—who, with his father, Ed, helped invent NFL Films, the league's primary mythmaking vehicle—admired both Leni Riefenstahl, infamous for her Nazi propaganda films, and Max Steiner, who composed the Marseilles-laden score for *Casablanca*, which certainly covers the waterfront of 1940s ideological wowsers. The intensity of this formidable propaganda apparatus was turned up full during the 2001 playoffs.

After beating Oakland in the snow game that closed their old stadium, the Patriots went to Pittsburgh for the American Football Conference championship game. Shortly before halftime, a Pittsburgh defender rolled into Brady's left ankle, spraining it so badly that Brady had to leave the game. Enter, for the final time as a Patriot, Drew Bledsoe. Four plays later, he threw a delicately timed ball to David Patten in the deep corner of the Pittsburgh end zone that gave New England a 14–3 lead it would never relinquish. Bledsoe got a game ball.

However, there never was any doubt that, as long as he could walk, and even if he couldn't walk well, Brady would be the starter against St. Louis. Even in his relief stint against the Steelers, Bledsoe had committed enough mistakes, and near mistakes, to remind Belichick why he'd made the switch in the first place. And, anyway, there was no kindling left to be lit under the argument. Bledsoe hardly had any constituency left, even among those who thought Belichick had handled him gracelessly.

The Super Bowl in New Orleans had been delayed a week because the NFL had played its full schedule of games despite going dark in the wake of the September attacks. It was the first sporting event ever formally declared a "National Security

Event" by the president of the United States. Even in less uncertain times, the Super Bowl is something like a militarized Mardi Gras. This one actually was. No less a figure than the national security adviser, Condoleezza Rice, was asked her opinion on the game's outcome. Unlike almost every football pundit, she told CNN's Wolf Blitzer that she thought the Patriots had a chance, if they could keep the St. Louis offense off the field. She also said she wouldn't mind being commissioner of the NFL one day.

The Patriots managed to maintain a reasonably normal atmosphere in what was an extremely strange context. They were twelve-point underdogs and very loose. One thing Belichick wanted to work on was an aspect of the St. Louis defensive backs he'd noticed when New England had played the Rams eleven weeks earlier. He noticed that, at one particular point on the field, the Rams did exactly the same thing every time. Their defensive backs fought receivers on the goal line, leaving wide swaths of the end zone open behind them, if the receiver could untangle himself to get there. As a defensive coordinator, he knew full well what a mistake this was. As a head coach, he knew even more clearly what an opportunity it was.

"We were running our out patterns down near the end zone, and the way St. Louis played their coverages, they really stopped on the goal line," Belichick recalls. "The defensive backs didn't back up into the end zone, so it was really hard to run an out. What you really want to do is run an out and up, because they're going to stop on that route and they're going to jump it."

While the Patriots stuck to their routine, there was the usual massive pregame extravaganza, which was as subject as everything else was to the febrile tectonics of the national mood. Roger Staubach, a Hall of Fame quarterback with Dallas but, more important in this context, a naval veteran of the Vietnam War, would toss the coin. Both the Boston Pops and Paul McCartney would play. Then, as the two teams prepared to be introduced to the crowd, it was announced that New England would eschew individual introductions; they had chosen to be introduced "as a team."

Given the complicated emotions surrounding the game, this decision resonated out through tens of millions of television screens. Perhaps deliberately, perhaps not, the Patriots had made a gesture aimed precisely at what the country most wanted to believe about itself. "The Patriots' behavior symbolized national solidarity," the author Rosabeth Moss Kanter later gushed. "At the beginning of the game, they ran out onto the field as a team . . . signalling their unity—The United Team Of America."

It would be the moment that first defined the Patriots in the era in which Tom Brady was the team's quarterback, and, even though he didn't know it at the time, it was where the image he would have to carry through his professional career was born— not the image he would create for himself but the image that would be created for him. What he saw in himself as basic—and relatively unremarkable—values were going to be hijacked by an anxious nation as incantatory spells to ward off an uncertain time.

Late in the first half, after New England recovered a fumble on the St. Louis 40-yard line, Brady drove the Patriots down to the 8 with only thirty-six seconds left in the half. On the next play, Brady saw the St. Louis defensive backs do exactly what he and Belichick had assumed they would do. They stopped on the goal line. David Patten broke to the sideline and then straight upfield, a shorter version of the play he'd run at a pivotal moment against San Diego. Brady laid the ball up, and Patten, tumbling backward, caught it, and New England entered halftime with a surprising 14–3 lead.

Surprising, that is, to everyone but their quarterback. While Brady and the Patriots were in the locker room preparing for the second half, U2 was evoking a storm of emotion in the Superdome by playing on a stage behind which was a screen displaying the names of all the victims of the September 11 attacks. Brady was struck by how normal it all seemed. The Rams had jumped the route, just the way he'd prepared for them to do, and he'd made his read and made his throw, just the way he was supposed to. For all the hype, it was still a football game, and he'd prepared for it well, and his team was eleven points ahead, the way it was supposed to be.

A couple hours later, after he'd led that John Madden–defying drive and Adam Vinatieri had won the game with his kick, Brady was standing on a podium, sparkly confetti falling on him like jeweled rain. Transported by the moment, Bob Kraft waved the Vince Lombardi Trophy and crowed, "We are all Patriots, and tonight the Patriots are World Champions!" which got a big hand but seems in retrospect to have been more than a little gauche. NFL Films was there, and, in their official film of the event, you see Brady catch Drew Bledsoe in an embrace. Brady's face seems ready to burst, but Bledsoe's is such a poignant mask of rueful complexity that it seems the two men are touching each other from different emotional dimensions. An arrival and a departure are both contained in that moment. Bledsoe would start the following season with a new job as the quarterback of the Buffalo Bills. Brady would start the next season with a new life as a national icon.

■ ■ ■

David Givens knew it was bad. The Patriots were trailing the Colts, and Givens knew that the short passing game was going to have to suffice for a running game that had stalled. He'd run a quick slant pattern on a fourth-and-one play, and, after the play was over, an Indianapolis defender named Mike Doss came in late and belted him, twisting Givens's knee. Not only did this knock another key New England player out for an extended period of time—he would not return for nearly a month—but it also resonated deeply with Givens, who would be entering free agency in the off-season and saw this latest injury in the context of all those injuries that had devalued his draft status when he came out of Notre Dame. "With me," he said later, "anytime I get hurt, I always tried to get back too soon." Part of this was the realization Givens had that even the slightest injury went down on the clipboards of the men who'd decide whether Givens would get the big payday at the end of the year.

"I barely made it into the league," he said. "I know that was why I was drafted late, so, whenever I get hurt, I'm going to want to get back as soon as I can."

The entire Indianapolis game was disastrous for New England. Once again, without a running game and playing always from behind, Brady found himself engaging in an on-the-fly redefinition of his football identity. He was throwing the ball too much, trying to make too many plays. In addition, there was something going wrong high in his right leg. It hurt when he pushed off. It hurt when he tried to plant it to throw. He would play with it. He would play through it. But it would change the rest of his season. And, because of the rigid policy the team had about revealing the details of its players' injuries, it would not be available for anyone to use as a public alibi, even assuming he was looking for one.

Meanwhile, on the other side, Peyton Manning and the

Colts were doing to the Patriots what the Patriots always had done to them—chewing up great gobbets of time with long, precise drives. On their second drive of the game, which began on their 32-yard line, the Colts took just over nine minutes to go sixty-eight yards. Flapping and gesticulating as though he were calling signals by semaphore, an odd quirk that makes Manning appear to be panicking whether he is or not, the Indianapolis quarterback delivered on a third-and-thirteen with a twelve-yard slant to Reggie Wayne, who'd beaten Duane Starks, a hapless New England cornerback coming to be seen as one of the great busts of the Belichick regime. That completion put the Colts in position to go for a first down on a fourth-and-one play from the New England 46.

It was the kind of moment against the Patriots on which the Colts heretofore had been guaranteed to fall off the stage and into the orchestra pit. Instead, Edgerrin James banged over right guard for two yards and kept the drive alive. James later would score on an identical plunge to put Indianapolis ahead, 14–7. They scored again—Wayne beating poor Starks for a second time to cap off a seventy-three-yard drive—and led 21–7 at the half.

New England got the ball to start the second half and immediately did precisely the wrong thing. Brady misfired on three consecutive throws to his tight ends—the first to young Ben Watson and the last two to the veteran Daniel Graham. The Patriots punted, and the Colts moved the ball right back down the field—sixty yards in eleven plays—to lead, 28–7. And then, on the next possession, after Brady had tossed a screen pass to Graham and the huge tight end had rumbled thirty-one yards for a score to cut the lead to 28–14, Belichick decided to roll the dice on an onside kick.

It was a measure of desperation—a tacit acknowledgment

that his defense, riddled as it was by injury, was unable to stop the Colts from moving the chains, and that the Patriots, who'd won three of the previous four Super Bowls with a balanced, mistake-free offense and an aggressive, play-making defense, would have to beat Indianapolis by outscoring them, the strategy that had always failed for the Colts when they'd tried it against New England. The onside kick was a statement, clear and unmistakable, that the New England Patriots were not at this moment what they had been only nine months earlier.

Whatever the theoretical and symbolic merits of Belichick's decision, the play was a hopeless botch. Adam Vinatieri failed to kick the ball the required ten yards for New England to recover it and retain possession. In addition, linebacker Monty Beisel, another off-season free-agent hire who was not working out very well, managed to be a full yard offside on a play that traveled only eight. The short kick plus Beisel's egregious penalty gave Indianapolis the ball on the New England 27-yard line. That the defense finally stiffened, surrendering only a field goal, was irrelevant. The score went to 31–14, and the Colts would wind up winning by a fat 40–21. By the end of the game, Belichick had sat Brady down in favor of Doug Flutie, the local legend who'd won the Heisman Trophy at Boston College twenty years earlier, and whom New England had signed in the off-season.

On the surface, Brady's numbers were solid, almost gaudy. He completed twenty-two of his thirty-three attempts, for 265 yards and all three New England touchdowns. His quarterback rating for the game was a glowing 121.4 out of a possible 158.6. (The quarterback rating is an abstruse calculation that figures in all the possible statistics, probably overweights interceptions within its parameters, and asks the unlettered football fan to believe in an assessment by which perfection contains decimal points.) His statistics were almost identical to those of Manning, who hit on twenty-eight of thirty-seven passes, for 321 yards and three touchdowns, and whose quarterback rating dropped to 117.1 only because he threw an interception in the second quarter to New England linebacker Mike Vrabel.

However, by his own remorseless internal calculations, Brady had failed. The New England offense had been outgained on the ground by a ludicrous 132 yards to 34. He'd had to throw too much, and the team had made dozens of little mistakes that would never show up in the statistics but that would stand out in that week's film sessions like Harpo Marx in the middle of *Il Trovatore*. Missed blocking assignments. Pass routes cut off early or simply run badly. Poor reads on his part.

Worse, he'd detected a kind of lassitude that he hadn't ever noticed on the New England sideline before. It seemed as though everyone was accepting the injuries as a legitimate excuse for playing spiritless, dreary football. Whatever leadership skills Brady had weren't working at this point. His confidence, always unbroken, no longer seemed transferable, and it galled him. Toward the end of the game, when Ben Watson had dropped a pass to conclude the last New England possession of the night, Brady, frustrated beyond endurance and his face contorted with anger, had screamed at his teammates on the sidelines and fired a cup of water at the ground.

Not only was this explosion inevitably picked up by ABC's ubiquitous cameras, but it was also caught on film by practically every still photographer working the game. It was a moment that was perfectly in character for the ferocious competitor who'd punched a hole in the wall back in San Mateo, but it seemed out of character for the cool, handsome Tom Brady, the guy on the magazine covers and in the goat photos, the guy who, only the night before, had appeared on *60 Minutes*, discussing how he managed to stay focused at critical moments. The conspicuously normal guy who told Steve Kroft that, if he could be anywhere in the world, he'd like to be knocking it around St. Andrews with his father.

One of the critical times for any celebrity athlete comes when the real person blasphemes against the created image. It can be relatively harmless—a profane tirade by a professed Christian, for example—or it can be the absolute end of things—the ur-text for the latter being, of course, the (probably) apocryphal story of the little boy confronting Shoeless Joe Jackson on the steps of the Chicago courthouse after the slugger had testified to fixing the 1919 World Series. By that standard, Brady's reaction, albeit magnified by television, was a benign example, but it was a look at the implacable forces that drove the actual person to achieve the success that had made the glossy image possible.

Out in South Bend, where he had taken the coaching job at Notre Dame the previous summer, Charlie Weis saw Brady's tantrum and it worried him. Not because of what people might think of Tommy. Weis couldn't have cared less about that. He knew more than most that, for all his success, Brady was still a work in progress, both as a person and as a quarterback. That Brady knew it as well was only part of the reason why Weis loved him.

"I would have told him that we didn't need him to put on a show here," Weis said. "See, that's the one thing he doesn't have to do anymore. I wanted to say, 'Don't one-up your teammates here,' just to get under his skin a little. There wasn't me there to tell him to shut the fuck up. He doesn't have me to dig him anymore. That's one thing he probably misses a little."

Outside the Indianapolis locker room, Peyton Manning talked for a long time about what an important win this was for the Colts, who were now 8–0 on the season. Previously, in this stadium, Manning had stood still for long disquisitions about how Bill Belichick and the Patriots had caused him to flounder and fail at the biggest moments possible. This was his first win against a Tom Brady–led New England team in six tries and, all in all, Manning handled it graciously. Down the corridor, in the New England interview room, people waited for Brady to come out and explain what had happened.

The room looks like the kind of lecture hall in which college freshmen regularly are anesthetized by European history or rendered senseless by *The Norton Anthology of English Literature*. Banked toward the rear are arcs of seats, each of which has one of those hinged, desklike apparatuses attached to one arm. There are blackboards, a big screen drawn down in front of the blackboards, and a podium set up in front of the screen. Sitting in the room after a game, win or lose, you half-expect Bill Belichick to come in and hand out that week's quiz.

He might as well have. Belichick's press conference was terse and relatively useless. There was nothing to say about the way the Patriots had played, and he said exactly that. Brady followed Belichick to the podium. He was in his usual postgame attire— a hooded sweatshirt over a dress shirt, and a crisp pair of jeans. His face was dark and serious. His eyes, which can take on a hooded quality that makes him almost inscrutable, were deep and black.

"There's not much to say," he began, his voice a featureless monotone, as though he were trying very hard to control its pitch and, through that, what he might say. "We got our butts kicked. We need to play better. We've got to fight harder. Give a lot of credit to the Colts. They played very well. We made too many mistakes. They were the better team tonight.

"That's it. Thank you."

And then, he was gone, the entire press conference having taken thirty-two seconds from the moment he walked in the door, and not being a conference in any real sense anyway, because Brady hadn't taken any questions. He would elaborate further the next morning, on his weekly paid radio appearance on WEEI, talking about the curious malaise that had descended on the team. But, on this evening, in the immediate aftermath of a terrible game, you could see the effort it took for him to stay locked within the first-person, plural, to stay within the place he always had been most comfortable, and the place within which he'd defined himself long before the larger world had defined him for itself, within the iron parameters of being a teammate.

5 | OTHER VOICES, OTHER LOCKERS

NOVEMBER 13, 2005: NEW ENGLAND 23, MIAMI 16
NOVEMBER 20, 2005: NEW ENGLAND 24, NEW ORLEANS 17
RECORD: 6–4

AFTER LOSING to Indianapolis, the Patriots went to Miami mired at 4–4. They'd beaten only one good team—Pittsburgh— since defeating Oakland on opening night. Fortunately, the AFC East had turned into the NFL's most conspicuous thrift shop. Even the tattered Patriots were better than perpetually rebuilt teams like the New York Jets and the Buffalo Bills. The only intriguing opponent within their division was the Dolphins, playing their first season under Nick Saban, a former Belichick assistant who'd come to Miami after a successful college coaching career at both Michigan State and Louisiana State. He'd won forty-eight games in five years at LSU, including an 11–1 season in 2003 that had won the Tigers the national championship.

The Dolphins played the Patriots even in a game of fits and starts. New England had cobbled together a running game behind Heath Evans. At six feet and 250 pounds, Evans is a squat throwback to the days when fullbacks looked like bowling balls, and he had played for Miami until Saban cut him the week before. He gave the Patriots just enough of a running game to take the pressure off Brady, who, visibly laboring, was having an in-

and-out afternoon. Sacked twice, he was wildly inconsistent, his timing clearly askew.

With five minutes left in the third quarter, New England was trailing 7–6, having mustered only two field goals by Adam Vinatieri. Out of the shotgun, Brady flipped a short completion to Evans at the Miami 42-yard line. In front of him, Dan Koppen got knocked a little sideways and then down, and Dolphin nose tackle Keith Traylor dropped all 337 pounds of himself on Koppen's right shoulder, dislocating it and tearing the rotator cuff. Koppen stayed down. Brady stayed with him, looking at his friend from behind the New England medical staff.

Koppen's would be the hardest of all the injuries that had pockmarked the New England season. Brady and Koppen had bonded from the day the latter arrived in camp as a fifth-round draft pick out of Boston College. Part of it was the fact that the two had followed similar career paths with the Patriots. Koppen's ascendancy had resulted in the team's cutting loose Damien Woody, a Pro Bowl center who took a fat free-agent offer from the Detroit Lions, just as Brady's play had caused Drew Bledsoe to be shuttled out of town. They were two people who'd identified themselves as underdogs and who understood the work it had taken to get them to where they were.

In addition, Koppen is simply funny. He's a natural deadpan comedian, a redhead who looks occasionally like a mischievous twelve-year-old. Charlie Weis thinks he looks like a pumpkin. He was the perfect antidote when it seemed the world was making too much out of a quarterback in his early twenties who'd already won himself a career. Koppen and Brady played hours of backgammon on the team plane, and Koppen came to realize what the quarterback needed and wanted most from his teammates was a sense of being one of them. When Tom Curran, the

perspicacious reporter from *The Providence Journal* who may
have been Brady's first real partisan in the media, arranged to
meet the quarterback for a social beer at a bar in downtown
Boston, Koppen came along, wearing a Santa Claus hat. Asked
about Brady, Koppen's reflexive answer, always, was "Why don't
you go talk to Tom?"

"Koppen's his boy," says Weis, who worked with Koppen almost as much as he'd worked with Brady. "He's one of those
guys who can get under Tom's skin, but in a good way." Weis's
wife, Maura, does not admit to many favorites among the athletes her husband has coached, but Brady and Koppen are two
of them.

And, most important of all, Koppen was a smart, aggressive
center. In Super Bowl XXXVIII, when New England edged
the Carolina Panthers 32–29, Koppen came of age. He was the
linchpin to a great Patriot offensive line performance that kept
Brady from being sacked even once by one of the best defenses
in the NFL. It was Koppen's job to make all the calls for the
offensive line, to adjust his linemates to what Brady would see
looking out over them. This communication is so important
that the Patriots hold a special camp every spring where the
coaches work only with the centers and quarterbacks.

"Tommy comes to the line of scrimmage, and he identifies
the [defensive] front," explains Weis. "Then Dan tells everyone
on the line, 'Okay, here's what we're doing.'

"One word might tell them all what they're doing. So Tommy
says, 'Okay, Mike's 54' (a call identifying the position of the middle linebacker). And then Koppen says, 'Swap.' It might be a run
or it might be a pass, or whatever. But once Tommy's identified
who the middle linebacker is, then Dan's the guy who tells the
offensive line, 'Okay, so this is how we're handling this.'"

The offensive line is the most obvious team within a team,

and the center functions as its quarterback. Its concerns are vital but curiously insular. One of the oddest sights on a football field is the huge offensive line, deep in its own territory in a loud and hostile stadium, holding one another's hands before the play to make sure their communication is immediate and clear. On some plays, Brady will check a running play into a quick, short pass, and Koppen and the linemen will remain blissfully unaware.

"It's just between Tom and the receivers," Koppen explains. "We have no idea. We just run the play that's called. We think we're running the ball. If the play called is off-tackle, we block off-tackle. I mean, we're five yards and a cloud of dust.

"We prepare by having a good week in the classroom. Our job in the meeting room is to learn the guys we're going against, how we're putting schemes together so we can get hats on hats. What we're doing is trying not to be surprised out there."

After Traylor dropped atop Koppen, Brady stood uncomfortably for a long time until they took his friend off the field. The metaphors were scattered now. Both Matt Light and Koppen were gone for the year—even though Koppen's return was announced in the press box, laughably as it turned out, as "probable," veteran left guard Russ Hochstein now would play center. For the rest of the season, Brady's blind side would be guarded by two rookies—Nick Kaczur and Logan Mankins—and his center would be someone playing out of position.

Gradually, the New England offense stalled. Trailing only 15–10, Miami crept back into the game. With 5:15 left, Brady threw a pass toward tight end Ben Watson on which Dolphin safety Yeremiah Bell made a great play, intercepting the ball near midfield. Miami marched to the New England 15-yard line. There, the Dolphin quarterback, Gus Frerotte, dropped the snap in the shotgun. It was just enough of a break in the play for the New England defenders to lose focus, and Frerotte picked up the ball and gunned it to Chris Chambers for a touchdown and a 16–15 lead with three minutes left in the game.

On the first play after the Miami touchdown, Brady spotted wideout Tim Dwight slanting deep across the middle and delivered the ball just beyond the fingertips of Miami's Reggie Howard, whom Dwight outfought for the ball and then ran fifty-nine yards to the Dolphins' 17-yard line. A game that had been vague and inconclusive suddenly seemed to be in sharper focus.

Ben Watson lined up on the left side of the formation. At six-three and 253 pounds, Watson is a bundle of extraordinary talent. Extremely fast for a man his size, he also possesses the soft hands of a wide receiver. Drafted in 2004 out of the University of Georgia, where he was enormously well regarded both for his football skills and for his commitment to charity work with a church near Athens, Watson had spent his rookie season injured and idle. He'd caught only two balls all year. He'd spent this year working on his blocking, especially his pass blocking, which he knew was the fastest way to get himself more playing time. Today, with the game on the line, it was coming to him.

He was supposed to break off toward the back corner of the end zone, "fading" his route. Brady would put the ball in the air long before Watson made his final move. The timing on the play had to be impeccable, a product of long, droning hours back in Foxborough. Watson made his break, jabbing his foot in the ground and spinning Miami's Lance Schulters in the opposite direction. He gathered in the pass, delicately touching both feet down in-bounds for the touchdown. New England led, 23–16, and would win the game by that score, even though the issue wasn't settled until the Patriot defense inexcusably almost let Miami score, giving up seventy-five yards in two minutes, only to have Chambers drop a Frerotte pass in the end zone with forty-one seconds left.

This was the twenty-first time in his professional career that Brady had quarterbacked the Patriots to a game-winning drive. It was the first one for Ben Watson, who'd caught the only two touchdowns New England had scored that day. Watson had run his route crisply, broken down the defense, but the play required that the pass be feathered to him. To Watson, it seemed like it hung in the air, in front of thousands of anxious faces, for far too long a time. "I was just waiting, waiting," he said. "I wondered if that pass would ever come down." After the game, Brady mentioned that Watson, as far as he was concerned, was working as hard as anyone on the team. But Dan Koppen was gone, and that was surely a hole. The season was changing on him now, it was changing on them all, and there wasn't anything he could do about it.

The podium was an issue for Tom Brady. In 2002, after the upset win over the Rams, Brady came into great demand. His weekly media sessions, usually held on Wednesdays, became such events that the crowd slopped over in front of neighboring lockers. His teammates couldn't get at their shoes or their pants, their iPods or their vitamins, their bling or their Bibles. The situation got more unwieldy after the wins in Super Bowls XXXVIII and XXXIX. So, by the beginning of the 2005 season, the whole, sprawling business was moved down the hall into the bunkerish, windowless room where Belichick met the press every day. Brady would take questions from behind the same small wooden podium the coach used.

He hated it. He fidgeted. He grabbed the podium so tightly that you could see his knuckles whitening. Every Wednesday,

Tom Brady—NFL superstar and national celebrity, renowned for his ability to remain icy under pressure—stood behind a podium and looked as comfortable as a reluctant mob witness. The New England media relations staff even offered to put a row of fake lockers behind him, the way yearbook photographers use those shelves that contain nothing but the spines of the Reader's Digest condensed books. It didn't matter. Brady was never going to make peace with the podium.

"I'm most comfortable with my peers, with my family, and with myself," he says. "The podium is way too formal. I think that's what coaches do. Players talk in the locker room. Some people are comfortable behind the podium. But I don't need to be the showstopper, the entertainer. I'd much rather be one of the guys."

This, of course, wasn't the whole truth. In the aftermath of that first Super Bowl, Brady enjoyed his first taste of being everybody's Tom Brady. He went to Disney World. He flew with Donald Trump, a new very close friend with whom Brady traveled to judge the Miss USA pageant in Gary, Indiana. He dated a few movie stars and a whole lot of people who weren't, a phenomenon that Trump made sure to point out to Michael Silver of *Sports Illustrated*. "If one thing stands out about Tom Brady," Trump told Silver, with the characteristic subtlety of a man who puts waterfalls in hotel lobbies, "it's that he loves those women. And, guess what? They love him, too."

"Tom was in vogue," recalls Charlie Weis. "He was the glamour boy, date all the supermodels and meet all the new rock musicians. And he was into that some after the [2002] Super Bowl." Weis watched all this with a combination of bemusement and concern. Everything Brady was experiencing off the field seemed to run contrary to everything he'd done in obscurity to succeed on the field. He watched Brady struggle trying to maintain a balance between enjoying his new life and drowning in it.

"You know, you can say all you want, but you know it's tough not to let all of that get into your head," Weis muses. "Even as levelheaded as he is. You know, to have them all chase you. I mean, the list was endless."

Brady was having trouble saying no to people and, occasionally, finding reasons why he should. That spring, his sisters Nancy and Julie moved to Boston not so much to look out for him as to give him a sense of being moored to something other than the celebrity that was enveloping him like a glittery carapace. They weren't clinging. They were just, sort of, around. When Tom Curran met Brady for a beer, Julie was the bartender who served them. His account of their conversation consists of Curran introducing himself to Julie Brady as a Patriots beat writer.

"Uh-uh," she replies, dropping a fish-eyed glower at him.

"His life changed," recalls Nancy Brady. "So many things that we take for granted—going to the grocery store, coming out to have a bite to eat for lunch, going out to get gas. I mean simple things that, for the rest of us, are sort of thoughtless, you know? At first it was kind of exciting, and we were always so protective of him anyway. I feel like the only people that do try to take care of him is his family. And I feel like we do guard him, you know, sometimes to a fault."

Brady has received so much credit for his "character"— a word that has been so drained of its meaning by the virtue-crat industry that it functions now primarily as an invitation to cynicism—that it's hard to remember that its development was far from inevitable, and that its maintenance requires just as much work as breaking down the Indianapolis defense. His sister Nancy has seen the effort close up ever since she moved to Boston to try to help her brother with it.

"These guys are such young guys, you know?" Nancy says. "I think that for the first few years, they're just trying to figure it out. How to get through the season. How to manage your life. How to manage all the outside things that, you know, you might want to do, but then, you do them and, all of a sudden, you realize, 'Wow. That took a lot out of me.' A lot of guys are just really prepared for playing professional football. They never have one inkling of how difficult it would be to be a celebrity.

"And that includes Tom. I mean, that was the farthest thing from his mind. He was so unprepared for it that I think it's still the hardest part of his job."

It was a human being, Nancy's little brother, who'd begat the quarterback, and it was a quarterback who'd begat the football star, and it was the football star who'd begat the celebrity, and his job now seemed to be to find a way to keep all of these evolutionary stages in balance with one another, lest the human being who'd been the basis for all of it become so distant and vestigial that he crumbled, taking everything else down with him.

It was an ongoing exercise in internal navigation. To master it, he used what had become the polestar of his competitive career. He would be a teammate, defining what that meant in his own terms based on his own experiences. Part of it was what he'd learned at home, which was why his sisters were in town. Part of it was the strategies that he'd worked out with Greg Harden at Michigan, and part of it was what he'd picked up on his own as he climbed the depth chart at New England. In fact, after the Patriots defeated St. Louis, Belichick specifically took Brady aside and cautioned him, not about the shallow perils of fame but, rather, about how it could alienate him from his primary constituency—his fellow players. On some cold December Sunday in Buffalo, Donald Trump wasn't going to be blocking on his blind side. It was advice that struck a deep and resonant chord in Brady, who'd been working to strike the mean between solitary performer and team player since high school. And it just so happened that the strategies Brady adopted to gain control of his life dovetailed almost perfectly with the way his coach thought a football team ought to be run.

"Tom adopted a leadership style by which he still has time for everyone," says Belichick, who at times sounds very much like someone who spent his formative years around the Naval Academy. (Belichick's father, Steve, was a longtime assistant coach at Annapolis.) "He doesn't put himself above anybody, above the equipment manager, above the guy on the practice squad, or above a defensive player. He has respect for them doing their jobs. He gets on people, not in an overly critical way, but still firm. I don't think he's ever shown up anyone, even though some guys might deserve it." And, just for a moment, Belichick's face flickers with amusement.

"It's different from my style," he explains, "just to mention one example."

In his 1908 masterwork, *The Philosophy of Loyalty*, the philosopher Josiah Royce explains that loyalty, in and of itself, is not necessarily a virtue. "If loyalty is a supreme good," he writes, "the mutually destructive conflict of loyalties is in general a supreme evil." Royce argues that being loyal to a cause that is destructive to loyalty generally in the world is a moral wrong. "In so far as my cause is a predatory cause, which lives by overthrowing the loyalties of others," he says, "it is an evil cause, because it involves disloyalty to the very cause of loyalty itself." In fact, Royce specifically cites fair play in sports as "a particularly good instance of loyalty," while decrying the "extravagant publicity" attendant to sports as their "principal evils."

And, of course, like Brady, Royce was a Californian transplanted to Massachusetts.

Royce argues that loyalty is a conscious choice, and he further argues in favor of what he calls a "loyalty to loyalty," by which personal loyalty is meant to serve the cause of loyalty in others. That's what Brady worked to fashion within himself while the centrifugal forces of his newfound fame were pulling him apart. He sought to keep connected with that part of himself that Elwood Reid had noticed—the person who could be good without being Too Good, who could keep his faith with his teammates even though he was more famous than any of them would be. In the ontological milk bottle that is the football player's soul, there is no mark darker or bigger than the one representing the sin of Pride.

In this, for example, because most football players are in alliance with one another even against the team that employs them, Brady had to find a way to be the public face of the New England Patriots without being seen within the locker room as the management's mouthpiece. He would try to arrange his life—in both its public and its private spheres—along the lines that Royce laid down when he wrote, "In so far as it lies in your power, so choose your cause and serve it, that, by reason of your choice and of your service, there shall be more loyalty in the world rather than less . . . In choosing and in serving the cause to which you are to be loyal, be, in any case, loyal to loyalty.

"Loyalty, then, is contagious. It infects not only the fellow-servant of your own special cause, but also all who know of this act. Loyalty is a good that spreads . . . Loyalty to loyalty is then no unpractical cause. And you serve it not by becoming a mere citizen of the world, but by serving your own personal cause."

This is very similar to the vocabulary that Brady developed to explain his place amid the changes his success was bringing to himself, and to the Patriots. And it explains a great deal about how the image of the Patriots as a selfless juggernaut, which was born in the team-as-a-team introductions before the Super Bowl in New Orleans, not only became general around the NFL but also became the template for other franchises. The loyalty there, real or imagined, became contagious.

It was very much a conscious choice for Brady, and not dissimilar to the one he'd made at Michigan when he determined that he would not blow up the team in his senior season. And he chose to be a teammate in such a way as to make sure his loyalty would be reciprocated, that it would be contagious throughout the New England locker room.

One of the first tests came five days before the start of the 2003 season. On Monday morning, the Patriots cut Lawyer Milloy, the stone-tough safety who'd been a stalwart on the defense that had helped beat St. Louis as well as one of the first New England regulars who'd seen the potential in the sixth-round pick out of Michigan with whom he eventually became running buddies around Boston.

"I think Tommy, at first, respected Lawyer as a player and then got to know him off the field, and realized how much they were alike," recalls Nancy Brady, who today lives in the Quincy condominium that used to belong to Milloy.

However, on a team that had come to believe in a certain image of itself, Milloy was a button pusher. In his account of the 2003 season, *Patriot Reign: Bill Belichick, the Coaches, and the Players Who Built a Champion*, Michael Holley quotes a confidential management memo in which Milloy is termed "a negative leader, sometimes." In addition, the safety was coming off a 2002 season in which his production had slipped just enough to attract the notice of the people who would owe him $4.5 million, a huge figure against the New England salary cap. The Patriots proposed a cut to $3.0 million; Milloy and his agent waved it off. On September 2, 2003, Lawyer Milloy was released.

It was a startling demonstration of the ruthlessness of NFL economics in the salary cap era, and a cold object lesson in the ultimate disposability of the commodities who play the game. The team was in an uproar. To prove that Providence or Whoever maintains a sharp sense of irony, Milloy signed with Buffalo, against whom New England would open its 2003 season. There he would be joining Drew Bledsoe, who was in his second year as the starting quarterback. All of New England's personnel doppelgängers were on display. During the introductions, Milloy, the last player to be introduced, danced his way across the field.

The Bills rocked the Patriots, 31–0, the worst opening day loss in franchise history. Brady threw four interceptions, one of which Milloy tipped to a teammate, and his old friend also roared through once to sack him. A week later, on ESPN's pregame show, analyst Tom Jackson told the nation that the Patriots hated their coach. Some of them doubtless did.

Brady was angry and shaken. But his public comments were muted. He was conscious, always, of the effect anything he said or did could have on his teammates. Professional football players have more to worry about as individuals than do any other athletes. Their careers are short. Retirement can be a nightmare of unresolved medical issues. The economics of their sport are heavily weighted toward the management side, thanks in no small part to the nature of the players themselves, who, for all the selflessness their sport demands, never quite have gotten the hang of standing up as a union. (From Michael MacCambridge's chronicle of the league comes a telling anecdote from 1974, when a former Cleveland player named Bernie Parrish embarked on a pie-in-the-sky One Big Union plan to unite all professional athletes. The NFL players were a millstone. "Football players," Parrish sighed, "act like owners.") Each football player is more purely a disposable commodity than is, say, the baseball player, whose money is guaranteed. They all know that. They all play the game—a rigid, structured, coach-laden game demanding individual sacrifice for a greater good—knowing that their careers could end with the next sack, the next tackle, the next passing route run across the middle. An unspoken conflict of loyalties—of players toward their teams, of players toward one another, of players toward their own physical well-being—exists within every football team, and it can be as destructive as all the others against which Josiah Royce warned.

In the wake of the Buffalo loss, Brady was more conscious than ever of how fundamentally fragile the team was. So were his teammates, all of whom had shared in the lessons about their insecure profession taught by what had happened to Milloy. However, Brady somehow managed, within himself, to navigate through the situation and to help create on the team a form of loyalty to loyalty in which every player's individual sacrifice was respected and honored by the effort and sacrifice of every other teammate, most especially those of Brady.

"We've got to play better," he said, after throwing four interceptions in a close loss against Miami, "and it starts with me." This was not simply leading by example, although that was the most obvious part of it. There was something deeper going on. The Vatican II fathers, who created the change in the Church of which Brady's father was a part, had talked about the general presence of the Spirit in the people of God, who were the Church. That articulation of a community of the faithful—loyal to one another and loyal to that loyalty—permanently changed everyone in the Church. In the family in which he was raised, Tom Brady learned not only how to be part of something greater than himself but also that there *was* something beyond the family, beyond the team—his father's Maryknoll instructors would have called it the Spirit—that made being part of such communities possible. It did not begin with him. It would not end with him. Even as his confidence always spread to his teammates, theirs always spread to him. Even as his enthusiasm always fired them, theirs always set him alight. He sensed something building around him, but his great gift was in realizing that he wasn't its source.

A month after the disaster against Buffalo, the Patriots beat the Tennessee Titans in Foxborough, 38–30. A makeshift offensive line, led by rookie center Dan Koppen, kept a good Tennessee defense off Brady, who was a solid but unspectacular seventeen of thirty-one for 219 yards, including a gorgeous 58-yard pass to Troy Brown. It was October 5, 2003. The Patriots would not lose another game for more than a year.

They won twenty-one games in a row, straddling the end of the 2003 season and the beginning of the 2004 one, including playoff games against the Titans and the Indianapolis Colts. They revenged themselves on Milloy and Buffalo, beating them to end the 2003 regular season by the same 31–0 score the Bills had dropped on them. In fact, as the streak went on, New England took a victory lap through almost the entire recent history of the franchise. In November 2003, with Bill Parcells in his first season as the head coach in Dallas, the Patriots shut out the Cowboys, 12–0.

They won thirteen games at home, seven on the road, and one, the Super Bowl in Houston, on a neutral field. They won two games in overtime, including a baffling life-and-death struggle against the second-year Houston Texans, 23–20, in Reliant Stadium, the same place where, two months later, they would outscore the Carolina Panthers to win Super Bowl XXXVIII, which was the fifteenth game in the streak. Against Houston,

Brady tied the game on a short pass to tight end Daniel Graham, a play on which the radio communication between him and Charlie Weis had broken down entirely. It may be better to be lucky than to be good, but it's undeniably better to be both.

The Patriots were good and they were lucky. They were basic and they were fancy. In 2003, they won a game in Denver at least in part because they deliberately took a safety late in the game. For much of the 2004 season, improvising against injuries, Belichick played Troy Brown in the defensive backfield, and the veteran receiver responded with seventeen tackles and three interceptions, including one against Buffalo off the perpetually beleaguered Bledsoe, who once used to throw him the ball on purpose. On the other side of the ball, in goal-line situations, Brady was just as likely to be throwing the ball to a linebacker, who'd come into the game to slum it for a while at tight end.

Anything the Patriots tried seemed to work, and the more things that worked, the more things they tried, even with the game on the line. And it didn't stop when the streak did, in Pittsburgh, 34–20, on October 31, 2004. A week later, while New England was crushing the St. Louis Rams, who'd never quite recovered from their loss in Super Bowl XXXVI, Adam Vinatieri threw the only touchdown pass of his NFL career, a four-yarder to Troy Brown out of a field goal formation.

For his part, over the twenty-one consecutive wins, Brady completed 412 of 690 passes for 4,953 yards. He threw for thirty-four touchdowns and threw only twelve interceptions. He threw for more than three touchdowns only once and never threw more than two interceptions in a game. And, because of these abilities to avoid the crushing mistake and to move the chains when he had to, the most impressive thing about the streak was that it was such a close-run thing. The first game was an eight-point win over Tennessee, and the last game was a 13–7 win at home against the Jets on October 24, 2004. Over the twenty-one games, the average margin of victory was nine points, which is probably not surprising for a team that won each of its three Super Bowls by only the three thin points provided by a Vinatieri field goal.

While the 1972 Miami Dolphins remained the only team to go all the way through a single NFL season without a loss, what New England did over those twenty-one consecutive games was inarguably harder, especially since, as Peter King observed in *Sports Illustrated*, that Miami team had changed only three players in its lineup from the previous season, whereas the Patriots had changed running backs, half their defensive line, most of their offensive line, and three of their linebackers between 2003 and 2004, and had kept winning anyway.

More to the point, it was this winning streak, and the third Super Bowl win over the Eagles at the end of the 2004 season, that cemented the Patriots—and with them, Tom Brady—as a public archetype. They no longer were the plucky underdogs who shrewdly introduced themselves as a team and brought joy to a wounded nation. Brady no longer was the scrappy sixth-round pick, elevated by injury into the spotlight. The Patriots were the very model of a modern major sports franchise, and Brady was being spoken of in the company of quarterbacks like Joe Montana and Terry Bradshaw.

On the outside, it was a giddy and ridiculous time. The notoriously cranky Boston media went so deeply into the tank for the team that some of its members may not dry off until the year 2525. Local television stations, and WEEI, the Boston sports-radio juggernaut, committed themselves to what amounted to gooey weekly infomercials for the franchise. Brady's contribution to WEEI was a Monday segment on the station's morning drive-time show in which the inevitably exhausted quarterback regularly sounded like a man emerging from a monthlong coma.

In some parts of the country, football is an organic part of the life of the community. There is a culture of football in those places that doesn't exist generally in New England, where high school teams regularly play in front of a corporal's guard of interested aunts and uncles, and where major college football is represented almost entirely by the Boston College Eagles. And, as for the professional team, what history it had was more of a comic opera than anything else and, for years, the primary local interest in the NFL was in betting on it. So it's probably no surprise that, suddenly and freakishly gifted with the league's signature franchise, and with one of the NFL's emerging signature players, the local sports punditocracy blew enough sunshine up the franchise's ass to light up the moons of Neptune.

The franchise was praised for its ability to maneuver deftly under the restrictions of the league's salary cap. (New England was the first dynasty of the salary cap era, which had begun in 1992, when a judge forced a settlement that tied a salary cap to the first form of real free agency the league ever had seen.) That a lot of this maneuvering meant the shuffling out of town of players who had been important to the team but whose salaries were becoming onerous was seen as further testimony to the wisdom of the New England front office. But that wisdom would have been entirely empty if it weren't for a culture that had simultaneously arisen among the New England players, which didn't have any more to do with a business model than it had to do with the architectural plans for Gillette Stadium.

Players took less money in order to stay longer in New England; in 2004, Matt Light signed a six-year deal at less than market value for left tackles, and Brady would do exactly the same thing at his position a year later. Linebacker Tedy Bruschi also committed to an extension rather than price himself on the free-agent market. "It's not," Light told *Sports Illustrated*'s King, "always about being the highest-paid guy." It would be a profound mistake, however, to interpret these as acts of loyalty toward the corporate institution that is the New England Patriots or even, primarily, toward their employer. They were acts of loyalty by the fifty-three human beings who made up the New England roster to one another, and to the loyalty itself that's arisen among them.

Brady insisted on being first among equals, and he wasn't even really comfortable with being first among anyone. He spoke, relentlessly, about the interdependence of the players. What elevates it above the usual locker-room tub thumping is the fervor with which Brady delivers the message. He's almost devotional about it, and, if these are clichés, then so are most prayers.

"We could have been better competitively out there, offensively especially," he said after one tough loss. "And I thought we could have done a better job of protecting our defense, and doing our part. I think that's just frustration as a captain of the team, you know, it's like, 'You're not leading us. You're not leading us.' I think that the frustrating part is that you're representing these guys and, if you look up, and you're way behind, it's a terrible feeling.

"Some guys have a routine, and you try to keep up with the routine that you've been doing for all these years, and, hey, if that's not working, maybe you change it up a little bit and try to dig deeper, and say, 'Guys, I'm going to do my part to prepare hard, to work hard, and just continue to try to improve.'"

Which was what players who came to New England during this time immediately sensed about the place. In 2003, defensive back Rodney Harrison came in from San Diego with a reputation as a vicious (and occasionally dirty) hitter. By the end of the season, having taken the departed Milloy's place as the competitive engine of the New England secondary, Harrison played one play of the 2003 Super Bowl with a broken arm before leaving, and he was weeping with gratitude to Bob Kraft in the Patriots' locker room after the game. The following season, Corey Dillon arrived from Cincinnati with a reputation for being one of the worst malcontents in the recent history of the league. He took a $1.5 million pay cut to join New England, in no small part because of what he'd heard about the team from players around the league. At the end of the season, having helped the Patriots beat Philadelphia in Super Bowl XXXIX, Dillon had run for 1,635 yards and twelve touchdowns, both career bests.

Neither man came to New England to be part of a business model. Neither came to New England to be anything more than a player among other players, to be part of a group of players who seemed to have figured out the solution to the conflict of loyalties that is present in every football team and that destroys so many good ones. In that solution, the quarterback remains the first among equals, but even the first among equals is nothing, more or less, than equal.

"Every quarterback," Mike Vrabel tells the interviewer on television, "can be defended."

Vrabel is the perfect example of how the Patriots built their team. He's an even more perfect example of the culture that developed within it, perhaps as much as Brady is. At six-four and 261 pounds, he's bigger than most linebackers, the last vestige in him of the defensive lineman that he was throughout his career at Ohio State. He's quick and startlingly athletic and, with his sharp features and a profile that looks like it was carved out of the Black Hills of South Dakota by Gutzon Borglum, Vrabel even looks a little like the ducktailed Continental soldier that adorns the side of his helmet. If you were putting together a prospectus for the football operation that is the Patriots, Mike Vrabel would be on the cover, if only as the logo.

Vrabel is the son of two school administrators from the sub-urbs outside Akron, Ohio. His parents kept a watchful eye out during Mike's recruitment, being wary of all those things that Elwood Reid describes in his novel. "I was concerned, early on," his father said later. "When he started being recruited by Ohio State, well, that's the big time. That can be overwhelming."

Nevertheless, Vrabel prospered in Columbus, even on a tal-ented team that sent a clutch of players to the NFL. A defensive end, he set a school record with thirty-six sacks and was named a first-team All-American in 1996. He also became something of an enforcer within the team, setting high standards for him-self and demanding them of his teammates. On one memorable occasion, when the team was running laps around the field, a highly touted freshman fell out. Vrabel finished his run, slipped away, and clobbered the rookie from behind.

Despite a strong college career, Vrabel was taken only in the third round of the 1997 draft, and he went to Pittsburgh, where he was switched to linebacker. By the time he'd learned his new position, he was buried on the Steeler roster behind two other star linebackers. He had his moments—as a rookie, he belted Drew Bledsoe, forced a fumble, and helped Pittsburgh beat the Patriots in a playoff game—but by 2000 he was so discouraged that his friends were worried he might give up football entirely, and Vrabel himself was contemplating law school.

However, Vrabel had long been on the radar screen of Scott Pioli, the Patriots' director of player personnel. The son-in-law of Bill Parcells, Pioli had been hired by Belichick when the latter was coaching in Cleveland. In 1996, when the team fired Belichick, prior to leaving Cleveland for Baltimore, Pioli stayed with the franchise, and he had first noticed Vrabel while scouting for Cleveland. Now, three years later, Belichick and Pioli saw in Vrabel the kind of player with whom they'd hoped to stock the Patriots. He was smart, coachable, and, yes, cheap. Vrabel signed with New England for a reported $5.2 million over three years.

Vrabel thrived as surely as Brady did in the opportunity society that Belichick had developed within the Patriots. Players are invited to camp because the team has seen something in them that it can use, and it's the players' responsibility to seize that opportunity. The franchise had reclaimed itself from its lunatic past. Belichick had reclaimed himself not only from the bad end he'd come to in Cleveland but also from the strange way it had ended for him with the Jets. Brady was a sixth-round pick, reckoned by the NFL savants to be less than Spergon Wynn. And Mike Vrabel's career looked to be dying on the vine.

Instead, he thrived, establishing himself first in the organized chaos that is special-teams play and then as the kind of intelligent, versatile player for whom Belichick can find good use in a number of situations. "When you tell Mike something, that's pretty much it," the coach says. "Maybe if he hasn't seen it before, he might miss it, but once he understands it, it's not going to fool him again."

Unleashed at linebacker, Vrabel quickly developed a knack for making big plays in big situations. In the Super Bowl against St. Louis, he went sailing untouched into the face of the Rams' quarterback, Kurt Warner, forcing Warner to throw up a soft balloon of a pass that New England cornerback Ty Law picked off and ran in for the touchdown that probably turned the game in the direction of the upset it became.

Two years later, against Carolina in Houston, Vrabel played a personal Super Bowl for the ages. He had six tackles and two sacks. In the second quarter, Vrabel hammered the ball loose from the Carolina quarterback, Jake Delhomme, and the fumble led to the first New England touchdown of the game. The play showed Vrabel reading the quarterback as quickly and precisely as a quarterback might read a cornerback. Delhomme had made as if to throw the ball, and then he'd brought it back down, a moment's hesitation that told Vrabel volumes. He knew that, behind him, the New England secondary had locked down the Carolina receivers, and that, while reloading, Delhomme had no idea Vrabel was coming. He chopped the ball free, and Richard Seymour fell on it. He made his play because teammates he could not even see behind him had made theirs first, sowing confusion in the quarterback's mind.

Most conspicuously, in the heat of a furious fourth quarter, in which the two teams would combine for thirty-seven points, and with New England trailing by a point, Vrabel came on offense as an eligible receiver on a second-down play from the Carolina 1-yard line. Weis sent in something called a "136 X Cross Z Flag," and Vrabel knew he wasn't in the game as a blocker. Brady faked a handoff to running back Antowain Smith, and Vrabel drifted across the middle of the field, just barely beyond the line of scrimmage and into the end zone. Brady threw him a good, hard spiral, and Vrabel, who hadn't caught a pass in well over a year, grabbed the ball, as he later told *Sports Illustrated*'s Peter King, "like it was my third child." After the game, as he was standing with his son in the riotous New England locker room, Vrabel had the little boy touch his shoulder pads. "Can you feel it?" Vrabel asked him. "Can you feel the vibrations? Can you still?"

"When you buy into something, and you believe in something that somebody's teaching you and coaching you, and it works, then you have no reason to second-guess or question what the people are telling you," Vrabel explained later. "It's silly to say that we don't have the players that everybody else has, because we do, but this team does understand what each other can do better than any other team I've been around."

Brady's success is deeply symbiotic with the success of the defensive team of which Vrabel—despite his occasional moonlighting as a receiver—is such a significant part. If he can keep the ball moving, then the defense can rest and resume its work with sufficient ferocity. At the same time, the active, ball-hawking style of defense preferred by Belichick, who saw in Vrabel exactly the kind of athlete best suited to that style, often arranges things so that Brady doesn't have to drive New England's offense very far for a score.

Each side understands the other. Belichick insists that, with his gifts for breaking down the opposition's defense on film, Brady could be a first-class *defensive* coach. After all, it's Brady's job to study film and to find flaws in a defense just as much as that's the job of a defensive coooordinator. Brady's just usually looking at the opponent's defense, is all. "He's got a doctorate in defensive football," the coach says. "He understands how a coverage should be played, and, if a team's not playing it that way, that there's a vulnerability there."

For his part, Vrabel has to know and understand quarterbacks. "It's about jamming receivers and getting in throwing lanes," he explains. "That's a tough combination when all of those things are working together back there, and you've got to throw the ball in rhythm and it's all timing.

"What we do is reactive to a certain point, but, if you've got a certain call, you have to adjust to whatever they're running. So the whole idea that you don't read anything, you just go, well, eventually, you're going to have to read where the ball's going, what the blocking scheme is. The guys who come off the ball, they still have to read and redirect [themselves], and get to the football." On the Patriots, offensive players like Brady have to understand what the defense is trying to do, and defensive players like Mike Vrabel have to be able to read and exploit weaknesses in offenses, starting with their own, every day at practice. And, of course, in Vrabel's case, he has to understand the offense because he's become such a quirky and important part of it down near the goal line.

In 2005, because of injuries and the retirement of Ted Johnson, Vrabel had been moved to inside linebacker. This move cut down on his ability to rush the passer as his responsibilities changed to the grinding, glamourless business of helping to clog the middle against an opponent's running game. Quite literally in most cases, this position meant exchanging a place at the top of the pile for one at the very bottom of it. But it still meant reading quarterbacks, parsing out the psyche of that curious breed. All quarterbacks, Mike Vrabel believes, can be had. Bearded the following day by someone who saw his interview on television, Vrabel laughs.

"Tom?" he says, conceding nothing. "Hey, we do a pretty good job on him, too."

At five-nine and 190 pounds, he's so small you might not notice him among the behemoths with whom he does his business. This impression holds until you look at his biceps, which you could very likely use to drive railroad spikes. Deion Branch becomes a football player at eye level.

New England found him on the second round of the 2002 draft, a water bug of a receiver from a pass-happy offense at the University of Louisville, where Branch caught 143 passes for 2,204 yards and eighteen touchdowns. He came out of a small high school in Albany, Georgia, as Anthony Branch, Jr. The Deion got hung on him as a testimony to his speed and dash, an homage to Deion Sanders, the bling-draped pinwheel of a defensive back who played for Dallas, San Francisco, and Baltimore. What flash there is to Branch, however, comes in short, quick bursts. He's a spark gap in the dense, cluttered spaces of the field and not a lightning bolt coursing down the sideline.

He is fast enough running in a straight line, but it's his ability to cut precisely and to accelerate instantly that made him attractive to the Patriots, who have based much of their passing offense on the ability of their receivers to make yardage after catching the ball—YACs as they're known on the scouting reports. In turn, this ability enables the team to take the greatest advantage of Brady's gift not only for delivering the ball to the right man but also for delivering it in the right place, so that the receiver can turn upfield and run. A quarterback whose throws require his receivers to turn back into the defense becomes both increasingly unpopular with them and decreasingly employable around the league.

"As a receiver, you have no idea where the defender is," Belichick explains. "You know where he was when you made your break, but it's up to the quarterback to control the receiver relative to where the coverage is. A good quarterback places the ball here, so I'm turning away from you. So, when I catch it, I'm running away from you. You don't want it there, where the receiver turns into the tackler, and he gets blown up."

What Belichick and Charlie Weis saw in Branch was a smart receiver who was quick enough to get open and tough enough to do it at precisely the right instant, a player who could coordinate the geometry of the game with his own internal clock.

"You tell a guy to run a route fourteen yards," Belichick says. "Well, that's great when there's nobody else standing out there.

Now, say, you're up at the line and the corner jams you before you get back in your route. Now, if you run fourteen, it's too late because the quarterback is back there holding the ball. You run that at fourteen and he can't wait. In that case, the receiver might have to run the route at eleven or twelve [yards].

"That's the receiver's time clock going off, saying, 'Fuck, it's time for me to come out of this break. I've got to get out of this break *now*. If it's twelve, it doesn't make any difference. The time has come. If I wait to run fourteen, it's not going to work because the quarterback needs to get rid of the ball.'"

Working with Brady, Branch developed a similar gift for the biggest stages. Against Carolina in his first Super Bowl, he caught ten passes for 143 yards. The following season, against Philadelphia, he had his true breakthrough game—catching eleven passes and gaining 133 yards. None of his receptions was longer than 27 yards, but all of them were critical. Branch was named the game's Most Valuable Player, the first time in three New England wins that Brady wasn't the MVP. Brady told people after the game how happy he was for Branch.

Branch was crucial to some adjustments that Weis and Belichick made during the game. In the second quarter, the Patriots went to four wide receivers. At the beginning of the second half, they moved Branch into the slot receiver's position, and he kept running his careful, modest routes down Philadelphia's throat, keeping the ball away from the Eagle offense. In the moving of the chains, the offense can fairly be said to be part of the defense, both units melding in their functions into one. Branch's best moment came with 13:44 left in the game. On the previous possession, Brady had hit on four passes in a row on a drive that ultimately put New England ahead, 21–14. Now, on a second-and-thirteen play from midfield, Branch broke out of the slot and down the middle of the field. Brady took a colossal—and, ultimately, illegal—hit from Philadel-phia's Corey Simon. His pass went high and just a bit short. Branch leaped and reached over Eagle cornerback Shelton Brown to pluck the ball away for a nineteen-yard gain that would help position Adam Vinatieri for the twenty-two-yard field goal that would prove to be the winning points.

Since that game, Branch had become a burgeoning star, eventually sharing with *The Boston Globe*'s Jackie MacMullan the story of his sons, Deiondre and Deiontey, born prematurely four years earlier back in Louisville. Deiondre had been struck almost at birth with meningitis and had become profoundly disabled. Branch had kept the story to himself for three years. Now, though, aware of the platform his skills afforded him, he grew in the use of his fame as surely as he'd grown into the role of caregiver for his boy. He used the story of his son to raise money and awareness on the issues of prenatal care.

On the field, he'd become Brady's prime target, the two de-veloping a form of unspoken communication based on the instant recognition of a situation and on a confidence in each other's abilities that amounted to two people with a common set of reflexes. Ray Berry had it with Johnny Unitas, and Joe Montana with Jerry Rice. Hit Tom Brady's knee, and Deion Branch's leg will kick. "Deion's open on every play," Brady says. "Every time you look, he's open. Every time I don't throw it to him, and there's an incompletion, I come back and he says, 'Hey, T, I was open.' So I have to find ways to get him the ball."

In February 2002, it was in the Superdome in New Orleans that the New England Patriots beat the St. Louis Rams, becoming the football team that stood for everything that a wounded country wanted to believe about itself. It was there that Tom

Brady first became a mirror in which the wounded country could look for everything it hoped was still there. There was a sad, determined unity surrounding the event. The NFL celebrated, among other things, the remarkable sacrifice made by a member of the Arizona Cardinals named Pat Tillman, who'd abandoned a lucrative contract in the wake of the September 11 attacks to join the army and fight in Afghanistan.

Now, three years on, Tillman was dead, killed by friendly fire in an incident about which the army could not seem to keep its story straight. His angry parents were publicly condemning the government. The Patriots now seemed to embody a unity in the country that was squandered and gone, and the Superdome had come to symbolize a feckless, helpless government, the place where desperate people went as a last resort against the fury of a hurricane. In 2005, a week after the Miami game, the New Orleans Saints came to Foxborough. Every game they played was on the road; their "home field" was in San Antonio. Their stadium was closed, a darkly iconic place in a drowned city, most recently seen on television as the vestibule to a graveyard.

It was not a prestige game for the NFL. The wandering Saints were 2–7, while the Patriots, at 5–4, were trying to win consecutive games for the first time all season, their roster as depleted by injury as it ever had been during Brady's time with the team. The Patriots would have to play without both starting running backs and without three wide receivers. They'd be missing three starters from the offensive line and starting tight end Daniel Graham. "You can feel sorry for yourself, and you can be discouraged, and whine and pout and complain, but that doesn't get you anywhere," Brady had said earlier in the week. "And the only way to dig yourself out of it is to realize what it takes to overcome all these injuries and start to think, 'Wouldn't it be great if we could turn this thing around?' That would make

for a great year, and it starts this week." Not even Brady, however, could have predicted the kind of emotional freight this conspicuously unglamorous game would carry.

On the Saturday night before the New Orleans game, while
watching a college football game at his home, Steve Belichick
died of heart failure at eighty-six. He had been a football lifer,
an assistant coach and scout who'd been hired and fired several
times, the way all assistant coaches are, before joining the staff
at the Naval Academy in 1956, when Bill was four. Steve had
stayed at Navy for thirty-three years, and Bill had tagged along
with his father from the time he could walk. At the end of the
Super Bowl the previous January, Steve had been standing next
to his son on the sideline when linebacker Tedy Bruschi had
doused them both with Gatorade. And, more recently, he'd become famous through the publication of David Halberstam's
book about his son, in which the relationship between Steve and
Bill Belichick is a pivot.

"It was one of the best moments of the entire Super Bowl extravaganza, filled as it so often was with moments of artificial
emotion," Halberstam wrote of the intergenerational dunking
at the end of the game, "because this moment was absolutely
genuine, father and son drenched together, emotion finally showing on the face of the son, usually so reticent about showing
emotion, as if to do so was to give away some precious bit of
control, to fall victim at least momentarily to the whims of the
modern media trap."

Bill Belichick didn't share his loss with his team before the
game, although the news began to filter through the stadium
and into the press box not long before kickoff. Brady and the offense started quickly. Beginning at their own 2-yard line, New
England launched a ninety-eight-yard drive in sixteen plays. On
the drive, Brady converted three third downs and a fourth down

with passes to three different receivers, including one each to Branch and to Ben Watson, whose role in the offense was increasing by the week. Brady first went to Watson on a third-and-ten from his own 15-yard line, covering twenty-nine yards with the kind of classic deep-out throw that always made Charlie Weis laugh at the people who'd questioned the strength of Brady's arm. The ball dropped deftly past the fingertips of New Orleans safety Dwight Smith and over Watson's left shoulder, so the receiver would have a chance to turn upfield and run.

And it was Watson to whom Brady went on the fourth-down play, waiting and waiting, checking down through his options, until Watson came clear to his left, having crossed the entire width of the formation to get there. Four plays later, Branch caught the touchdown, a two-yarder on which Brady and Patrick Pass sold a play-action fake so well that you could see the New Orleans linebackers dance just a bit, forward and back, like men unsure of their footing, until Branch was alone in the end zone.

Vrabel caught the next one, in the second quarter, after New England had taken advantage of a short New Orleans punt to start a drive on the Saints' 48-yard line. Again, Brady sold the fake, this time to Heath Evans, who folded himself at the waist as though he'd taken a hook to the ribs. Again, the New Orleans linebackers looked as if they'd suddenly stepped into a mire. Vrabel slipped crisply through the confusion and caught the third touchdown pass of his career. The third touchdown, in fact, in as many catches, which prompted more than a few people to wonder whether NFL defensive coordinators didn't have more in common than they'd care to admit with Wile E. Coyote. Sooner or later, one of them had to figure out that Vrabel wasn't a decoy.

The Patriots were riding Brady's arm, more than they would

have liked to do, and certainly more than he'd have preferred. On three occasions, with only the most perfunctory attempts at deception, they sent receiver Andre Davis simply sprinting down the sidelines and Brady threw the ball as far as he could. They were straight, schoolyard fly patterns, no chaser. And one did connect, a sixty-yard touchdown, a gorgeous midline incision through the New Orleans secondary that gave New England a 21–7 lead. After Brady's carefully dissecting defenses one slice at a time, this was something akin to a surgeon entering the operating theater waving a scimitar.

But the New England defense struggled to hold on, especially the secondary, which was still a hodgepodge. It was made up of untested rookies, such as the speedy Ellis Hobbs, and free-agent acquisitions who looked increasingly as though they'd been drawn from the bad-risk pool. The New Orleans quarterback, Aaron Brooks, a cousin of Atlanta star Michael Vick, threw for 343 yards, the third straight quarterback to light the Patriot defense up for more than 300 yards. He got the Saints all the way back to 24–17, and he moved them all the way down to the New England 22. From there, Brooks took two cracks at tying the game, but Hobbs defended one pass into an incompletion, and safety Eugene Wilson made a leaping interception on the other to end the game.

"I think both teams were playing hard," Brady said. "They have a very physical defensive line. Those guys were playing hard all day. And it is a good group of linebackers." He'd had a solid day—fifteen of twenty-nine for 222 yards and three touchdowns without an interception, so his quarterback rating—as always, apparently calculated on an abacus that was a bead or two short—was 111.6. But the postgame atmosphere was freighted with common grief.

"Personally," Bill Belichick said, "I coached this game with a heavy heart. Yesterday, my father did what he enjoyed doing. He went and watched Navy play and he watched them win. Some of his former players were there. He had dinner, and I spoke with him after the game. And, like he normally does Saturday night, [he was] sitting around watching college football, and his heart just stopped beating. So, I'm sure that's the way he would have wanted it to end. He went peacefully, which was unusual for him." With that, Belichick left the team for most of the following week.

For Deion Branch, father to a handicapped son, and for Tom Brady, the devoted son to a devoted father, the notion of losing a father resonated profoundly. "That just shows you what kind of man he is, the fact that he could still focus on this game and coach the team to victory with all this lingering on his mind. It's hard, man," said Deion Branch, who was learning all the time that playing in pain doesn't necessarily mean the physical.

"I guess when I do lose my father, I know how tough it will be," Brady mused after the game. "I just can't imagine, as a person, to not allow that out, to hold that in like he did."

They all had one another, and Josiah Royce was right about loyalty to loyalty, that it is both sustenance and balm, and that it is a kind of path through even the most painful distraction. A careful person could follow that path and avoid the force that Royce specifically cited in regard to big-time sport as the primary enemy of the loyalty that teammates must have to the loyalty between them: "Extravagant publicity."

CHARLIE AND MAURA WEIS met on the Jersey Shore, a courtship off of some old doo-wop record. The Shore was what the East Coast had in place of all those beach blanket movies from California, except that people named Funicello were a lot more common there than in the homogenized California of the United States of Disney.

"I was dragged out by my girlfriends to a place called Leggett's," Maura Weis says. "And we had dinner, and I saw two guys looking over at us and I was telling my girlfriends how creepy they were. I said, 'Like, they're just staring.'

"The next thing you know, they're over here talking with us, and Charlie said he was a football coach and I thought, 'Who'd want to date a football coach?'" Undeterred, Charlie took Maura and all her friends out to dinner later that week. "When we were out to dinner," she recalls, "Charlie was saying how he was very fortunate and that God was really good to him, and that's when I realized that there was some deeper connection with Charlie."

They married not long after, and they followed Charlie's career up through the ranks. They came to New England when Charlie joined Bill Belichick's staff after the latter took the Patriots job in 2000, just in time to start to work with a rookie quarterback from Michigan on whom Dick Rehbein was very high. Maura Weis was one of the first people to know what her husband thought the Patriots had. "He told me, 'Maura, this kid could be the best ever,' and I was struck by that because he never talked like that about anyone," she says. Later that year, at a dinner for the quarterbacks that Weis hosted at his house, Maura fell into conversation with the youngest of them.

"He asked about my daughter, who has special needs, and my son," she recalls. "I realized that this was just a caring individual. He's got that kind of personality that, when he talks to you, you feel like you're the only person in the room, you know?"

For years, Charlie Weis's weight had been a cause for concern, not only for its very real effects on his health but also for its purported effects on his career. He was a successful NFL coordinator, which is considered to be the last rung on the ladder leading to a head coaching position in the league. But there was a feeling abroad in the league that Weis might not project an image on the sideline with which the average NFL team was comfortable. In an attempt to alleviate the problem, Weis checked himself into Massachusetts General Hospital for gastric-bypass surgery during the first week of June 2002. It was supposed to be an overnight procedure, done laparoscopically, and he was supposed to be home in twenty-four hours. He decided to tell only a few people about the surgery, and one of them was Brady.

The next morning, the quarterback showed up to visit. "He was coming by because I was supposed to check out that afternoon," Weis says. "He was just stopping by, just so he didn't have to listen to my shit for him not stopping."

But overnight, something had gone dreadfully wrong. In the early hours of the morning after the procedure, Weis had begun to bleed internally, and he'd lapsed into a coma. He was moved into the surgical intensive-care unit. Maura went with him. "I guess I was in with Charlie," she recalls, "and they told me that somebody was there to see him, and I went out and it was Tommy.

"He didn't know what to expect, and I had kind of been in shock myself from this whole thing because they called me at six in the morning to tell me he was bleeding. Charlie was intubated and he was really in bad shape."

Brady and Maura went into the small, dimly lit cubicle where Charlie lay unconscious. Maura explained to the quarterback what had happened, and what was being done for her husband now. After a while, the doctors came in to do some sort of procedure, and the two of them went back to the waiting room. "He looked at me, and he was, like, 'Am I okay?' And I said, 'Yeah, why?' And he said, 'I felt like I was going to pass out in there.'

"He said blood usually gets him queasy, and he doesn't really like to look at blood, and there was plenty of that there for him to see, and I thought, you know, I just didn't realize how young he was until he said that. I was, like, 'Oh, my God,' and so he kind of made me keep it together for him.

"He made me stronger because I knew he was young, and I didn't want to cry in front of him. I didn't want to freak out. I probably held myself together more because he was there."

For the next forty-eight hours, Charlie lay close to death. He received the last rites of the Catholic Church twice. Brady stayed with Maura Weis. He was there early in the morning, and he left only when they threw him out. Something instant and instinctive caused him to invest himself in Maura, and she in him, each holding the fear and the doubt at bay for the other's sake, supporting each other against the long, fluorescent isolation of the ICU.

"It was weird because, we were there so long, I can remember not knowing whether the sun was out or not," Maura re-calls. "And I got to know the nurses when the shifts changed and all." Several academic studies have been done on the effects of long-term ICU stays, not only on the patients themselves but on their loved ones and caregivers. It can be a grimly insular busi-ness; several studies refer to "ICU psychosis." One night, when Charlie had to go in for another surgery, Tom and Maura went to dinner. Brady asked Maura how she and Charlie had met, and she told him about the club on the Jersey Shore and the creepy guy who'd come over to talk to her.

"That shows you how smart he is," Maura says. "It brought me around to the really good times. Then, we went back over, and he waited until the doctors came out of the surgery, and, you know, I was really upset, and I was quite mad at the doctors, so he really kind of calmed me down through that. Even though he didn't know me, he knew how fired up I was about that whole thing."

At last, some of Charlie and Maura's friends and family were able to get to Boston from around the country, but Brady remained constant. Charlie drifted in and out of consciousness for the next eighteen days, and Brady was there every day, talk-ing to the coach even when the latter was unconscious, jiving with him about how much Weis would hate what they were making him wear, if he had only been awake to see it. Later, when Weis finally was awake and out of danger, Brady told him how happy he was.

You're not going to be that happy in a few months, Weis growled at him.

"Tommy came to me and said, 'Do you think he'll be nicer afterwards? Maybe not yell as much?'" Maura Weis recalls. "We were both, like, 'Nah. That's not going to happen.'"

Brady stayed with Weis throughout his lengthy rehabilitation period. At first, Weis was foggy and vague, and inchoately depressed. (To this day, he remembers almost nothing about the eighteen days in which he was in crisis.) During training camp, Brady visited him every night when practice was over for the day. Four years and change later, and two Super Bowl championships on from that endless month, Weis is at Notre Dame, on a foggy day in early winter. He's getting ready for his first bowl game as a head coach in a conference room two blocks from the big stadium that Tom Brady cased for its mystique on his way back to Ann Arbor.

"When I got out of the hospital," Weis says, "here's a guy who came over to my house every night just to hang out with me for an hour, just to lift my spirits up. I stayed alive because of my family. I fought to stay alive because of my family. But I got better faster than I should have because of football, and he spearheaded that.

"I never really went in really, really close to a player, because I'm the same guy who's going to have to be just tearing into him later. But, from the day I went into the hospital, our relationship changed."

It was Maura who'd filled Charlie in on everything that had happened while he was "away," including the most surreal moment of them all. It was the second night, not long after it had been determined that Charlie would have to go into surgery again. Maura was talking to the doctors, holding herself in check with only the greatest effort. Brady was with her. Just at that moment, as the machines beeped and hummed and whirred in the perennial twilight of the ICU, as the doctors whispered while everyone else's nerves screamed, one of the nurses asked Brady for an autograph.

Later, he told the woman, his voice barely carrying over the song of the machines. Maybe we could do it later.

Except for those measured on a scoreboard, or by the number of increasingly garish rings one can accumulate, the great rewards of a successful football career often come hooked to unsolvable dilemmas. Are they owed to the player for past performance, or are they owed to him as a kind of promissory note against further greatness in the future? This is most keenly felt, always, in the negotiation of a player's contract, when the management-tilted structure of the NFL makes it easy for a team to argue the point either way, depending on its immediate competitive needs and its situation vis-à-vis the league's salary cap. Except for quarterbacks, there's virtually no such thing as a franchise's signature player anymore in the NFL. The Patriots have been notably cold-eyed about shuffling popular but expensive players out of town. Lawyer Milloy was the first of them. Before the 2005 season, the team let All-Pro cornerback Ty Law go to the New York Jets.

Celebrity can work that way, too, but in the opposite direction. Generally, it arrives ex post facto, and clearly as a reward for services already rendered. (There are exceptions, of course. The golfer Tiger Woods was famous long before he won anything, and the tennis player Anna Kournikova became famous without ever winning anything.) This means that the sugar can come at an otherwise distasteful time. Already in 2005, Brady had hosted *Saturday Night Live*, and he'd been profiled not only by ESPN's *SportsCentury* but also on *60 Minutes*. He had been the lead in a commercial that went into heavy rotation during breaks in the games in which he also was playing. And now he was here, in the crepuscular light of the Gillette Stadium press box, the empty field below him green and empty and oddly alien to the business at hand. He was being photographed because *Sports Illustrated* had named him its Sportsman of the Year.

A tiny stylist fussed with his hair. A slightly taller person fussed with his wardrobe. A local camera crew wandered around in the shadows, so that Brady was in the position of being filmed while being photographed, a tangled ball of meta-media that would have delighted Marshall McLuhan. The photographer was Walter Iooss, Jr., a legend from *Sports Illustrated*'s glory days, immortalized by his former colleague Dan Jenkins as "Shag Monti" in Jenkins's transparent roman à clef about the magazine, *You Gotta Play Hurt*. Iooss/Monti is portrayed as a character somewhere between a photographic genius and a roadie for the Grateful Dead. As they worked, Brady talked to Iooss about the goat photo that had accompanied the *GQ* story that had kicked off this season. "I'm telling you," Brady said. "There must have been a thousand goats there."

All of this is a reward for the previous two seasons, the ones that ended with Super Bowl victories. However, the honor is coming down on him in the middle of a season in which only the dreadful AFC East is keeping the New England Patriots from sliding into mediocrity, and from doing so in such a way as to presage the several years of mediocrity and rebuilding that are forced upon every franchise by the gimmicky system through which the NFL maintains its parity. This particular moment, for example, in which he was being celebrated for having beaten Philadelphia and Carolina in consecutive Super Bowls, and for having helped establish New England as the league's most formidable franchise, came only a few days before Brady and the Patriots fell to one of their most signifying losses of their current season.

With Belichick having missed most of the week's practices

attending to his father's funeral services, Kansas City ran the Patriots off the field, 26–16, in a game that wasn't nearly that close. The Chiefs piled up a 26–3 lead in the middle of the third quarter, and they coasted from there. The New England defense again was a muddle, surrendering 119 yards to KC running back Larry Johnson and 323 passing yards to Trent Green, staving off a complete rout only by stiffening inside their own "red zone"— the area from their 20-yard line to the goal line—three out of four times in the first half, forcing the Chiefs to settle for a field goal.

And Brady had one of his worst days as a professional quarterback. He threw four interceptions, three of which banged off his intended receivers. In the first half, he connected on only seven of eighteen throws, and he was intercepted twice, which gave him a quarterback rating of 15, approximately the rating achieved by the average mark throwing footballs into a peach basket at a carnival. Both of those interceptions were on overthrows, although Deion Branch did manage to tip the second one. There was clearly something wrong with him. Brady was stepping gingerly into his passes, as though he were unable to get his feet firmly enough under him to work his touch on the ball. His passes kept sailing on him. He looked tentative, as though he were hurt and fighting as hard not to show it as he was to move the chains. He concluded the game trying to rally the team but ended the last two New England drives with interceptions.

The loss left New England at 6–5 for the season, but there was some dry rot in those numbers. The team was 2–5 against opponents with winning records, and it had been soundly thumped on three of those occasions, most notably against Indianapolis. The measure of how much New England benefited from its weak division was the fact that, even with the loss in Kansas City, the Patriots led the AFC East by two games.

On the plane coming home, Brady teared up thinking about the game. "It was a killer," he said. "Yesterday was just frustrating because it was a great opportunity and we didn't play the way we're capable of playing. I didn't play the way I'm capable of playing. Anytime the quarterback doesn't play the way he should, well, I'm glad we don't go through it too often or I wouldn't get much sleep." The honors were coming and his team was stuck in the mud. This put how he'd defined himself as a competitor somewhat at odds with how he had to define himself as a celebrity athlete. The rest of his public life would be measured by how well he managed that conflict within himself.

"It is not fun when you throw four picks," Brady continued, clinging closely to the empirical calibrations of the game. "It's like you've been kicked in the stomach, and it doesn't go away for two or three days. It puts you right back in your place. Just when you think you've got it all figured out, you find out you still have to try to get better."

Already, Brady's daily life was being steadily drained of the ordinary. For example, he'd come of age as a celebrity athlete in the age of the picture phone. It used to be that anyone who wanted an autograph or a photograph or a handshake would have to muster the gumption to come up and ask. Now, Brady would go to lunch, say, with his sister, and she'd look up and see someone standing behind her brother, waving, while someone else pointed a cell phone at them from across the room.

"He's struggling with how to live his life normally, trying to find that balance of being true to himself and of being the role model that everybody wants," Nancy Brady says. "I mean, we have no private space. We have no private time. If we were to come out for lunch, and we just want to have a nice afternoon, and we have ten people come up to the table, he's uncomfortable every time."

She talked about this at a seaside restaurant south of Boston, a bustling place tucked into the same apartment complex in which her brother lived when he first came to the city. People around her table are pretending not to be aware of what she's talking about, and failing very badly at it.

"And he asks me, 'Do I sign and, you know, get it over with because it takes less time than to explain that I'm just trying to have lunch with my sister?' I was so upset that I wanted to leave before they came to take my order," she explains. "At what point do you say, 'Okay, not any more'? That's my thing. I'll say it, because I'm extremely upset, because I think there are limits on what people have a right to do."

It would have been easier if Tommy had been born a jerk, Nancy thought. If he'd spent his entire life spoiled and arrogant, so that, when his career permitted him even greater heights of jerkitude, nobody would have expected anything more. He could have blown off people at lunch without being concerned in the slightest. Nobody would have been surprised if he'd actually gotten in a fight with the guy at the gas station who wanted him to stick his head in the car to say hello to the guy's children, and then got angry when Brady told him he'd do it after he finished filling his tank.

But he couldn't slug the guy. That wasn't who he was, and it definitely was not who people thought he was. Confronted by public rudeness, to say nothing of public boors, Brady's range of options was limited not only by his own virtues but by the image that had arisen out of them. But he also would not lock himself away, which made him different in a way from many of the Boston sports heroes who'd come before him, who discovered that the city could be the biggest small town in the world. Great players here are considered common property—civic institutions, like the Swan Boats in the Public Garden or the perpetually cranky MBTA. Ted Williams hated the place so much that he didn't become a local icon until long after he'd retired. Larry Bird spent his early years as a local icon in seclusion or in southern Indiana, which is much the same thing.

Brady would not withdraw. He would not become a monk. When he dated Bridget Moynahan, an actress who starred with Will Smith in *I, Robot*, their coupling became regular grist for the local gossip mills. In a time when even the most profanely gaudy athlete can wrap himself in Scripture as though it were a floor-length mink, Brady wore his family's conspicuous Catholicism lightly, if at all. He would define what a normal guy is and try, as best he could, to live up to that. Which was how the whole thing about his cruising the Net for porn started.

It began with a piece of reportorial trickeration. Brady told the author of the *GQ* piece, David Kamp, that, in all respects except his job, he was a normal twenty-six-year-old guy doing normal twenty-six-year-old things. "Like surf the 'Net for porn," asked Kamp. "Normal stuff," Brady replied, a non-denial denial that was good enough to go bouncing through the media wind tunnel as an explicit confession for a week or so. It was a minor kerfuffle at best; the goat photo was a much bigger deal. But it was an indication of the edge Brady had come to walk as a public person, and the ceaseless tension between who he was and who he'd come to be to everyone else.

"He needed the opportunity to excel, and he knew he could once he had it," muses Charlie Weis. "And, by excelling, he's trying to handle it as best he can, even though he hates the invasion of privacy. That's the thing he hates more than anything else, because he loves to be one of the boys, and he can't be one of the boys because you'll read about it the next day in the gossip columns of the *Herald*.

"Look, they all have egos. *We* all have big egos. *We* all think we're pretty good at what we do. But Tommy's not abrasive. That's why he's so good with his team. He never acts like he's above the team. That's not to say he won't go at people, because he will, but he doesn't do it as though he's above them."

It was easier in the locker room. He knew who he was as a football player. He'd known it before a lot of putatively smart football people had figured it out. He was a quarterback, but, most of all, he was a teammate. He was good at being a teammate. "The reason for all of it is because we've been successful playing football," Brady insists. "Tom Brady, the person, doesn't win these awards. I just don't want to lose what we've accomplished. Sitting there, losing a game like that [in Kansas City], you're heartbroken, really. You're tearing up because you let people down. You let your teammates down. That's not something you get over easily."

He'd always thought of himself as a work in progress, taking nothing for granted, because that always had been the safest way to go. He had lived a long time on intimate terms with the possibility that football would end for him. He'd looked it in the eye when he was recruited out of Serra and during all the confusion and controversy at Michigan. It was right there in front of him as his name slid slowly through the first day of the NFL draft and well into the second. It fairly bellowed at him when he arrived in the National Football League as a fourth-string holder of a clipboard.

He knew what the end of his career would feel like, better

than anyone else ever would. He would not be summed up before he was ready to be, and he would not be summed up by anyone else. So he gave *60 Minutes*, which regularly asks the subjects of its profiles for at least a day's worth of time, only a couple of hours, and he made sure that Deion Branch was a big part of the segment. He didn't participate in ESPN's *SportsCentury* feature at all, because that sounded to him too much like a retrospective. He was still too young for a book about him. His celebrity was a work in progress, too. He would treat his celebrity in the way that Orson Welles once had Charles Foster Kane talk about love. Here's to love on our own terms, Kane toasts, because those are the only terms anyone ever really knows.

In many ways, Brady became a careful, cautious public figure, but a public figure nonetheless. For example, to watch him be so completely flummoxed by a question about his Irish heritage was to see him gingerly avoiding an easy answer less because it might be wrong and more because the easy answer might sound insincere, all the while knowing that virtually any easy answer, however insincere, would redound to his credit. And, since most Boston schoolchildren with Irish heritages can rattle them off almost from birth, this moment was the plainest proof that, as beloved as he'd become in Boston, Tom Brady was indeed from those dim places beyond the Charles.

Even during his *60 Minutes* interview, in which he talked about the perils of being recognized in a public place, Brady couched his answers gently, talking about how the peripheral vision he uses in the pocket to avoid onrushing defensive linemen he can also use to spot people coming at him from the blind side, pens and paper at the ready. He talked about how hilarious his friends from back home found the whole thing. He said there was no place he'd rather be than playing golf with his parents, which made people wonder how Ms. Moynahan felt about that. Ultimately, he told Steve Kroft, "You can't have the football fame without the other stuff. So, in a lot of ways, I've created this myself."

He found a way to deal with what was coming at him through a part of himself that always eluded people who only thought they knew him. He was endlessly curious. At Serra, he'd taken an architecture class, losing himself in the minute technical details of construction. He loved figuring out how things worked, and why they worked the way they did, and his curiosity was a part of that interesting mind that Elwood Reid had glimpsed at Michigan. The curiosity was part of the reason he was so very good at breaking down defenses while looking at films. He saw how the pieces fit, and he was able to recognize when they didn't, and why they didn't. Off the field, as he became more successful, he determined to study other successful people in other fields, to see how they put their lives together, and to see how all the pieces worked. It was why he and Bob Kraft talked at length about how Kraft ran his other businesses. It was why Trump so fascinated him.

"He's smart enough to know that the profile from being a star quarterback gives him an advantage," explains Jonathan Kraft, Bob's son and the president of the Patriots, "but he'll be intensely driven to be good at whatever his craft is. Tom would immerse himself in whatever it would take to be good at something, to develop a strategy to succeed at it."

The destructive side of celebrity is inertial. You can get lost in pointless motion or you can get mired in isolation. But learning was something Brady knew how to do. It was a way to keep his life moving so he wouldn't find himself, at forty-five, locked away in a trophy room. It was also a way to keep his life moving in a specific direction over which he had some control. In April

2005, when he went off to New York to host *Saturday Night Live*, he involved himself in all aspects of the production. He talked to the cast members, and he chatted up the writers. He sat through the long, grinding midweek meetings, in which forty-five or fifty proposed skits are winnowed down to the handful that actually are performed on the show. Part of this was the fact that he is incapable in any enterprise of not being a teammate. But it also reflected his genuine desire to learn.

"In the meetings," recalls Lorne Michaels, the creator and producer of *SNL*, "he was willing to express his opinion. I found him open and thoughtful, and he pretty clearly was open to what we thought might be funny for him to do. He was very interested in all the steps of the process of putting the show together. He came to play, as they say." However, there was a skit involving the Philadelphia Eagles, whom the Patriots had defeated in the Super Bowl two months earlier.

"He was open to everything," Michaels explains. "But he was worried about the stuff with the Eagles, that it might be disrespectful. He was willing to make fun of himself, but I got the feeling he didn't want to be mean about anyone else."

On the show, Brady's opening monologue poked fun at his clean-cut image. He was required to sing a mock-boastful song that not only included the immortal couplet "I won the Tour de France / without wearing any pants" but also had him singing the praises of "my sweet behind." Later, in a how-to skit about sexual harassment—"Be Handsome. Be Attractive. Don't Be Unattractive"—he was filmed walking through an office in his briefs. In New York to watch the show, Nancy Brady, who hadn't seen her brother on any stage except a football field since he'd been in an eighth-grade production of *The Wizard of Oz*, was stunned.

"I was caught off guard when he decided to do *Saturday Night Live*," she says. "I mean, I thought it was great, but I was surprised, you know, him appearing in his tighty-whities and all.

"I didn't go to any of the dress rehearsals, because I wanted to see it live, and he comes out in the first act, and he does the whole song and dance, and I was laughing and cheering and I just couldn't believe how he really threw himself into it, and the fact that he was so amused and whatever they asked him to do, he would do it, and that he didn't take himself so seriously."

Brady had begun to control his brand, as the marketing people would say. But, by instinct, he also seemed to know that the first order of business was not business at all. It was to recognize what was authentic and what was not. It was to recognize what was authentic in yourself and what was authentic in those things you were being offered for a piece of yourself. And the best way to do that was to see how all the other parts of this new world worked, at your own speed and on your own terms, while hanging on to first principles—which, in Brady's case, were those of being a teammate—because without them, none of the rest of it would be possible or right.

Constructing a career this way is to build one in which every untoward rumor takes on added weight, in which every whisper is a scream, like a curse in a cathedral. The path that Brady had chosen is not the easiest journey to make or the simplest life to lead. It's full of contradictions. It's potholed with paradox. But it's still the truest path across the public landscape, because it recognizes that, while that celebrity is what this country adopted when it gave up on thrones, it's also what this country adopted when it gave up on the stocks.

■ ■ ■

The National Football League has its headquarters in a black, faceless building in midtown Manhattan. There's the usual post-9/11 security check in the lobby, and, when the elevators finally let you out on the seventeenth floor, you're greeted by huge photographs from the previous Super Bowl. On this day, Tom Brady is everywhere around the NFL's main lobby, Philadelphia Eagles tumbling uselessly at his feet. Next to the main reception desk is the permanent Lombardi Trophy, surrounded at its base by a championship ring from every Super Bowl. You can measure the growth of that event, and the growth of the NFL along with it, through the decreasing practicality of those rings for the purpose of actual human adornment. By the 1980s, the damn things looked like radiator ornaments.

The NFL has marketing in its DNA. Pete Rozelle, the most towering figure in the history of the league (and, arguably, in the history of professional sports), came out of the postwar explosion of the wind industries—advertising, public relations, and mass communication—and, as Michael MacCambridge recalls in his history of the league, it was Rozelle's vast network of personal contacts in all three fields that was responsible for the NFL's first breakthrough successes in the late 1950s and the 1960s. Moreover, as MacCambridge also points out, in 1963 Rozelle talked the various league owners into starting up NFL Properties, a revolutionary concept by which the pennants, jerseys, and various paraphernalia associated with the teams would all be produced, marketed, and sold under a single, leaguewide umbrella. (These products eventually would include, of course, team umbrellas.) MacCambridge argues that even the relatively thin early profits of NFL Properties were far less important than was the effect of NFL Properties in branding the league and extending its reach.

Of course, the profits did not remain thin for long. In 2004, they were big enough to cause a squabble between the rich owners and the very rich owners. At issue was the long-standing policy of dividing the profits from licensing and team apparel equally among all thirty-two NFL teams. That he managed to renew the agreement to do so is considered one of the great achievements of Rozelle's successor, Paul Tagliabue, who retired after the 2005 season. So, when somebody sells Tom Brady's jersey, the money comes to NFL Properties and thence to all of the league's teams. Buy a New England Patriots shirt bearing the number 12—even one of the spiffy pink-and-white ones that have become increasingly popular in middle schools—and you're also helping out, say, the Seattle Seahawks.

His office tucked deep into the NFL complex, Phil Guarascio markets the league surrounded by so many NFL-themed gewgaws that he appears to be running the Pete Rozelle Memorial Preschool. He's slim and dark, and he seems to crackle with a kind of urgent energy. Within the first five minutes of stepping into his office, Phil Guarascio will attempt to give you something.

He came to the NFL from General Motors, where he signed golfer Tiger Woods to his first major contract. He talks about athletes as "platforms" through which various products can be marketed. "One of the truisms in marketing these days is the notion that everything is a platform," he explains. "A lot of the trend in marketing personalities these days is to look at them as platforms. A lot of great athletes, the younger, newer athletes, like Andy Roddick and the Williams sisters, they want to be seen as entertainment platforms.

"The great ones, the ones who really represent extreme value for marketers, tend to be people who are self-possessed but not really full of themselves. They have an appeal to men and women, and they can cut across age-groups. They can represent different things to different age-groups and cohorts, but do it in a way that stays within their brand. It's hard to find those kinds of people."

Brady caught the NFL's marketing people as much by surprise as he caught everybody else in the league. His "brand," such as it was, consisted only of his being the successful quarterback of a Super Bowl championship team. While that certainly was more than enough for the Patriots—and, very likely, quite enough at the time for him—it was just an embryonic stage in how he could be marketed. "He's absolutely a work in progress," Guarascio says. "What makes you a platform starts with what you do on the field, and there are some athletes who can actually rise above that, and he may be one of them. If the Patriots have a bad year, or they fall into the middle of the league somewhere, Brady might be one of those guys who can rise above that.

"If I were marketing Tom Brady, and I was looking toward the future, I might do some things differently to build up his personality value outside the game, as opposed to relying on the exposure he gets from being part of a winning team."

If the podium was a problem for Brady because it set him apart from his teammates, it's hard to imagine that being considered a "platform" is altogether comfortable. Brady has been as cautious with his commercial endorsements as he has tried to be in the locker room, and in his public pronouncements. While he has been able to pick up endorsements from Gap, Nike, and Sirius satellite radio, as well as the Visa campaign, the success of the Patriots didn't translate into increased endorsement opportunities for his teammates. Ironically, according to many people in marketing, the very thing that New England had come to symbolize—meritocratic egalitarianism among teammates—made the other individual players less marketable than the quarterback.

"He's done a good job so far managing his brand," Guarascio explains. "Clearly, he needed the platform more than some of the more extroverted guys did. I don't think of him necessarily as a shy guy, just a little more introspective than a lot of them are.

"I would say, to look at him, All-American with an edge, an edge toward hipness and coolness, and understated elegance, low-key, but there's that edge there, when he gets into the red zone, there's that steeliness, that 'Fuck you, we're going to get this in the end zone' thing. Sort of a Cool Hand Luke thing. A guy people like, but who you don't fool with. If I were managing him, I'd exploit that." That there is an actual human being under discussion here seems oddly beside the point.

Every public person makes peace with the artificiality of his or her public existence. There are athletes who give themselves over so thoroughly to their public brands that they become indistinguishable from them. They become Commodity People, shiny and perfect, round and edgeless and slightly inhuman. Michael Jordan was like that, and Tiger Woods seems well on his way. In almost every case, the process of converting the private person into a vehicle for public consumption of everything from soda pop to cardinal virtues is the creation of something artificial that can never evolve but only shatter entirely. This is how we end up with athletes who are purely platforms, loyal to their brands and not to their teammates. You can freeze yourself there, as though the primitive tribesmen were right all along about what happens to your soul if you allow someone to take your picture.

The Visa commercial campaign that debuted during the opening night telecast of the game against Oakland was a measure not only of how cautious Brady is about the commercial aspects of his personality but also of how stubborn he is about bringing his own definition of himself as an athlete into every enterprise in which he becomes involved. He will not be summarized. He will not be frozen in place. It's his first big commercial, and he's not lounging on the beach in Cancún, tossing back a beer surrounded by what appears to be the Cinemax late-night starter kit. Instead, he's the straight man, sitting in what looks like a candlelit restaurant, an actress who is not the actress he's dating sitting next to him, and surrounded on all sides by his actual offensive linemen, all in full uniform, including helmets.

They get laughs just by sitting there. They tell all the jokes. In the second commercial of the set, which ran later in the season, the linemen—the metaphors—overrule the director and hijack the entire production, and Brady says hardly anything. It was more than an effective spot. It was a demonstration of the star as teammate, as clear a one as any that ever happened on the field, and that the demonstration further cemented Brady's "brand" in that regard seems more natural than any marketing contrivance could be.

"They probably hadn't seen each other in a couple of months," recalls Jimmy Siegel, a mystery novelist and producer who created the spots for Visa. "And you felt that they liked each other and that he was happy to have them around. I think it made him more comfortable as opposed to having it be just him and this girl on the set. Here he is, surrounded by his buddies, his offensive linemen, and I think he was happy to share the spotlight with them, too."

They shot the commercial over two days on a soundstage south of Boston. Brady committed to one day of shooting, so they filmed everything they needed from him for both commercials on the first day. His teammates heckled him mercilessly from off camera. When someone blew a line, Brady would whisper, "Red zone," to get things back on track, and all of them quickly grew acclimated to the hurry-up-and-wait process involved in shooting any film, even a television commercial. And the linemen turned out to be a comedy troupe.

"They all had sort of a different character that came out," Siegel explains. "[Tackle Tom] Ashworth was sort of that sad-sack face, and Koppen was so good because he's always rolling his eyes, kind of a wise-guy kid thing. Matt Light was sort of the straight man of the bunch, and Brandon Gorin had this kind of solidity to him."

Siegel noticed that Brady was far less loose than his teammates were. "He was probably a little stiffer than all five of the linemen were, which was part of the surprise," Siegel says. "He was sort of the focus of things, and he was only there for the one day. It's hard to be natural on camera for a lot of people. It wasn't hard for the linemen, which was amazing, but it was a little hard for him." They, after all, were all wearing uniforms. Brady was the guy in the suit.

This tailgate is a Time—which is what Massachusetts politicians throw whenever they must once again run for office. Since Massachusetts politicians never stop running for office, this means that any social gathering at the center of which you find a politician is a Time. A Time is usually a fund-raising dinner, but it can be a fund-raising lunch, a fund-raising trip to the ballpark or, yes, a fund-raising wake where, very likely, Jimbo, Jr., will be shaking hands over the departed Jimbo, Sr., preparatory to a run for the Governor's Council.

For almost three decades now, Congressman Marty Meehan has thrown tailgates at Patriots games. His district a hodgepodge northwest of Boston, a living legacy to gerrymanders long forgotten, Meehan has tailgated at both Patriots stadiums, and he has tailgated for very good Patriots teams and very bad ones. On this afternoon, there were steak tips and shrimp and cold beer, and plenty of time to eat and drink, and there was an odd lot of politicians, journalists, and everything in between, swapping lies under a tent on a rise above the stadium.

At the beginning of January 2004, just after the Patriots had defeated Indianapolis for the AFC championship, Meehan relayed a request from the White House to Jonathan Kraft, whom Meehan had invited to attend President Bush's State of the Union address later that week. (This was largely a matter of courtesy for all concerned, since Meehan is a Democrat, and the Krafts are well-known benefactors to a variety of liberal causes.) The president, Meehan told Kraft, would like Tom Brady to be his guest as well. Moreover, Brady was invited to sit in the box in the House gallery reserved for special guests of the president.

Kraft and Brady flew down together, and Kraft mentioned that he was happy to have had a chance to win two Super Bowls. Brady scoffed. He had no intention of going to the Super Bowl and losing. "It wasn't like, 'Yo, man,'" Kraft said. "It was more like the way he said it, the thought of losing never crossed his mind." They didn't talk about football for the rest of the day.

When they got to Washington, Kraft and Brady met Meehan at a White House reception before the speech. Meehan was struck by how at ease Brady was in the unfamiliar setting, how he seemed to lock in on whatever person was talking to him. He's got it, Meehan thought.

Not long thereafter, Brady was whisked away to join the president's special contingent. It turned out that, for all the honor of the invitation, Brady had been invited to attend the address as a visual aid. There was a passage in the speech in which the president called for strong action to be taken to combat the use of illegal performance-enhancing drugs in professional sports. Just as the applause for the line rose, the national television cameras cut away to Brady in the gallery. It was clear that he was there not simply for who he was. He was a prop, a character in a commercial not his own.

Now Tom Brady is one of the least oblivious people on the planet, and the State of the Union address is approximately as spontaneous a production as the Rose Parade, so it beggars belief that Brady didn't know why he was there, or to what use he was going to be put. However, Jonathan Kraft thought Brady was uncomfortable about it the whole flight back. But he also had soaked up the experience. His curiosity was piqued by another new world that football had opened up to him. "On the way home, talking about the speech, we didn't talk about the game at all," Kraft said. "We talked about the Middle East, and about the tax cuts that [Bush] had made after 9/11. He didn't profess to be smart about it. He was more posing questions [rather] than giving opinions."

He had to know he was being made an icon in that moment, for a specific political purpose, and in the context of a specific issue—performance-enhancing drugs—in which suspicion was regularly treated as fact, every rumor took on significance, and about which every hint could become a headline. It was at that speech, in that moment, in the context of a volatile issue touching close on Brady's own profession, that the discussion opened up about Tom Brady and his possibilities as a political figure. Increasingly, politics is covered as a glorified sporting event anyway, complete with television hecklers, most of whom have law degrees. The only real difference between the panel discussions that end every night of the national political conventions and, say, FOX Sports's weekly NFL wrap-up package is that Terry Bradshaw is a much funnier hick than Zell Miller.

And the country's politics always have been celebrity-sodden. The Republic already has coped with the realities of Governor Arnold Schwarzenegger, Governor Jesse Ventura, and Congressman Sonny Bono. Jim Bunning, the old Phillies pitcher, is a senator, and Jim Ryun, who once ran the mile faster than any other American, is in Congress, all of them following the lead of Bill Bradley, the former Knick and former senator who ran for president in 2000.

For its part, the NFL had launched the careers of Jack Kemp and of Steve Largent, a Hall of Fame receiver who served as a congressman from Oklahoma. In 2006, former Washington quarterback Heath Shuler ran for Congress in North Carolina as a Democrat, and Lynn Swann, the former Steeler receiver and the most famous football player out of Serra High School not named Tom Brady, geared up to run for governor of Pennsylvania as a Republican on the platform that he was, well, Lynn Swann.

He was a consultant's Christmas goose—stuffed full of focus-group platitudes and automatronic catchphrases. His knowledge of most of the issues was wafer-thin, and Swann appeared to have begun thinking about the race approximately eleven minutes before announcing his candidacy. One NFL-savvy political pundit proposed that Swann get his fellow Pittsburgh Hall of Fame receiver John Stallworth to run as a Democrat, so as to take the pressure off Swann from the left side the way Stallworth used to do on the field in the 1970s. Tom Brady never has approached a major decision in his life as obviously unprepared as Swann was to run for governor. But, Swann was famous, and that was enough.

And Brady himself told *ESPN* magazine that his "craziest ambition" was to be a United States senator, which touched off widespread speculation as to his party affiliation, and whether he would run in Massachusetts or in California. Brady dodged all the questions with a smile, but the buzz was serious enough to set the tireless folks at Thesmokinggun.com to digging. They discovered, embarrassingly enough, that, while Brady had registered as an independent in both California and Michigan, he'd apparently never actually voted.

"People say he's a Republican, but I'm not so sure," Marty Meehan said as snow began to fall. "I do know that you can watch him in a room, and you can see him learning from the people he's talking to, and focusing on them." Meehan compared Brady's gifts in this regard with those of Bill Clinton, which is like comparing a kid pianist with Mozart.

Snow is iconic to the franchise now. It brings back not only the win over Oakland in the last game in the old stadium but also a win over Miami two years later, in December 2005, in which the fans tossed handfuls of snow in the air in perfect time to the syncopation of Gary Glitter's "Rock and Roll, Part Two." (On the official NFL Films video of the game, the tossing of the snow looks like the explosion of thousands of personal fireworks displays.) Now, as the game began against the Jets, the first snow of the season fell gently through the lights as though, all around the stadium, a curtain was parting.

The Patriots put the Jets away in a workmanlike fashion, 16–3. With the New England defense relatively healthy for the first time in weeks, the Patriots kept the New York offense off the field long enough for Adam Vinatieri to kick three field goals. New England had twenty-four first downs to twelve for the Jets, and they had the ball almost seventeen minutes longer. For his part, Brady kept the chains moving in the snow. He completed twenty-seven of his thirty-seven throws for 271 yards, but he didn't throw for any touchdowns. In fact, Brady ran the ball himself four times, including a three-yard gain on the last play of the game. Even in the best of times, and in the best of weather, his running style is ungainly, but he looked stiff and unsure of himself. He seemed to be dragging one leg behind him.

His best pass was probably the twenty-five-yarder he'd thrown to Ben Watson, the baby-faced tight end from Georgia who, it seemed, was improving by the hour. Watson could always run and he could always catch, but his blocking was demonstrably better, particularly on passing downs. And he was doing everything with tremendous confidence. He was running his routes strongly, and asserting himself more forcefully as a blocker. His play was allowing Watson to blossom fully as a teammate. Not long after the game with the Jets, while Brady was surrounded at his locker, talking about having been named Sportsman of the Year, Watson snuck into the media scrum and, using a plastic bottle for a microphone, asked Brady what he thought of the improvements the Patriots obviously had made at the tight end position.

"I probably wouldn't have done that last year." Watson laughed. "He's a great player, but he's a cool guy. I mean, he's Tom Brady, and he's the quarterback, so he's an important part of the team and a well-known guy. But, as a teammate, he's just cool."

In 2004, when he was hurt and he was young, it would have been unthinkable for Watson to interrupt the quarterback this way. But he'd done the work in practice, and now it was beginning to show itself on the field, and Ben Watson was free to act like Tom Brady's teammate, in the fullest sense of the word. The quarterback could be his straight man, if just for a moment, as though they were the only act on the stage.

PART 3 A TOUGH TIME TO GO SLEDDING

7 | TREATMENT DAYS
DECEMBER 11, 2005: NEW ENGLAND 35, BUFFALO 7
DECEMBER 17, 2005: NEW ENGLAND 28, TAMPA BAY 0
RECORD: 9-5

HE WAS HURT, and then he got hurt again.

Sometime in the middle of the season, probably right around the game against Indianapolis, Brady had been diagnosed with a hernia high on the right side—a tearing of the stomach wall that, because professional athletes seemed to represent what epidemiologists call a "cluster" in regards to this particular injury, had become known recently as a "sports hernia." (Donovan McNabb, his rival quarterback from the previous Super Bowl, also had suffered from one.) It had drastically limited Brady's mobility, and it had played havoc with the delicately calibrated throwing motion on which he had labored so hard since the first days at Tom Martinez's camp back home. The injury would require surgery, but that would wait until the season was over. Consistent with team policy, the hernia was kept secret from anyone outside the official Patriots family. It had happened subtly; Brady hadn't missed a down because of it. It was an internal injury in every sense of the word. The policy, of course, denied Brady a very legitimate excuse for why his passes fluttered and sailed, occasionally to people wearing the wrong uniforms. But it's unlikely that he would have availed himself of it publicly in any case.

The next injury, however, happened in plain view. New England went to Buffalo after beating the Jets at home. At the end of the first quarter, the Patriots took over on their own 20-yard line. On the first down, Brady whipped the ball to Ben Watson for eleven yards and the Buffalo secondary seemed to sag. Over the next eight plays, Brady hit Watson three more times, the last of them for fourteen yards that got New England all the way to the Buffalo 3-yard line. On the next play, Brady called his own number. He took a short step backward after taking the snap, then threw himself toward the end zone. As he did, a Buffalo defender rolled in and cracked his left shin.

Brady scored the touchdown, but he got up very slowly and walked to the New England bench like a man dragging a great weight behind him. The NBC broadcast crew immediately went on point. The cameras stayed on Brady as the Patriots medical staff worked on him. He got up and strolled around, testing his leg. He didn't miss a down.

Meanwhile, as the afternoon snow began to roll in off Lake Erie, the Patriots were wrecking the Bills, whom they'd edged by only 21–16 at home back at the end of October. It was the first time in weeks that the team had anything resembling its full roster together, and the New England defense was in particularly full roar, harassing the Buffalo quarterback, J. P. Losman—in favor of whom, it should be noted, the Bills had shipped Drew Bledsoe off to Dallas, where he'd been reunited with Bill Parcells. The Patriots held the Bills to a ludicrous eighty-six total yards in the first half.

For his part, Brady came back in the game and, in the face of his injuries, played with an almost giddy recklessness. He appeared to be trying to cure his injuries by defying them. On two occasions, he scrambled for good yardage. And, with fourteen minutes left in the first half, as New England sent Deion Branch on a reverse around the right end, Brady got himself out in front of the play and threw himself into a full body dive—leading with his throwing arm—that took Buffalo safety Troy Vincent down and out of the play. The play gained ten yards, but it was called back because Brady was penalized for having thrown an illegal block. Brady was briefly outraged.

He had a solid day, twenty-nine of thirty-eight for 329 yards and a pair of touchdowns. He also threw two interceptions, both of them in or near the Buffalo end zone. In the fourth quarter, with the Patriots so clearly on their way to what would end up as a 35–7 victory, the mood on the sideline was as light as it had been in weeks. Belichick lifted Brady for backup Doug Flutie. However, the most compelling statistic of the game, because it measured both Brady's willingness to sacrifice himself and the dominance of the New England defense, was the fact that Tom Brady alone outgained the Buffalo Bills on the ground, seventeen yards to fourteen.

The Patriots were now 8–5, and the road to the playoffs was a clear one. All they had to do was dispatch the lame, the halt, and the crippled from the AFC East. If they could beat the more formidable Tampa Bay Buccaneers on the following Sunday in their only remaining game outside the division, so much the better. But wins over the Jets and the Dolphins would put them where they wanted to be. All they had to do was get healthy and stay that way. The playoffs are an entirely different season, with dynamics all their own. Few teams knew this better than the Patriots did.

Over the ensuing week, the injury Brady had sustained against Buffalo dominated the news at the New England training facility. Brady was limited in what he could do in practice, and severely limited in what he could say about it. "You guys know that Belichick doesn't like me talking about this stuff," he said. "He gave me strict instructions to keep quiet, so that's what I'm doing."

But Brady had been hurt, and now he was hurt again. That week his father came to visit from California. Late one night the elder Brady came downstairs and saw his son sitting in the bluish half-light of the living room, an air cast on his injured leg. He was having God's own trouble getting out of the chair. It hurts, Dad, Tom Brady told his father. It hurts pretty bad.

Tuesdays are treatment days. The players come in and submit themselves to the ministrations—manual, mechanical, and, more than occasionally, pharmaceutical—of the team's medical staff so that they can prepare to go out and play another game of a collision sport with injuries that the average journalist wouldn't sustain outside a car wreck, and that would put the average stockbroker in bed for a month.

"I done played with dislocated kneecaps every day, so I been there, broken fingers and all that," explains Corey Dillon, the New England running back who seemed to be breaking down physically in this, his ninth season in the NFL, seven of which had him taking gratuitous punishment for some truly terrible teams in Cincinnati. "Hey, man, that's the norm. It's a brutal game that we play. It's not for the meek. Nine times out of ten, you're going to be playing when you're hurt. I'm going to play in a neck brace, if I have to.

"You can't take these injuries lightly. I mean, they're serious, but you got to tolerate it if you want to play. That's up to the training staff, when you're ready. Then, you go for it. Only I can deal with the pain I'm in."

It is a deal they all make with themselves, that the game inevitably will break them down physically because the human body was not designed to play football at the level at which it's played in the NFL. Close up, the average collision is startlingly loud, an almost inhuman noise, as though something huge, made of plastic and metal, has been dropped from a great height and has shattered right in front of you. When Brady says the hit that incapacitated Drew Bledsoe was the loudest he'd ever heard on a football field, he is saying a great deal.

And the effect of all these collisions on all these players only recently has been subjected to serious, longitudinal studies. In the past, the NFL's safety measures, such as they were, most often were a case of the right things being done for the wrong reasons. In 1947, Michael MacCambridge writes, the league adopted its weekly injury reports—the ones with which the Patriots now so bedevil the rest of the league—as a move toward transparency for the benefit of the people who bet on the games. The face mask first appeared as a halftime improvisation to protect Cleveland quarterback Otto Graham, who'd been smacked in the chops during the first half of a game in 1953. The league was egregiously slow to respond to complaints by its players concerning the dangers of artificial turf throughout the 1970s and '80s. The National Football League Players Association never had the clout in those days of its counterpart among major-league baseball players. Football players played football, period.

The situation has gotten better. For example, a number of player agents, led by the überagent Leigh Steinberg, seized upon several well-known cases to force the league to take seriously the consequences to its players of repeated concussions. Still, though, in 2004, just before New England beat Carolina in the Super Bowl in Houston, the *Houston Chronicle* published a story about the astonishing human toll that professional football takes, and not merely upon the players, whose blood and bone and sinew are the media from which the NFL draws its art. According to the newspaper, a study revealed that 65 percent of NFL players retire with some sort of permanent injury; that the suicide rate for active and retired players is six times greater than the national average; and that 78 percent of NFL players are unemployed, bankrupt, or divorced within two years of leaving the game. The art of the NFL depends in no little measure on what can be called voluntary self-destruction.

Consequently, every player makes a deal with himself, tacitly or otherwise, early in his career. Ultimately, it's the deal with himself that Elwood Reid couldn't strike, and it's the deal that his fictionalized self, Elwood Riley, turns down in *If I Don't Six*. It's a bargain that encompasses their families, too; Galynn Brady stopped having fun at football games when her son was carried off the field at Michigan. But it is primarily a gamble a player takes with himself, using his future for chips.

Two decades ago, Steve Grogan broke his leg playing quarterback for the Patriots as the team was driving toward the franchise's first Super Bowl. He was so anxious to be part of it that he had the doctors take the cast off two weeks early. He haunted the training room, doing whatever he could to get ready to play, forcing his body so he could pretend it had healed. One day, he found himself sitting next to Tony Eason, the young quarterback who'd replaced him, and who already had developed a reputation among his teammates for being overly concerned about his body.

"He goes to me, 'Why are you doing this?'" Grogan recalls. "And I told him it was because I wanted to play football, and he goes, 'Well, aren't you worried about how your body's going to feel when you're forty?' And I said I already knew my body was going to feel bad when I was forty, and I said, 'That just goes with the game.'

"And his response to me was, 'Man, when I'm forty, I just want to be able to jog and play tennis and have fun and not be worried about being physically handicapped.' I looked at him and I said, 'Man, you're in the wrong business.'"

Grogan's well past forty now. Balding and lean, he looks like someone in terrific shape. But there are periods of lost time in his career, when he got hit in the head and misplaced the next several minutes. "We had a lot of head injuries when I played," he recalls, "and nobody worried about it too much. Once you could count the fingers, you were back in the game, you know?

"I think I picked up the paper the other day and I was reading where a player retired, and I'm reading that he's cranky, that he's got short-term memory loss, and he has trouble sleeping. I handed the paper over to my wife, and I told her that's what'd been happening to me the last fifteen years, so don't blame me anymore. It's the concussions."

Grogan's life is bounded by the limits of the old vaudeville joke:

PATIENT: Doc, it hurts when I do this.
DOCTOR: Then don't do it.

If he does certain things, his neck is going to be killing him the next day, so he tries not to do any of them. If he keeps his left knee in certain positions very long, it's not going to work for him when he tries to stand. "You adapt," he says.

Steve Grogan was reckoned to be one of the toughest players who ever played in New England. In Super Bowl XX, against the Bears, his teammates nearly mutinied against Eason, preferring to play with and behind Grogan. His injuries—and his willingness to play through them—were his ultimate bona fides.

"If you sign up to play professional football, you know what can happen, and you don't think about it, because you're twenty-five or thirty years old and you're out there in front of sixty, seventy thousand people," Grogan muses. "You don't really think about it. You go out there and throw your body around and you don't worry about what happens later. And, even talking to some of the guys I played with, and we're all having physical problems of some kind, we'd all go back and do it again tomorrow or, maybe, the day after."

There is no stranger presence in an NFL locker room than that of the Piss Patrol—two elderly men who look like the winners in an Elks Club whist tournament. Their job is to visit a team and supervise the mandatory drug testing required of all NFL players. Basically, the Piss Patrol sit outside the shower room and bathroom facilities to make sure that players don't try to finesse the league's comprehensive urinalysis program. They bring to their grim task all the essential and obvious good humor of those terra-cotta soldiers buried with Emperor Qin in China.

It would take Arthur Miller to imagine the conversations these stoic guardians have with their families upon leaving for a business trip. ("Goin' up there to Foxborough. Nice town, Foxborough. Gonna check out the defending champions.") They are, perhaps, neither liked nor well-liked. In any event, they are there to make sure that football remains drug-free. Or, at least, free from all those drugs of which the NFL disapproves, because, after all, in the strict etymological sense anyway, there's no such thing as drug-free football. Remove all the various pain potions that are part of a player's daily life, and the average NFL season would be approximately two weeks long.

The essential argument that the NFL—and, indeed, all professional sports—makes is that it is proper to take certain drugs to make your performance possible, but improper to take certain drugs to make your performance better, or to make you feel better in the aftermath of a game. This, it is argued, is for the sake of the player's health. That there is a fundamental moral incoherence here through which you could run a fullback is rarely addressed. If anything, it has been ignored even more thoroughly as the national feeding frenzy over performance-enhancing drugs increasingly seems to look less like a public-health issue and more and more like a moral crusade. The drugs the NFL allows are those that enable players to compete despite injuries that in the real world likely would keep them in street clothes. It's all figured into the bargain each player makes with himself and with the game.

All season, the Patriot locker room had been full of medical comings and goings. The most momentous one had come in October, when linebacker Tedy Bruschi returned to the team. Shortly after the Patriots had beaten Philadelphia in Super Bowl XXXIX, Bruschi had collapsed from a stroke. His career seemed to be over at thirty-two. He had won three Super Bowl rings. Given his enthusiasm and the intelligence he brought to the position, any team at any level would have hired him as a coach on the spot. He had all the money he'd ever need. He came back to the game anyway. For three weeks after his return, there had been a crowd three deep around his locker. And everyone in the unruly scrum tore up the language trying to find a way to gently frame the question "But what if you die out there?"

Things had settled down around Bruschi after about a month. He was still a sought-after spokesman for the defense, but that had been the case even before the stroke. He'd even suffered a run-of-the-mill NFL injury to his leg. He was now just another player with physical problems through which he'd have to play.

It was another way for him to realize he belonged. His life was normal again.

They were all walking a bit more slowly. Dan Koppen was back, a new surgical scar running down the back of the shoulder he'd injured in Miami, ending his season. His natural ebullience seemed to be drained from him. The light in his blue eyes was gone, and he seemed to be walking through the locker room in an alternate dimension, a place where the sounds of his teammates could not reach him. A stocking cap pulled low over his eyes, he looked very young and immeasurably sad.

David Givens was just happy to be back on the field. While he'd been sidelined, he'd watched the tape of the Indianapolis game over and over again. It was a fourth-and-one and he'd just run a slant route, and Mike Doss of the Colts had slammed into his leg. Every time he watched the tape, the shot he'd taken looked cheaper than it had the time before. He got angrier and angrier, until he couldn't watch the tape anymore. "It was a dirty play," Givens said. "You could see that on the tape, but what can you do?"

He'd returned against the Jets, running so gingerly that his family back in Texas even noticed it on television. Now, though, as New England prepared to play the Tampa Bay Buccaneers, 9–4 playoff contenders from the National Football Conference, Givens was feeling free for the first time in over a month. He was ready for this season, which had come to mean so much to him professionally, to start again.

"I'm a terrible patient," he said with a laugh. "No, really, you do not want to be around me when I'm not playing. But I was so excited when I felt like I could come back. It's a kind of happiness I can't explain to you."

Of course, the injury that prompted the most discussion—and, therefore, the least information from either the team or the player in question—was the one Brady had sustained to his left leg during the game a week earlier in Buffalo. (The preexisting hernia remained a closely kept secret.) His practice time during the week had been limited, and he'd chafed at that. However, on Sunday, the Patriots came out and played their best game of the season.

They thrashed Tampa Bay, 28–0, truly igniting their home crowd for the first time since Indianapolis had thrashed them here on that Monday night in November. Eight days before Christmas, it was bright and warm, with the temperature pushing forty degrees at kickoff, a perfect day to play. Almost from the start, the New England defense confused and harassed Chris Simms, the young Tampa quarterback whose father, Phil, had called signals for the New York Giants when Bill Belichick had been there as an assistant to Bill Parcells. The first two Tampa drives ended with Simms being sacked by New England linebackers.

With a number of previously injured players returning, the Patriots—and Belichick—seemed liberated. On their first drive, they got hopelessly giddy in their play calling. On a third-and-one, Brady tossed the ball to offensive tackle Tom Ashworth, who'd reported into the game—along with the inevitable Mike Vrabel, perhaps functioning as Ashworth's decoy—as an eligible receiver. Television viewers could see that, behind the cage of his face mask, Ashworth's eyes got as big as saucers, but he hung on to the pass and stepped delicately into the end zone for the first touchdown of his career.

Once that worked, it seemed like everything did. The defensive front seven slammed Tampa's star rookie running back, Carnell Williams, into virtual invisibility. Williams gained only 23 yards, and the Buccaneers gained only 138 total yards on the day. They hardly threatened at all after the moment shortly before halftime in which Vrabel blasted Simms loose from the football. The fumble led to a touchdown pass from Brady to

Givens and a 21–0 New England lead that might as well have been three times that.

On offense, healthy at last, Givens had a terrific afternoon, catching six passes for 137 yards and a touchdown. But the most signifying pass was one that Brady had thrown him in the first quarter, one that had echoes of a special practice session all the way back at the end of training camp. Brady's mechanics had gone screwy on him, so he'd flown Tom Martinez east to try to see if they could puzzle out what had been going wrong.

"It's like the car's running smoothly," Martinez says. "When it goes bad, they don't always know what's wrong. It's always been up to him to contact me. I don't interfere. When he feels it's time for a tune-up, he's got a dime and he knows the number, so I've always left it up to him."

Martinez was thrilled. It was his first time at an NFL training camp. Brady introduced him to Deion Branch, and the three of them worked after practice, looking for the tiniest flaws in Brady's technique. Gradually, the quarterback's form returned and he began hammering the ball in to Branch with increasing confidence. One of the last passes they worked on was an in-and-out corner route, on which Branch would slash toward the middle of the field, pivot, and then sprint for the corner of the end zone. The play required a powerful, well-timed throw, and the fact that Brady was willing to try it convinced Martinez that his work on that occasion was finished.

With 14:10 left in the first quarter against the Buccaneers, Brady stepped into the shotgun on third down and sent Givens on exactly the same route on which he'd ended his practice with Martinez back in August. Givens ran the route perfectly, splitting cornerback Juran Bolden and safety Dexter Jackson, and Brady threw a bullet, the tip of the ball spiraling so fast that there seemed to be a hole right there in the daylight. The thirty-two-yard completion led to Ashworth's touchdown, but it also did a great deal to convince the Tampa Bay defense that it was in for a long afternoon. Afterward, Buccaneer cornerback Ronde Barber specifically cited the pass as the game's early turning point.

Brady was twenty for thirty-one for 258 yards and three touchdowns, which was probably the best he could have expected, given the fact that his injuries had kept him from putting in a full week at practice. "I mean, you practice," he explained. "You just try to prepare mentally, but it's hard because you love to be able to take the snaps. I like taking the reps and, when [I'm] not able to do that, it becomes a little more challenging."

There was almost a note of regret to his voice, that he'd missed a week of practice that he'd never get back again, that there was an opportunity that had been denied to him by his physical shortcomings, and that he'd gotten a very brief and very limited look at what life without the game would be like. Practice was a joy and a refuge, and he hadn't been able to lose himself in it the way he liked.

"I certainly have had better weeks," Brady said. "It was a long week, and I wasn't able to prepare on the practice field as many days as I would have wanted to. And I always want to play, and the only way I'm not going to play is if the doctor tells me I can't play. So, believe me, me playing is exactly what I would expect of everyone else on this team, if you can find a way to play. For me, injuring my leg, it's different than if I'd injured my arm or something like that. I mean, I don't move very well, nor do I move very well when I'm completely healthy, so I guess I'm used to that."

What Brady said reads more banal than it sounded at the time. After all, as simple repetition, all prayers are mere clichés. It's the faith you put in them that makes them sacred. It's the authenticity of that faith that makes them prayers.

8 | BUNKER MAN

DECEMBER 26, 2005: NEW ENGLAND 31, NEW YORK JETS 21
JANUARY 1, 2006: MIAMI 28, NEW ENGLAND 26
RECORD: 10-6

HE WAS going to be alone for Christmas. His girlfriend, Bridget, was off making a movie in Canada; they'd been a bicoastal couple all season, if you counted the beaches along Lake Ontario as a coast. And Nancy was going home to San Mateo for the holidays. Her decision was rather sudden, and it caught him up short. "I felt bad," Nancy said. "This was the first holiday that I was not here, since I moved here. He was happy that I was going to go home, but I felt bad because we really hadn't talked about plans, so I just wound up taking off." He spent Christmas Eve and Christmas Day at the homes of various teammates. On the day after Christmas, Brady and the Patriots went down to New Jersey to play the New York Jets.

On September 20, 1970, almost seven years before Tom Brady was born, the Jets and Joe Namath went to Cleveland to play the Browns on a warm Monday night. It was the first NFL game ever played in prime time, and it was the opening night of one of the great carnival acts in the history of both television and professional sports. If it did nothing more than bring to the country the inimitable presence of Howard Cosell, ABC's *Monday Night Football* would have to be reckoned as one of the most significant breakthroughs in the history of the entertainment side of the medium. At the apogee of its popularity and its influence, which unquestionably was during the days in which Cosell, Frank Gifford, and Don Meredith were its broadcast team, *MNF* was the first regularly scheduled sporting event that was perfectly self-contained.

In terms of its public profile, the crew was as far beyond the average network sportscasting drones as the Rolling Stones are beyond a third-rate cover band in a Holiday Inn lounge. It arrived in a city the way a rock tour would, with Cosell, the Giffer, and Dandy Don standing in for Mick, Keith, and Charlie Watts. And, if the whole thing eventually turned into a vodka-sodden vipers' nest, it already had broken so much new ground that the NFL—and the televised sports that the league had come to drive before it—would never be the same.

The games even looked different on Monday night. They were sharper and more vivid—taking on, as Michael MacCambridge puts it, "an exquisite, saturated sheen." The *MNF* package affected everything about professional football. Every Monday night, it was the only NFL game being played, so it gave the players on the participating teams a national stage all to themselves, as opposed to the ordinary Sunday schedule, which was split up fifteen ways.

"When you play on Monday night," New England receiver Troy Brown said, "you know everybody's watching. You make a mistake, and you hear about it from all your friends."

Cosell's halftime highlights—almost always done completely off the cuff and almost always brilliantly crafted—set a new standard. (MacCambridge even quotes John Madden to the effect that, while coaching the Oakland Raiders, Madden used to use Cosell's weekly highlights to augment his scouting.) *MNF* even helped the gamblers, giving the ones who tapped out on Sunday a whole series of get-even propositions on the next night. In almost every sense, *Monday Night Football* was one of the last manifestations of the genius that had allowed the late Pete Rozelle to turn the NFL into the great, gravitational sun around which all professional sports came to revolve.

Now, after 554 shows, this game between New England and New York was going to be the last Monday night game broadcast by ABC. Starting in 2006, the package would be seen on ESPN, the giant, writhing octopus of sports media and ABC's corporate sibling in the Disney entertainment empire. The shows likely still would look good but, as highlights from the golden years played on the huge screens at either end of Giants Stadium, it was hard not to believe that the cutting edges of *Monday Night Football* long ago had been filed away, and its rough places made smooth, and that this process would only continue in its new home. All you had to know about *Monday Night Football* on ESPN was the fact that, for more than a decade, Chris Berman, one of the cable monolith's signature personalities, had been doing an NFL highlights package by burlesquing Howard Cosell. Now, it seemed, *Monday Night Football* would come to play in that Holiday Inn lounge after all.

Campfires burned all over the parking lots at the Meadowlands, and the tailgating went on long after kickoff. Given the historical import of the evening, and given *MNF*'s long history as a magnet for lunacy—something with which the New England franchise had become sadly familiar down through the years—officials of the vast sports complex had determined that no alcohol would be served during the game, so many of the patrons stayed outside, serving themselves well into the game. On the New England sideline, Belichick explained to Brady that the Patriots would begin the game by running the ball almost exclusively. Brady understood, but he was as unhappy about it as any quarterback would be.

The Patriots called seven straight running plays on their opening drive, which ate up more than eight minutes on the clock and ended with Brady tossing a one-yard touchdown pass to Mike Vrabel. This was no longer a case of Vrabel's drifting surreptitiously and unwatched into the secondary. He made a serious inside move, lost one of the Jet linebackers, and snagged a good, hard throw from Brady for the first of his two touchdown catches of the night. By game's end, Vrabel's career record as a receiver read eight catches, all of them for touchdowns. He was apparently unstoppable.

The Patriots piled up a solid 21–7 lead in the first half, their defense playing well for the fourth consecutive week, holding the Jets to a paltry twenty-eight total yards over the first thirty minutes of the game. The Jets wouldn't record a first down until the third quarter was nearly over, and then only because New England's Richard Seymour picked up a strict-constructionist roughing penalty against the New York quarterback, Brooks Bollinger.

Significantly, though, Brady was visibly laboring, his legs undermining his ability to throw the ball with touch and confidence. In the first quarter, he threw a balloon of a deep out toward David Givens, and Ty Law, Brady's former New England teammate who'd signed with the Jets shortly before the season began, jumped the route and took the ball back seventy-four yards for a touchdown, a longer version of the pivotal play Law had made in the first half of the Super Bowl in New Orleans against the Rams. Law was gone the moment Brady threw the pass, but the quarterback gave chase anyway. At about the New York 10-yard line, dragging his left leg like dead weight, Brady pulled up, and Law scored.

It became a game about moving the chains, no more and no less. Cosell would have been merciless. Meredith would have been singing by halftime. New England never let the New York offense out of the bog, surrendering a late touchdown that merely tailored the final score to a semirespectable 31–21. For his part, Brady found Deion Branch on a five-yard square-out in the third quarter to push himself over four thousand passing yards in a season for the first time in his NFL career. (Drew Bledsoe was the only other New England quarterback to throw for that many in a single season.) Afterward, Brady stood with Bridget, who'd come in for the game, and he talked for a long time with Bill Harris, the former Michigan assistant who'd recruited him but who had left before Brady enrolled. In the concrete chill of the bowels of the stadium, Brady caught Harris in a hug and kissed him on the cheek. Heads swiveled. Brady and his movie-star girlfriend walked away down the hall.

His 185 yards on the night was his low for the season, and, for the third straight week, Belichick lifted him for safety's sake after the game obviously had been decided. The last real *Monday Night Football* game, the league's primary star-making vehicle for more than three and a half decades, had as its most significant personality a man in a gray sweatshirt who was willing to have his quarterback throw passes to his linebackers, as long as both of them had proven to his satisfaction that they were worthy of his trust, and who would take this rough, choppy game as a win and go along with it to the following week. The last star of *Monday Night Football* was a coach.

"You try to get the team as prepared as possible," he'd say not long afterward. "What should we be doing? I don't think this is the time to go sledding."

Every so often, as the season goes along, Bill Belichick eschews his morning press conference, at which he usually looks like a man undergoing a root canal with a butter knife, and brings the assembled press into one of the classrooms inside Gillette Stadium in which his team usually gathers to study film. He cues up the film himself, and, wielding a remote control the way coaches once wielded only a whistle, he spends an hour or so bringing to life a lot of the jargon that he throws around on a daily basis.

Today's lesson is Joe Montana. On the screen, Montana and the 49ers are working against a New York Giants team from the 1980s, a team for which Belichick designed the defense while working on the staff of Bill Parcells. Belichick is pacing back and forth, starting and stopping the action on the screen, as animated as a kid with the latest PlayStation.

"Look at this. These are the kind of plays that used to drive us crazy," he says, flipping the film off for a second. "You blitz. You come free, and he still gets the ball off. Defensively, later, you're sitting with your players, and you look at the film, and you say, 'Well, you're doing what I told you to do, and they hit it in there anyway.' It's tough.

"We've got perfect position here [on the San Francisco receiver]. But the ball's in a perfect spot, and the guy catches it and falls forward, and he gains six yards and the ball's on the nine-yard line. You can't give up six yards down there, so you're doing everything you can, and the son of a bitch just throws a perfect pass.

"Or, look here," he says, cuing up another play from the same game. "It looks to me like they had the pattern called to the other side, and we'd taken that away. So he went back to the other side and [Jerry] Rice ran a curl, and Montana saw the defender on the inside of the curl and led Rice to the outside of it. That's what you have to do defensively, is take everything away that you can. If you get beat by good execution, you've got to keep pushing your execution to the highest level. That guy's in the Hall of Fame, and that's why he's there."

Eventually, the obvious question arises. After all, Tom Brady and his father probably were sitting in the stands watching the very game that Belichick is showing right now. Over the previous four seasons, the comparisons between Brady and Montana have flown thick and fast, especially since Brady and the Patriots won their third Super Bowl, leaving Brady only one behind the San Francisco quarterback. At the question, something in Belichick seems briefly to go blank and unremarkable, as though he's been idly asked for the key to a private code. His answer comes out of some deep vein of iron banality.

"Tom's a good quarterback," he says. "He does a lot of things well. It's hard to compare players from different eras who played in different systems. Tom does a lot of things well. He makes a lot of good plays. He makes a lot of good throws."

Brady and Belichick are inextricably linked—a coach who was about two losses away from being a retread, and a quarterback whose career might have died on the vine anywhere else. In Belichick, Brady found a coach willing to take a chance on him without the reservations that had dogged him at Michigan. And, having taken a chance very much like this one once before, in Cleveland, Belichick found a quarterback who seemed worth the risk. Without Tom Brady as his quarterback, Bill Belichick was 41–57 as an NFL head coach with a 1–1 record in the playoffs. Brady became the starter in the third game of the 2001 season, and, from that moment until the beginning of the 2005 season, Belichick's teams went 48–14 with a 9–0 playoff record, including three Super Bowls. Without each other, they both might be journeymen, their careers truncated for any one of a dozen reasons. They were first joined in serendipity; they are bound now by what they've come to mean to each other.

"He's one of the most mentally tough guys I've ever been around," Brady says. "He's a guy that expects us to come to work every day and put everything else aside, whether it's off the field or whatever you did last week. He doesn't care about it. He just wants you to continue to move on and make improvements."

"Put it this way," Belichick says. "Without Tom Brady, I wouldn't have accomplished a fraction of what I've accomplished. There is simply no other quarterback I'd rather have than Tom Brady. I can't say any more about a player than that."

Belichick is a man of public contradiction whose charisma extends to the door of his locker room and no further. His press conferences are monuments to authoritarian impatience, but his private politics are reputedly quite liberal, and he has a well-known jones for the music of Jon Bon Jovi. He can armor himself with monosyllables against the outside world, but, within his very small circle of trust, he can laugh at Mike Vrabel's dead-on imitation of him, and even mark one particularly bad loss by bringing a shovel to the next practice and burying the game ball.

He can be ruthless with a player's career, whether that's shuffling a star like Lawyer Milloy out of town after having praised him lavishly throughout training camp or cutting some poor special-teams scrub for missing a single play, but he can watch game films and explain not merely the mechanics of a football game but the art within those mechanics as well.

His office is at the end of a long corridor that winds through the east side of Gillette Stadium. It is book-laden but relatively trophy-free. There is a small paperweight on the front of his desk, a testimonial from one of the several honorary degrees he's received now that he's reckoned to be a managerial genius. "Building teams of player-leaders," Rosabeth Moss Kanter calls it, although Knute Rockne would probably chuckle. It was the old Notre Dame coach who, despite being himself a self-promoter of Barnumish proportions, once wrote, "Psychology has its place in football, but not to the extent that football fans believe. Otherwise, schools would be turning over the coach's job to the professor of philosophy. Whenever I hear the football coach referred to as a deep and serious thinker . . . pardon me, if I smile."

Belichick is a defensive coach whose career was saved by a quarterback, which is ironic but not necessarily paradoxical. "It's still the quarterback that everything has to go through," says Belichick. "I mean, in terms of the franchise and selling tickets and everything, that's a whole different ball game, but the quarterback's got to be the guy everything you want to do on the field goes through, regardless of what his personality is."

The one immutable thing about him is that he believes a football player is a football player is a football player. Adam Vinatieri, Belichick always says, isn't a kicker. He's a football player. Linebackers and tackles should be able to catch touchdown passes. Defensive ends should be able to lead the blocking in a goal-line offense, and he ought to be able to put a wide receiver back there at cornerback, because receivers study defensive techniques as hard as the defensive players who use them do, or they should, at any rate, if they're going to play for him. At some level of his football mind, Belichick doesn't think in two platoons.

"In Tom's case," he explains, "what he knew in 2001 was considerable. What's he's learned in subsequent years has added on to that until, now, he's got a doctorate in defensive football. He understands what they're doing and, if they're not doing it, why they're vulnerable. That's what Tom's great at; he understands how a defense should be played."

It was something Belichick noticed about Brady straightaway. They both looked at defenses the same way. They could both see deeply into the opposing schemes, one or two moves ahead. They could see the opportunity present in the space between how a defense should be played and how an opposing team, or an opposing player, actually played it.

"At the end of the play," Belichick says, "you could say, Tom, what happened on that play? Why'd you throw it there? And he'd answer, 'Well, I went back and I got my read, and the linebacker flashed in front of him, so I couldn't throw it then, and then I got pressure from that side and came off it and hit my check down.' Then, you'd put the play on film, and everything he said happened, happened.

"A lot of guys, believe it or not, can't tell you what they saw. They don't see the defense. They look at the receiver. They throw it to the receiver because they think he's open, and, eventually, that's going to get you into trouble. They're open now, but they're not going to stay open because that window's closing. A lot of guys will come over and tell you, 'Well, I saw the corner playing off him,' and you go back and look at the play, and the corner's not that far off of him. Or, they'll say they saw the linebacker go to one side of the field and he really didn't. He went straight back. The quarterback just made up his mind before it happened that this was what was going to happen, and he didn't really confirm it. He just saw what he wanted to see. With Tom, when I asked him about things like that, the answer was never 'I don't know.' What he said he saw happen was always what had happened."

They worked for hours together, eliminating as many variables as they could, fortifying themselves against the impermanence that's so basic to the game. You try to find as many things as you can that you can rely on because, by its very nature, football exists in a world of fragility. Careers are fragile. No player can count on being healthy for an entire season. Success is fragile. The NFL counts as a fundamental basis for its success the fact that it makes it as hard as possible for the same teams to be good year after year. The league's vaunted parity masks a calibrated volatility with which every NFL player—and, most especially, every NFL coach—comes to live. Professional football is a lifetime education in the immediate and the temporary.

Belichick had an early lesson in all of this in Cleveland, where he lived through an experience so otherworldly that it's hard to imagine it happened to a team other than the Patriots. His benching of Bernie Kosar marked him lousy with the Cleveland fans even though it was the right thing to do at the time. His guarded, gloomy mien was an unsettling departure for the perennially optimistic Browns fans. And then he got caught up in one of the most singularly unsettling departures in the history of the league.

At the beginning of the 1995 season, Cleveland owner Art Modell announced that he would be uprooting the Browns and moving them to Baltimore, where, of course, they'd be replacing the Colts, who'd been uprooted and carted off to Indianapolis a few years earlier. At least the Colts blew town all at once. Belichick had to spend an entire season as the most visible employee of a lame-duck franchise. That he managed to win five games in a season in which the Browns played with, as Bob Dylan once sang, "one foot on the highway and one foot in the grave," looks in retrospect like the coaching job of the decade. He got fired at its end, though, his last game there concluding in a near riot when disgruntled Cleveland fans took it upon themselves to dismantle the old Municipal Stadium and hurl the pieces of it onto the field.

Brady, of course, learned at Michigan that his career was a delicate balance of his work and other people's opinions, and then he got a graduate-level education in that subject when the entire NFL passed on him five times before Belichick and the Patriots gave him his chance. Once Brady seized the opportunity, it was Belichick who helped drive him to succeed further, pushing him and prodding him, keeping him in constant forward motion, as a football player anyway. Which, as it happens, was how Brady was most at ease with himself, and it was how he kept fame from petrifying him, or celebrity from summing him up before he was thirty. Belichick was the face of an audience that didn't want Brady to sell it credit cards or save its soul.

For Belichick, Brady now was a great constant in a season in which there was something unmoored about him. He'd reportedly separated from his wife, and that had made the papers. He'd lost his two principal coordinators; Charlie Weis had gone off to Notre Dame, and Romeo Crennel, who'd been Belichick's Belichick on defense, had taken the job as head coach of the Browns team that the NFL had dropped in Cleveland to replace the one that had beaten feet to Baltimore. And his father had died in the middle of the year. There was a drift to the way he was in public—strange, muted moments in which he groped for what he wanted to say.

Even when he was being gruff, and uncommunicative, and impossible, he seemed less settled in what he was doing. In a season in which his quarterback hadn't been well since the halfway point, and in which his team had been bedeviled by nagging injuries, there was pain enough in the ellipses of what he said to make you believe that Bill Belichick might be playing hurt himself.

Somehow, the Miami Dolphins managed to stagger through the AFC East and arrive in Foxborough on the first of January,

2006, for the final season game of the regular season with an 8–7 record. A win in Foxborough and the Dolphins would finish the season at 9–7, which would be a considerable accomplishment for the rookie head coach, Nick Saban, and his young team. He was a Belichick acolyte, as firmly a member of the extended Belichick coaching family as Belichick once had been part of Bill Parcells's. In 1991, Belichick had hired Saban to coordinate the Browns defense in Cleveland. Saban brought to Miami all the management principles he'd learned from Belichick, including the bunkerlike mentality regarding public comment about virtually anything. However, Saban also got the Dolphins playing hard, which was quite enough to make Miami what passed for a contender in the AFC East.

"It was a pretty special group of coaches, and I knew that at the time," Belichick recalled of his stint in Ohio. "I told the owner that several times, too. I don't think the quality of the coaching staff was the major problem in Cleveland. I do take pride in that. I learned a lot from them. I learned a lot from Nick. I know he said he learned things in Cleveland, but I might have learned more from him than he did from me." In fact, after the Patriots beat Carolina, Belichick went to Baton Rouge to study how Saban, then the coach at LSU, worked with the talented defensive backfield that would win Saban a national championship.

Consequently, as Miami came to Foxborough there were several levels of intrigue to what otherwise might have appeared to be a relatively meaningless game for the Patriots. They had clinched a spot in the postseason, and they knew they would be playing their first playoff game at home the following weekend. However, with the Cincinnati Bengals losing their final game, if New England beat Miami, the Patriots would host the Pittsburgh Steelers, a brutal, physical team that New England had only barely edged in the third game of the year. If the Patriots were somehow to lose to Miami, then their first-round opponent would be the Jacksonville Jaguars, a manifestly easier matchup for a team that needed as many of those as it could get.

Brady started the game, his eighty-seventh consecutive for New England. He played three series of downs, took nineteen snaps, was intercepted once, and completed three of the other eight passes he threw, one of them for a touchdown to Deion Branch. He then left the field for the rest of the day, along with a whole clutch of the other New England regulars.

On the sideline, Brady was in constant motion and constantly in conference with Matt Cassel, the rookie quarterback from Southern California who'd replaced him for the afternoon. "I'm always trying to put my two cents in," Brady says with a laugh. "My quarterback coach said, 'God, you're a pain in the you-know-what when you're on the sidelines,' because I'm always chipping in. But it is a different perspective. Things happen awful quick out there."

Cassel's college career had been even more star-crossed than Brady's. He'd had to play backup to two consecutive Heisman Trophy winners. Now, he was watching what he'd been studying come to hostile life all at once in front of him. "There was a lot of buildup before the game," said Cassel, "but I was anticipating that. Once I got into the rhythm of the game, things started to slow down a little bit. I got hit back under my chin a few times, which I deserved, because I made the wrong 'Mike' [a linebacker] call."

Cassel played gamely, even after Miami's Reggie Howard popped him in his own end zone, knocking loose the ball for what became a safety. The game bristled with oddities, from Brady on the sideline to the first dropkick the NFL had seen since 1941. In the fourth quarter, after Cassel hit Tim Dwight for a nine-yard touchdown, Belichick lined up the third-string quarterback, Doug Flutie, in the shotgun for the conversion, and Flutie, who is perhaps the last football player alive who can still drop-kick, nailed one through the uprights. "The way they celebrated, I thought they'd won a Super Bowl," said Miami's Jason Taylor, one of Brady's closest friends in the league.

Friendships in the NFL can begin most strangely. Belichick found Saban because he hired him. Brady and Taylor cemented their friendship the way modern athletes will—at a fashion photo shoot in Los Angeles. They were both young and handsome and famous, and they were able to joke with each other from out of a common context. They were more alike than they were different, and the fact that they played directly opposite each other seemed, at best, good for a laugh or two.

"I heard that Dan Marino and Bruce Smith used to have that kind of friendly rivalry," explained Taylor. "I met Tom when we were doing an event for Zegna. We keep in touch during the year, and we talk once or twice a month. I take care of him when he comes to Miami." Brady first met Taylor, however, at the bottom of a pile that had assembled itself on Brady's head during his first season as a starter.

"I remember that pile," Belichick said. "It was right before [Taylor] scooped up that fumble and jogged into the end zone down there in Miami, and we had, like, ninety yards of total offense.

"I think, as a quarterback, if you have a guy after you twenty, thirty, forty plays a game, there's no sense getting him any more antagonized than what he already is. So, I think you'd be best served to be respectful, pat them on the back, and see if you can slow them down a little bit."

Even though Cassel nearly brought New England all the way back from 25–13 in the last nine minutes of the game, the 28–26

Patriot loss was all but forgotten between Flutie's dropkick and the imminence of the postseason. "It's the best I felt coming out of a game in a long time," Brady said. "I don't think I got hit today, which is great.

"It's different when you're not playing. You get cold. I looked over and I said, 'God, is it always this cold out?'"

It certainly seemed as though a collective decision had been made to try to arrange to play Jacksonville, and not Pittsburgh, the following week. Belichick denied it several times after the game. Nobody heard a cock crow.

9 | ENDGAMES

THE LAST playoff game the New England Patriots lost had been in January 1999, when they went down to Jacksonville and got beaten easily, 25–10, in a wild-card playoff in which New England was led by backup quarterback Scott Zolak and coached by Pete Carroll. Two days earlier, Michigan, with Tom Brady backing up Brian Griese, had beaten Washington in the Rose Bowl to win the national championship.

It was three years before New England played another play-off game, and they won that one, beating Oakland famously in the snow on Adam Vinatieri's kick. Since then, they had won nine of them in a row, and Brady had been the starting quarter-back in all of them. In five years, he had gone past Terry Bradshaw, who'd won five playoff games in a row for the great Pittsburgh teams of the 1970s, and he'd become, by winning percentage, the greatest playoff quarterback of all time.

The postseason is a radically different context from the reg-ular season. Beyond the singular importance of each game—any loss ends the season, after all—there is a ferocious collision between the accumulated knowledge of the long regular season and the relatively limited time you have to bring all that infor-mation to bear on a particular opponent. Bill Belichick talks about how the "volume" goes up, and he is not necessarily referring to the extraneous noise surrounding the postseason, although that certainly is a factor as well.

"Your preparation and all of those little situations—third and short, second and long, red area, backed up—all of those situations, the volume within them has grown, and you're defending more, and they're looking at you and saying, 'Well, they played this before, and now they're playing something else.'

"They're playing against four things instead of two that you've shown. At this time of year, all that preparation and that volume, it puts a lot of mental pressure on players not only to handle the multiple things that we are doing but to handle the multiples that they throw at you."

Which is why, even though some coaches are wary of going a week without a game at this time of year, most teams contend seriously during the regular season to secure a first-round bye in the playoffs. The bye allows them not only to rest their injured but also to prepare for that first playoff game in a more relaxed and thorough fashion. In each of the previous two seasons, both of which had ended with victories in the Super Bowl, the Patriots had had the first week of the playoffs to rest and recuperate. This season, however, they had not played well enough to earn the luxury of a week off.

Brady's talents for preparation and analysis make him uniquely suited for the atmosphere surrounding the playoffs. It's a good time for anyone who's a quick study, and who can translate what he sees on film to what he must do as swiftly as Brady can. So much of the coolness remarked upon by his teammates comes from Brady having studied film intently enough to learn all the possible contingencies that might arise, and from Brady's ability to recognize these in an instant. Both the volume and the velocity of the preparation were increased. It helped, however, that he had come to adopt Belichick's philosophy that each game—playoff or not—was to be prepared for as sui generis. That helped Brady focus during his brief time to prepare for each week of the playoffs, and to filter out the extraneous chatter that increases week to week, culminating in the Wagnerian cacophony of the Super Bowl. Brady might have won nine consecutive playoff games, but it was healthier for him to look at them as nine one-game winning streaks.

This season, however, he and the Patriots would be playing their first playoff game on Saturday night having ended the regular season only the previous Sunday. "We're trying to squeeze two days into one, because it's a short week for us," Brady said. "The pace speeds up. I mean, it speeds up anyway, but especially with the short week.

"I think anybody looking back seventeen games ago is only setting himself up for failure. I'm looking to see what we can do this week. It's a one-game season for us, and it's all about what we can do in preparation so that we can ultimately go out and execute during the game. We're not going to win just because we show up. I think that's ridiculous. If we don't go out and play the way we're capable of playing, we're going to be sitting at home Monday, and I don't want to be doing that."

More to the point, Brady's previously overwhelming success in the postseason had allowed the rest of the teams in the league to create for one another a Tom Brady to worry about before they took the field against the real one. So much of the reason for why he'd done what he'd done in the playoffs was that he believed he could do it. Now, somewhere, buried in their minds under all the preparation and scheming, his opponents believed it as much as he did.

The credibility Brady had established over the previous four seasons allowed him (once again) to throw the respect card down on the table. "I think we've been disrespected more than any other team in the league this year," he said, aiming this nonsense as always over the heads of his immediate audience and toward his teammates beyond. "I think we've been given up on by a lot of media people, a lot of fans, even our own fans, and if there's one team that feels it's disrespected, it's us." However, if any team had a right to come into the game with a chip on its shoulder the size of a sequoia, it was Jacksonville, if only because everybody in the league believed that New England so preferred to play the Jaguars that the Patriots had gamed their way into doing so against the Dolphins.

It was obvious why Belichick might have wanted to finagle the Patriots into a game with Jacksonville. The Jaguars were a defense-intensive team with quarterback troubles. Byron Leftwich, the tall, athletic gunner the team had drafted out of Marshall University in 2003, had missed the last five games of the season with a broken ankle. His backup, David Garrard, had stepped in, and Jacksonville had won four of those five games, finishing the year at 12–4. Now Leftwich was at least marginally ready to play again after missing over a month. Meanwhile, there was more than a little talk that Garrard might be able to do for Jacksonville what Brady had done for New England in 2001. Brady had created a competitive archetype that now worked for him as well as his receivers did. He could now create quarterback controversies on opposing teams without even being there.

No matter who quarterbacked the Jaguars, with his defense finally healthy and playing very well, Belichick faced in Jacksonville the enticing prospect of a team led either by a young quarterback who would be playing his first playoff game both injured and rusty, or by a fifth-year quarterback playing his first playoff game as the sixteenth game of his NFL career. Leftwich would start, limping, but he would be playing with one eye out for the New England linebackers and the other one cast back over his shoulder to see if Garrard was warming up.

"I would not be happy [if Garrard came in]," Leftwich admitted. "But I can't think that way. I can't even allow myself to think that way just because everybody's saying I'm going to be rusty after five weeks off. I guess we'll all find out on Saturday night."

Nothing started smoothly for either side. The first New England possession of the game was a complete burlesque. They picked up penalties on their first two plays from scrimmage, and then Brady hit umpire Chad Brown right in the head with his first pass of the game. The first half evolved into a struggle between the two defenses. The New England schemes were baffling Leftwich, but Brady was taking a fearsome beating from the Jaguars' talented defensive line and linebacking corps. After muffing a couple of easy scoring chances, including a certain touchdown pass that went through Deion Branch's fingers, the New England offense went into a shell. If the Patriots had played things any closer to the vest, they could have called signals with a defibrillator.

On the last New England possession of the first quarter, Brady scrambled to the left and was flung to the ground on second down, and he was sacked on third down when his pocket broke down completely. Never nimble outside the pocket, Brady seemed at this point to have lost some mobility within it. On fourth down, in an attempt to shake themselves loose from their lethargy, the Patriots chose to try to pick up a first down, but Brady juggled the snap in the shotgun, and he tossed the ball safely away, limping off the field to the sideline.

Confident that his defense could hold the Jaguars for as long as it had to do so, Brady finally got the team moving in the second quarter. Tim Dwight returned a punt to the Jacksonville 37-yard line. Throughout the first half, when he wasn't running for his life, Brady had found his passes sailing on him again. Now, though, his spirals were tightening. He hit David Givens with a pass on the Jacksonville goal line, but Givens got hit and lost the ball, and Brady screamed vainly for a call. After Corey Dillon banged over the left side for four yards, the Patriots caught the Jaguar linebackers being overly aggressive. Anxious to rush Brady into bad decisions, the Jacksonville defenders committed themselves too recklessly. Brady gave the ball to running back Kevin Faulk slanting behind a linebacker while Logan Mankins sealed off Jacksonville defensive end Paul Spicer. The side cleared out, and Faulk ran the ball all the way to the Jacksonville 15.

Three plays later, Brady sold the Jacksonville defense with a pump fake to Ben Watson in the left flat and, as linebacker Mike Peterson stepped toward Watson, Troy Brown snuck in behind him to the middle of the end zone, and Brady nearly threw the ball through him for a touchdown and a 7–0 lead. On the replay, Brady's fake looks like a perfect trompe l'oeil. He follows the motion all the way through, and he doesn't look toward Brown almost until the ball leaves his hand. This was the way it had been all season—excellence on the Scan button. It would be there, and then it would disappear, and then it would be back, play by play, possession by possession, and, ultimately, game by game.

The touchdown was enough to give New England a 7–3 halftime lead, and it was clear at this point that the defense was perfectly capable of making that thin margin, or any other lead the Patriots might muster, stand up until well after Valentine's Day. In the third quarter, Brady engineered an eighty-one-yard drive that took 6:42 off the clock, ending the march with a feathery, play-action pass to Givens, slanting into the end zone from the right side. Often, on plays like this, Brady fairly sprints down to jump into the celebratory scrum. ("My job is to catch him, most of the time," Dan Koppen once explained, "so he doesn't fall on his face.") This time, though, Brady walked very slowly and didn't get there until well after the rest of his teammates did.

The game finally broke open at the end of the third quarter. On a third-and-thirteen play from New England's own 37-yard line, Jacksonville sent a linebacker in on a blitz, and tight end Watson spotted it as soon as Brady did. Watson adjusted his route, and Brady slipped the ball to him underneath the defense. Watson turned upfield, lighting out for the end zone.

"When Ben started running down the sidelines," Brady said, "I started looking around for flags. I always look around to see if there are any flags, because that's a pretty crappy feeling. That was an incredible play. We haven't had one like that in a long time."

For weeks, Brady had been talking about Watson's startling athletic ability, and now it came to vivid life. Three Jacksonville defenders converged on him, and Watson fought all of them off, including Gerald Sensabaugh, a safety who tried to knock Watson out of bounds at the last moment and looked, instead, like a man running full speed into a wall. It was the longest touchdown pass in the team's playoff history. For his part, Brady was able to jog downfield to rejoice. The game ended, 28–3, the tenth consecutive playoff win for New England, keeping the team undefeated in the playoffs for the twenty-first century.

Now, they knew they would be traveling the next week, but they didn't know where. They would play in Indianapolis or they would play in Denver, and they'd lost decisively to both teams already. For the next twenty-four hours, until the Sunday games decided their schedule, Belichick and the coaches would cram for both possible opponents, for Peyton Manning and the Colts, who'd lost only one game all season, and for the grinding running game of the Broncos.

"If we go to Denver," Belichick mused, "then my feeling is that it might be the earlier game so, if that's the case, we'll probably get that one on Saturday. We won't know for sure until the second game tomorrow night."

As it happened, Pittsburgh beat Cincinnati, sending New England to Denver, and depriving the punditry in and around the NFL of another weeklong Brady-Manning extravaganza. This would not be a matchup of archetypes—the collision between Bradys and Mannings of the mind that had become something like a medieval morality play to the irrational partisans of both men. This would be a football game blessedly drained of the vicarious.

Instead, Brady and the Patriots would go to Denver and play a team that had roughed them up badly in the sixth game of the season. It was not the showpiece game that the league and its television partners might have preferred, but it pitted Brady against a defense, led by the brilliant cornerback Champ Bailey, that had proven to be notably unimpressed by his reputation. Denver hit people, hard and early, and it played extraordinarily well with the lead.

"My parents asked me the other day, 'Do you get nervous before games anymore?'" Brady said. "I told them, 'Mom and Dad, you know, I've played a lot of football.'"

Champ Bailey jumped the route.

Champ Bailey jumped the route and ran the other way.

Champ Bailey jumped the route and ran the other way, and the season was over.

Champ Bailey jumped the route and ran the other way, and the season was over, but not for at least one more play, because young Ben Watson threw one of the greatest individual efforts that anyone had ever seen across Invesco Field, and then the season was over. Nobody believed it was over, and nobody played like it was over, but it was, right there, when Champ Bailey jumped the route and ran the other way, all the way, almost.

On the evening of the game, the moon hung huge and low and bright over the Rockies, and the sky softened into an almost perfect parfait. The night was clear and warm, and nothing at all like it should have been in Denver in the second week of January.

These two teams had a longer history with each other than they had with anyone else. On September 9, 1960, as part of that lunatic rich-man's experiment known as the American Football League, Denver and the then Boston Patriots met in the first game for either franchise, with the Broncos beating the Patriots, 13–10, in front of 21,597 curious onlookers at Boston University. As the years went by, and the Patriots staggered through seasons of garish misfortune, Denver became one of the AFL's signature franchises, their old Mile High Stadium one of the upstart league's most famous home fields, notable for how the Broncos would run onto the field through what looked like a rodeo chute. The last vestige of the old place is a huge white bronco that rears up from the very top rim of Invesco, Denver's new stadium, which has all the amenities of a modern stadium but only half the charm of an old one.

This was the second time the two teams had ever met in the playoffs. All week, with the New England defense having now put up strong efforts five weeks in a row, the primary focus around the Patriots was how to keep Denver from playing from ahead. Back in October, the Broncos had piled up a 28–3 lead, and, while New England had come back to make a game of it, it was not an experience any of them wanted to repeat. Given a big enough lead, the Broncos' running attack would move the chains, chew up the clock, and force Brady and the Patriots to try to make big plays. In turn, this would allow the Denver defense to pour itself relentlessly against the makeshift New England offensive line.

"When you're down 28–3, not a lot feels good," Brady said before the game, reflecting on the previous game against Denver. "That's a team that likes pressure, that really lives on pressuring the quarterback. It was just too much to overcome. We dug ourselves too deep of a hole and just couldn't fight our way out of it.

"They're fast and they're smart and they're tough, and they're very disciplined. For a team that blitzes as much as they do, they don't blow hardly any assignments."

Almost from the very start of the game, it seemed that the huge mountain moon had moved into the House of Screwball. The first quarter was strangely stagnant. Denver's running game was stalled, and Brady didn't hit anything with a pass except the ground. The only real excitement came on the opening possession when Denver safety John Lynch, a ferocious hitter that Denver had picked up from Tampa Bay before the 2004 season to energize its already talented secondary, began jawing with Brady, who went back at Lynch, pointing and gesticulating. Six minutes later, as Belichick tried to pick up a first down on a fourth-and-one from the Denver 36-yard line, Lynch belted Brady from the blind side, and the pass fluttered to the ground well behind tight end Christian Fauria.

The first real change in the game's momentum came in the second quarter, when New England's defense stuffed a Denver drive at the New England 3-yard line. On fourth down, Denver's

Jake Plummer, a quarterback whose reputation for brilliance and erraticism chased him out of Arizona, instead tried to loft a gentle "fade" route over New England's Asante Samuel to Ashley Lelie. It was a strange call. Denver, after all, had had one of the most reliable short-distance running games in the league for more than a decade. Samuel defended the play superbly, choking off the drive.

Four minutes later, Samuel stepped in front of Lelie at the New England 11-yard line and intercepted a Plummer pass. (Samuel had to wait a few minutes while the referees consulted the replay to see if he'd caught the ball within the field of play. This would not be Samuel's last brush with the referees this evening, but it would be by far the happiest, as his interception was upheld.) On the first play from scrimmage, Brady rolled out to the right, the pocket moving with him, and all of them moving away from the pressure coming from the right side of the Denver defense. He spotted Andre Davis, streaking down the middle of the field, having beaten Bailey to the inside. The fifty-one-yard completion eventually resulted in a Vinatieri field goal that gave New England a 3–0 lead. It would be the only lead they would have all night.

However, as beautiful as the throw to Davis was, it signified a great deal about what came after it. On second down, Brady got hit hard again, and, on third down, he overthrew Deion Branch on a relatively easy toss in the left corner of the end zone. He looked choppy and out of sorts, his rhythm syncopated all wrong now both because of his injuries, and because of the relentless Denver pressure, especially over the left side of the New England line.

For a while, it appeared that New England was going to make the 3–0 lead stand until halftime. However, with two minutes left, and after picking up a first down on the play, running back Kevin Faulk ran the ball into someone's knee in the middle of a pile, and Ian Gold, a Denver linebacker and a former teammate of Brady's at Michigan, fell on it, giving the Broncos a first down at the New England 40. On the next play, Plummer sent Lelie streaking down the left sideline. Samuel ran with him, long dreadlocks flopping out of the back of his helmet. As the pass came down, the two of them got tangled up reaching for it, neither one gaining a clear advantage, although, were this a boxing match, it looked as though Lelie might have been ahead on points. Even though he thought there was no infraction on the play, Lelie shrewdly threw his hands in the air in mock exasperation. Across the field, standing under the goalposts, back judge Greg Steed let his flag fly, calling Samuel for interference.

Belichick melted down on the sideline. Samuel stood in the end zone, hands on his head, dumbstruck. It was an utterly ridiculous penalty, but it gave Denver the ball at the New England 1-yard line, where the Broncos this time eschewed finesse, punching running back Mike Anderson in behind the big beef for a 7–3 lead. The stadium was still buzzing from this sudden turn of events when Todd Sauerbrun, who'd kicked the ball off for Denver, managed to knock it loose from Patriot rookie return man Ellis Hobbs. The improbable fumble allowed Denver to close the half on a fifty-yard field goal from Jason Elam, and Denver left the field leading, 10–3.

Brady's first half was unremarkable. Except for the long completion to Davis, he had done little more than survive. He'd completed seven of his fifteen passes, none of them for touchdowns, and he'd missed several open receivers. More to the point, for him and for all the Patriots, the game seemed ominously the reverse of how the Patriots had played in important games ever since Brady had taken over at quarterback. They were making mistakes. Worse, they were making them at the worst possible times. Whatever the opposite of opportunism was, they suddenly were afflicted with it. They were stuck for the moment in the role they'd forced on Indianapolis, and Carolina, and Philadelphia. Denver wasn't playing particularly well, either, but, suddenly, New England was the 2001 St. Louis Rams, a defending champion caught up in a close game but playing like it was four touchdowns behind.

The third quarter began promisingly. The defense forced a punt, and Brady marched the Patriots fifty-eight yards in five minutes to the Denver 14-yard line. There, however, on a third-and-two, Brady bounced an easy pass for the first down in front of Branch, and New England settled for another field goal to cut the Denver lead to 10–6. That partially missed opportunity didn't seem so important when, after Denver again failed to move the ball, New England again drove it back, this time all the way down the field until they were set up with a first down at the Broncos' 10-yard line.

Brady was sharp on the drive, hitting four passes in a row. On the first of them, he stepped into the face of a furious rush and found Troy Brown down the sideline for thirty-three yards. He then hit Branch for twenty-six more at the end of a "flea-flicker" on which he'd taken a tossback from Dillon. It was the finest bit of sustained offense that New England had been able to muster the entire game. Dillon even managed to bang out a crucial five-yard gain in the middle of it, a lonely bit of success for the anemic Patriots' running game.

Branch caught a pass on first down that got the Patriots to the Denver 5-yard line, but David Givens dropped the next ball. On third down, Brady read a blitz from Denver safety Nick Ferguson, and he got chased out of the pocket, running left to right parallel along the line of scrimmage. In front of him, Brown broke out and up toward the back right corner of the end zone.

Brady thought he saw Champ Bailey move inside to pick up another Patriot receiver, and he threw the ball toward Brown. But
he never had his feet under him—it all starts with the feet, Tom
Martinez had said, long ago—and the ball had just enough air
under it for Bailey to read the throw, wheel back in front of
Brown, and take off with the interception. Brady was hit on the
play. Lying on the ground, he heard the roar of the crowd and he
knew very well what had happened.

On the other side of the field, tight end Ben Watson saw the
interception. He wheeled and set off in what seemed like a fruit-
less pursuit. Later, when what happened was replayed on television a half dozen times, you could see Watson create the angle
he would need, a long hypotenuse from the Denver 5-yard line
to the New England 2, fashioned out of pure speed and a desire
not to give up on the play. All the improvements that Watson
had made over two years with the Patriots, all the heat he'd
taken from Belichick and the other coaches, and all the patience
he'd had to have, learning how to play for this impossible man,
Watson threw all of that into this sprint. Bailey was just beginning to slow when Watson finally closed the angle, blasting
Bailey so hard that the ball came loose.

"Had to be another Georgia guy to make that play," Bailey
laughed later.

It was an astonishing feat of raw athleticism, and it might
have changed the game for good. Had the ball bounced out of
bounds in the end zone, New England would have taken over at
its own 20-yard line. However, the officials ruled that Bailey had
fumbled the ball on the field of play, giving Denver a first down
just shy of the Patriots' goal line. Belichick vainly sent the play
to be reviewed, but it stood as called. Denver slammed Anderson in on the next play for a touchdown, and now they led 17–6.

The interception had been a fourteen-point swing in the

game. Denver now had the working margin that New England had been dreading throughout the previous week. It also seemed to crack something in what heretofore had been New England's smoothly professional competitive personality. The Patriots sideline grew restive. After Anderson's touchdown, linebacker Willie McGinest furiously pursued linebacker Larry Izzo on the New England sideline, and the altercation got so heated that Mike Vrabel had to separate his two angry teammates. Nothing that had sustained the Patriots over the previous five years seemed to have accompanied the team to Denver.

Still, though, the defense managed to keep the Broncos from running out the game entirely. As the fourth quarter began, Brady moved the team again deep into Denver territory. On a third-and-five, Troy Brown broke loose at the Denver goal line, but Brady threw the ball five feet over his head. And then, as if to prove conclusively that everything was misaligned in the New England universe this night, Adam Vinatieri blew a forty-three-yard field goal, the first one he'd missed in thirteen attempts. At which point, things came completely unglued. The normally sure-handed Troy Brown muffed a punt on his own 15-yard line, and the Broncos walked in for an easy score and a 24–6 lead.

Brady had one great moment left in him. On a play on which he was flattened by Denver's Gerard Warren, he somehow found Branch slashing in from the left side for seventy-three yards. On the replay, Brady goes down like a rag doll, his head bouncing hard off the turf. For a second, as he lifts his head, his eyes are vague and unfocused as he takes a brief stroll down what the old boxing writers used to call "Queer Street." Then you can see his face brighten again. Givens caught the Patriots' last touchdown pass of the year, a dart in the back of the end zone. It cut the margin to nine points. Denver added a late field goal, and Tom Brady had lost the first playoff game of his career, 27–13.

They'd lost the game the way they'd won so many others. They had been forced into a situation where they had to throw the ball. A team that had built its fearsome reputation in the playoffs on relentless defense and on relentlessly moving the chains had played an erratic game. They had committed turnovers and hadn't forced them. Before this game, they'd turned the ball over twenty-one fewer times than their opponents had in the previous ten playoff games. Here, they turned it over five times, including three fumbles, all of which led to Denver scores, and Bailey's killer interception.

They'd outgained the Broncos 420–286, and they'd shut the Denver running attack down to a paltry 96 yards. Brady had thrown for 341 yards, but he'd missed several open receivers at bad times. The Patriots had made all the big mistakes, and winning statistically while losing on the scoreboard felt every bit as empty to them as they'd maintained it was when they were on the other end of things.

Football teams move like small armies do. In the New England locker room, the players talked in low voices while the noisy business of packing up the season went on all around them. Ben Watson accepted congratulations on his great effort on Bailey's interception but said he wished it had come in a winning game.

Brady came into the interview room outside the locker room. He looked fresh and scrubbed. He limped a little, but he was far more animated than he had been during the thirty-two-second press conference against Indianapolis. He talked about Bailey's play. "If I had led Troy more toward the back of the end zone, maybe he could have made the play," he said. "It's part of playing quarterback sometimes. You make those plays, and sometimes you don't.

"It's only about a half hour ago, but you think about all

those plays we could have made in that game, and it's just very disappointing. You keep trying to rally and rally, and then that final gun sounded. I guess the reflection will have to come in the next month or two."

He turned to leave and stopped halfway down the small flight of stairs that led off the podium.

"Thanks, you guys," he said. "For everything."

They were all milling around down the hall, all the Patriots and their families, the season over a month sooner than the last two had ended. There were a number of children running around, lightening up the mood considerably. Linebacker Matt Chatham scoured the vicinity for a case of beer and, finding one, wandered off toward the team bus with it. His parents nearby, Brady was standing with Bridget in the middle of what was becoming an Irish wake, introducing her to the various relatives and friends of his teammates who had come to the game, taking each person just above the elbow and looking right at them, smiling easily, owning the space around him the way people say he always does.

Statistically, it had been his finest year ever. Counting the two playoff games, he'd completed 369 of 593 passes for 4,652 yards and thirty touchdowns. For long stretches, he had been all the Patriots had offensively, and he'd played half the season in real pain, the way football players do. Moreover, he had weathered his first year as a truly famous person. He'd gotten through *Saturday Night Live*, and the goat photo, and TOM SURFS FOR PORN! He'd even survived all those honors that had come his way based on what he'd already accomplished.

On the field, he'd done well enough in those moments when he was the only one standing still to keep the rest of his life moving. He was still fashioning it on his own terms, without becoming petrified by his own success or frozen in his own celebrity, and he knew he had because he knew how much this loss would come to hurt him over the next few weeks, when he was playing golf or doing interviews. As the crowd thinned a little around him, he spotted someone who'd come to him about five months earlier, wondering about writing a book that Brady had decided he wasn't yet old enough to be part of.

"Hey," he said. "Thanks for being around, okay?"

The team bus was warming up, and, little by little, the New England Patriots climbed aboard. From the outside, you couldn't see in much past the first row, where a nose tackle named Vince Wilfork was digging into a bag of fried chicken. Tom Brady kissed his mother. He kissed his father. He kissed someone else's mother. He kissed his girlfriend, the movie star. Slowly, he walked up the stairs into the bus. You could see him through the windshield briefly, and then he was gone, into the undifferentiated darkness of the bus, where his teammates were.

AFTERWORD

THE 2006 New England Patriots season formally began on a soft June morning that cracked open what had been a dripping and muddy springtime. The team gathered in Foxborough for its annual mandatory minicamp. The camp was closed to the general public, and the media coverage was subject to restrictions so rigid that, if Bill Belichick had shown up in full camouflage and sprayed his defensive backfield with gunfire, nobody would have been allowed to report on the carnage. Even in the season's very first moments, some things about the Patriots are always in midseason form.

Some key players were absent. Neither Dan Koppen nor Rodney Harrison was yet fully recovered from the injuries that had ended their 2005 seasons, and Deion Branch was holding out in a contract squabble. Moreover, a number of familiar faces were gone forever. Veteran linebacker Willie McGinest, who had played on all four New England Super Bowl teams going back to Bill Parcells, signed as a free agent with the Cleveland Browns and his old defensive coordinator, Romeo Crennel. Receiver David Givens finally confounded all the anonymous clipboards surrounding his career by scoring a big payday with the Tennessee Titans. And, most stunningly, at the end of the previous

March, Adam Vinatieri, the placekicker who was the only player close to Tom Brady as the iconic figure in New England's great run of success, signed a five-year, $12 million contract with the Indianapolis Colts. Vinatieri would now be called upon to apply the punctuation marks to drives led by Peyton Manning. Whatever minor deities watch over the National Football League, they're obviously gifted with a deft touch for irony.

Brady spent the offseason getting healthy. His hernia was repaired and the leg injury that had hobbled him after the game in Buffalo finally healed. Immediately prior to the opening of minicamp, he played golf with George H. W. Bush and Bill Clinton in Maine. A week later, at a charity tournament sponsored by the team, Brady reacted to losing a long-driving contest by helicoptering his driver a good distance from the tee. He was ready, people thought, to compete already. On August 17, however, an unremarkable day in the middle of an unremarkable camp, Brady's entire public persona was blindsided.

The Associated Press and the New York *Daily News* reported that morning that Brady's name was among those of ten to twenty athletes listed on a subpoena served by the federal grand jury sitting in San Francisco on one Greg Anderson, the physical trainer for Barry Bonds, the San Francisco Giants slugger, who was being investigated for possible perjury and tax evasion in connection with the BALCO sports-doping scandal. (Anderson already had served time in connection with the BALCO case and also had been jailed for refusing to testify against Bonds.) The BALCO case was a kind of foul counterpoint to everything that was happening in sports. The morning's headlines—BRADY LINKED TO BALCO FIGURE—were accompanied by a kind of sotto voce chorus calling up how he'd gone to the same high school as Bonds, how skinny Brady looked in all those photos in the Michigan media guide, and how he sat there in the congressional gallery, a kind of living prop, when George W. Bush mentioned this very issue in a State of the Union address, and the cameras had cut to Brady while everyone applauded. Because of who he was, and because of who he'd allowed people to believe him to be, Brady had built a public life in which bad news always was amplified by the good, where every whisper was a scream. He got surrounded coming off the practice field. He admitted having called Anderson, once, about the possibility of arranging a workout when Brady was back home in San Mateo, an account that Anderson himself confirmed. The workout never happened and the two men never had met.

"I think any time for an athlete you're even mentioned in something like this, it's disappointing," Brady told the scrum of reporters. "But it was a long time ago, I was back in the Bay Area and I wanted to work out for a day, I knew he had a gym, I called and he wasn't around. That was about it.

"Something like that, that's nothing I stand for. I represent a lot of things, and certainly fair play and me trying to be a role model for children, that's what I'm all about." There was something very fragile about him in that moment. The moment passed. The fragility seemed permanent.

On the field, as Brady worked with new receivers like Reche Caldwell, whom the team had signed to replace Givens, and old ones, like Troy Brown and Ben Watson, there was a lot of early June in his throws. He hit some passes, and he missed some others. His mechanics were off just enough to disrupt his timing, especially on the deep-out patterns. And he was throwing the ball to strangers, too.

"Over the years, you develop a rapport with guys," Brady explained. "There are certain ways I look at Deion and read his body language coming out of routes where I can really throw the ball early and anticipate it. Until you really throw enough of those passes where you can start understanding that, you're always hesitating a little bit."

He'd come over after the morning session and been swarmed by the assembled media. Even more than before, Brady is the face of the franchise, a franchise already picked as a Super Bowl competitor by those preseason football magazines that come out roughly when the crocuses do in the spring. He talked about the players who had left, and he talked about Branch, whom he expected to see in camp as soon as the two sides in the contract dispute stopped flexing at each other. "I'm probably less worried about Deion than I am about myself," he said. He had not liked the way he'd played in the first formal practice of the 2006 season. He had not liked it at all.

"I'm just going to have to come out here this afternoon," Tom Brady said, "and try to find a way to do it better."

NOTE ON SOURCES

Except where indicated, all direct quotations in this book come from my own interviews. Several of the sections—including the ones on Mike Vrabel, Adam Vinatieri, and the Manning family—rely to some extent on work previously published in *The Boston Globe Magazine*, *Esquire*, and *GQ*.

A number of books were immensely helpful, chief among them Michael MacCambridge's magisterial history of the National Football League, *America's Game: The Epic Story of How Pro Football Captured a Nation*. David Halberstam's *The Education of a Coach* is definitive on the topic of Bill Belichick and his relationship with his players, particularly his quarterback. Michael Holley's *Patriot Reign: Bill Belichick, the Coaches, and the Players Who Built a Champion* contributed a great deal to my understanding of the recent success enjoyed by the New England Patriots, while David Welky's essay collected in *The Rock, the Curse, and the Hub: A Random History of Boston Sports*, edited by Randy Roberts, remains the best short summary of the team's strange backstory. The anthologies *Tom Brady: There's No Expiration Date on Dreams*, published by Rich Wolfe and *The Sporting News*, and *Greatness: The Rise of Tom Brady*, published by *The Boston Globe*, were also invaluable resources.

The Patriots have become a case study in management skills, which is how they figure into Rosabeth Moss Kanter's *Confidence: How Winning Streaks and Losing Streaks Begin and End*. My understanding of the Second Vatican Council comes primarily from the theology department of Marquette University, the work of the Council fathers, and the writings of Garry Wills, especially *Why I Am a Catholic* and *Bare Ruined Choirs: Doubt, Prophecy, and*

Radical Religion. I drafted Josiah Royce onto the Patriots roster with the invaluable assistance of *The Philosophy of Josiah Royce*, edited by John K. Roth, and *The Loyal Physician: Roycean Ethics and the Practice of Medicine*, by Griffin Trotter. The debt I owe to Elwood Reid's *If I Don't Six* should be obvious from page one, and nobody should write a book about any football team without first reading *About Three Bricks Shy of a Load*, by my friend Roy Blount, Jr.

ACKNOWLEDGMENTS

THE GRATITUDE comes to rest first on Portola Drive in San Mateo, California, with Tom and Galynn Brady and their children. Thanks to them, to Nancy Brady, and to young Tommy, the quarterback, who was always curious about the project and who did not get in the way. Thanks also to his representatives, Don Yee and Steve Dubin. Thanks also to Stephen Pope of Boston College, whose insights into his California cousins, and into the Catholic faith they share, were invaluable.

Over the course of the 2005 season, I was the guest of the New England Patriots. My hosts included Bob and Jonathan Kraft, as well as the members of the team's media relations staff: Stacey James, Michelle Murphy, Casey O'Connell, and Jared Puffer. Bill Belichick gave his word that he'd be there after the season and he was. Thanks also to Scott Pioli and Virj Najarian. Inside the locker room, special thanks go to Dan Koppen, Corey Dillon, David Givens, Deion Branch, Ben Watson, Richard Seymour, Mike Vrabel, and Adam Vinatieri.

At *The Boston Globe*, my current professional home, sports editors Don Skwar and Joe Sullivan sent me to Super Bowls XXXVIII and XXXIX, at which the idea for this book first germinated. Thanks for picking up the tab.

Covering the New England Patriots is not the easiest beat in daily sportswriting, and my work was made easier by the contributions of the team's regular press corps. This begins with my colleagues at the *Globe*: Ron Borges, Nick Cafardo, Jerome Solomon, Jackie MacMullan, Bob Ryan, Mike Reiss, and Amalie Benjamin (welcome to The Show, rook). It includes John Tomase, Michael Felger, Karen Guregian, and Steve Buckley from my alma mater, *The Boston Herald*. Thanks also to Mark Farinella, Glen Farley, Eric McHugh, Jim Donaldson, Alan Greenberg (for all the rides), Steve Burton, Dan Pires, Chris Collins, Mark Ockerbloom, Laura Behnke, Wendy Nix, and Mike Giardi. And special mention goes to Tom E. Curran of *The Providence Journal,* Tom Brady's original amanuensis, mulching king of the Ocean State, for helping to broker the idea to the subject. Fairways and greens to you always.

At *Sports Illustrated*, editor Terry McDonnell assigned me to write the essay accompanying Brady's selection as the magazine's Sportsman of the Year, which allowed me to hone some of the themes on which I elaborate at length here. Thanks also to *SI*'s Michael Silver and Peter King, and especially to Rob Fleder, my old Tishman Building running buddy.

I would be remiss if I didn't specifically applaud several intrepid archivists: Bob Hyldberg, who tracked down the summary of Harpo Gladieux's epic 1970 performance against Miami; Aaron Schatz of Cold Hard Football Facts; and Brendan Hughes, who has devoted himself to an exhaustive history of Tom Brady's college career, which can be found at http://home.com cast.net/~thetaildragger/Pats/TB by any and all obsessives.

Around the NFL, thanks go to Harvey Greene of the Miami Dolphins, Craig Kelley of the Indianapolis Colts, and all the other media staffs of the opposing teams on the Patriots' 2005 schedule. In New York, Greg Aiello, Brian McCarthy, and Phil Guarascio were my hosts during my visit to the mothership. Coach Tony Dungy of the Indianapolis Colts was equally generous with his time during my visit to Indianapolis.

Tracing the arc of Tom Brady's career required a visit to all of its various station-stops. At Serra High School, Mike Peterson was a helpful and willing guide. Thanks also to Bob Ferretti, Patrick Walsh, Tom McKenzie, Randy Vogel, Kevin Donohue, Russ Bertetta, and Ralph Stark. Bob Vinal tracked me down on the phone. And Tom Martinez took time over breakfast to demonstrate the flaws in my personal throwing motion, and to discuss his most famous pupil.

In Ann Arbor, I am indebted to Coach Lloyd Carr, and to Dave Abloff and the rest of the sports-information staff. The book is immeasurably better for the insights of Mike DeBord, Brad Canale, and Greg Harden. Champions of the West, all of them. Thanks also to John Heisler at the University of Notre Dame. Also in South Bend, Coach Charlie Weis was generous with an early morning in winter, and I am extraordinarily grateful for the willingness of Maura Weis to discuss the worst three days of her life. Thanks also to Stan Parrish of Ball State University.

Tom Brady quickly became the favorite young football player of a great number of old football players, most of whom were happy to talk about why that's the case. Thanks to Terry Bradshaw, Roger Staubach, Jim Plunkett, Steve Young, and Bart Starr, as well as to ex-Patriots Steve Grogan and Steve Nelson, who continue to grace the strange history of their franchise by being the most honorable parts of it. Archie Manning remains the kind of gentleman on which the South built its reputation. Another one, Raymond Berry, saw the connection between Brady and his old partner, John Unitas. And Bob Gladieux continues to laugh when he tells his tale for the two hundredth time, and we should all be grateful for that.

Paul Perrillo was invaluable over the course of the season, both as a colleague around the beat and as the fact-checker for much of the manuscript. Salient points, sir. Any mistakes that remain are my own, except for the one made by all of you sports editors who haven't yet hired Paul. That one's on you, folks.

Congressman Marty Meehan throws a good parking-lot bash, and Jimmy Siegel not only writes a fine suspense novel, but also is the best film director of offensive linemen who ever lived. And thanks also to Elwood Reid, for remembering what it was like and, especially, for writing the way he can. And to Mountaineer Mike Tomasky, for his encouragement. And to everyone at Mulberry Studios in Cambridge, Massachusetts, for their transcription skills, especially on a tight deadline. And to the Benincasa family of Napoli Pizza in Watertown, Massachusetts, once again, for the use of the hall.

This book has its deepest roots, oddly enough, in Eric Alterman's Altercation website, which was my adopted home on the Internet for several years, through the good graces and encouragement of Doc Eric I. It was within the extended Alter family that I came to know Eric Rauchway—Doc Eric II—who not only taught me how to pronounce "Czolgosz" correctly, but also introduced me to Thomas LeBien at Farrar, Straus and Giroux, who took a big chance on a project that was more than a little amorphous at its beginnings. Of course, thanks to Vince Young and the rest of the 'Horns; I caught him in a very good year. I owe him a plate of ribs at Stubbs—and a Shiner Bock—for his grace and his patience. Thanks also to June Kim, Elizabeth Garriga, and the rest of the FSG depth chart. We drafted very well.

Everyone at the relentless juggernaut that is the David Black

Literary Agency knows that I love them madly. For further details, please consult the dedication page.

Doug Most, Susanne Althoff, Anne Nelson, and the rest of the staff at *The Boston Globe Magazine* were enormously patient with the time it took for me to complete this project. I guess my chores around the place have been piling up. I'll start on the lawn this afternoon.

At home, I continue to be amazed by the courage and patience of my wife, Margaret Doris, whose fingerprints are on all the best parts of this book, and by the ongoing wonder that are Abraham, Brendan, and Molly. Damn, I'm lucky. I have more bench strength than any man deserves.

CHARLES P. PIERCE
WINTER/SPRING 2006